Wales is the best choice for holidays and breaks – there's so much to see and do in this beautiful part of Britain. And, for those looking for accommodation, this guide contains the best choice of hotels, guest houses and farmhouses.

These pages contain everything from modern seaside hotels to great-value guest houses, elegant country house hotels to traditional farmhouses, and excellent places to stay in towns and cities which are ideal for business stopovers as well as pleasure.

This is a complete guide to finding and booking accommodation in Wales. You'll find information on Wales's many attractions, followed by a comprehensive listing of places to stay.

C O N T E N T S

Whilst every effort has been made to ensure accuracy in this publication, the Wales Tourist Board can accept no liability whatsoever for any errors, inaccuracies or omissions, or for any matter in any way connected with or arising out of the publication of this information.

Designed and published by the Wales Tourist Board, Brunel House, Cardiff CF2 1UY. Written by Roger Thomas Freelance Services. Printed in Britain by KNP. Distributed overseas by the British Tourist Authority. Copyright © 1991 Wales Tourist Board. ISBN 185013 036 1.

Wales is a breath of fresh air. Explore its green heartlands, where the busiest sight you're likely to come across is the friendly hustle and bustle of market day. Wander along endless beaches with only the sound of sea birds and surf for company. There's so much uninterrupted, unspoilt coastline and countryside in Wales. Along the coast you'll discover sandy bays, clear seas, sheltered coves and airy headlands.

The great outdoors

You could spend an entire holiday exploring one of Wales's three National Parks. The wide, open spaces and grassy flanks of the 519-square-mile Brecon Beacons National Park; Pembrokeshire, the only coastal-based National Park in Britain or the Snowdonia National Park, a glorious, undiscovered region of forests, lakes, remote moorlands and mountain-backed seashore.

Country Crafts

Craft skills are more than alive in Wales – they thrive here. Craft workshops which welcome visitors are dotted throughout the country – so stop off on your travels at a pottery, woollen mill, woodturner's, leatherworker's, candlemaker's, jeweller's or slate workshop. If you want to see a number of different craftsmen working together, then visit one of Wales's many craft centres.

SOUTH PEMBROKESHIRE COAST

Attractions for all

Castles are the one thing you simply can't miss. Over 100 are open to visitors, so you're never far from powerful medieval fortresses such as Conwy Castle or evocative ruins deep in the country, such as Cilgerran on its wooded bluff above the looping River Teifi. As Wales's castles come in all shapes and sizes, so too does the kaleidoscope range of attractions here. There are parks dedicated to wildlife, butterflies and the countryside, narrow-gauge railways and spectacular showcaves and forest visitor centres.

Where to stay

Wherever you stay, you'll be closer to a host of attractions. And, with the help of this guide, you'll find *your* ideal accommodation. A quick flip through these pages will convince you of the variety of good accommodation in Wales – and don't forget that this book is just as handy for the business person looking for a place to stay.

POTTERY MAKING AT MAENTWROG

BALA LAKE NARROW GAUGE RAILWAY

Eventful times

There's always something happening in Wales. Throughout the summer there's a packed programme of events – everything from music festivals to medieval days, craft fairs to guided walks along the coast. Spring, autumn and winter are also eventful times. There are prestigious arts festivals, celebrity performances, sporting events – and don't forget market days, the best free show of all, when the country comes to town.

Celtic heritage will be celebrated throughout the year as part of a Celtica festival. And 1991 sees a very special event coming to Wales when the Cutty Sark Tall Ships Race starts from Milford Haven in July (full details on page 7).

To give you some flavour of the times ahead we've listed some of Wales's events on these pages, and also described a few events in more detail. For full 'what's happening' information, call in at a Tourist Information Centre when you arrive or contact the Wales Tourist Board for a free events leaflet.

EVENTS 1991

JANUARY	
2	Winter Pops
Brangwyn Hall, Swansea

FEBRUARY	
24	John Lill Piano Recital
Bodelwyddan Castle, Bodelwyddan, Clwyd

MARCH	
6	Bangor-on-Dee Races,
Bangor-on-Dee, Wrexham
15–17	The Welsh Beautiful Homes and Garden Exhibition, Margam Park, Port Talbot

APRIL	
12	BBC Welsh Symphony Orchestra Concert
Brangwyn Hall, Swansea
22–27	Newport Drama Festival 1991
Dolman Theatre, Newport

MAY	
4–6	Llandudno Victorian Extravaganza
Llandudno, Gwynedd
17–19	Llangollen International Jazz Extravaganza
Various venues, Llangollen, Clwyd

JUNE	
14–22	Cardiff Singer of the World (Provisional)
St. David's Hall, Cardiff
19–24	Criccieth Festival of Music and the Arts
Memorial Hall and other local venues,
Criccieth
22–23	Welsh Game and Country Pursuits Fair
Gelli Aur, Llandeilo, Dyfed
22–28	Barmouth to Fort William Three Peaks
Yacht Race. Start: The Quay, Barmouth

JULY	
15–13	World Harp Festival
St. David's Hall and other venues, Cardiff
19–21	Colwyn Bay International Folk Dance
Festival, Colwyn Bay
20–27	Fishguard Music Festival
Various venues, Fishguard

AUGUST	
3–10	Llanwrtyd Wells Festival Week
Llanwrtyd Wells
8–10	Welsh National Sheep Dog Trial,
Dollgellau
17	Celtic Fun Day
Welsh Folk Museum, Cardiff

SEPTEMBER	
2–22	Dylan Thomas Festival
Various venues, Swansea
15 September–6 October	Cardiff Festival of Music
St. David's Hall, Cardiff

OCTOBER	
5	Gwyl Werin Caernarfon, Caernarfon
12	Rugby Union World Cup 1991
Wales v Australia,
National Ground, Cardiff

NOVEMBER	
2	Concert by Brecon Cathedral Singers/
Gwent Chamber Orchestra
Brecon Cathedral, Brecon
23	The South East Wales Brass Band
Championship Contest
Parc and Dare Theatre, Treorchy

DECEMBER	
31 December–1 January 1992	Nos Galan Road Races
Penrhiwceiber and Mountain Ash

Llangollen International Musical Eisteddfod
9-14th July 1991

A colourful, cosmopolitan gathering of singers and dancers from all over the world in the beautiful little town of Llangollen. A unique festival first held in 1947 to help heal the wounds of war by bringing the peoples of the world together.

Royal Welsh Agricultural Show
22–25 July 1991

Four days of fascination – and a show that attracts a wide audience to Llanelwedd, Builth Wells not just from the farming community but from all walks of life. One of Wales's premier events, held in the heart of the country, covering all aspects of agriculture – and a lot more besides.

Royal National Eisteddfod
3-10 August 1991

Wales's most important cultural gathering, dating back to 1176, and held at a different venue each year. A festival dedicated to Welsh, Britain's oldest living language, with competitions, choirs, concerts, stands and exhibitions. Translation facilities available. This year's event will be held in Mold.

Brecon Jazz
16-18 August 1991

The streets of Brecon come alive to the sound of summer jazz. A great three-day jazz festival with a wonderful atmosphere. Over 80 concerts by bands and solo performers held throughout the town, both indoors and in the open air.

Llandrindod Wells Victorian Festival
17-25 August 1991

The Mid Wales spa town of Llandrindod celebrates its Victorian past. The festival includes street theatre, walks, talks, drama, exhibitions and music – all with a Victorian flavour.

Celtica 1991

Celtic heritage spreads its net far and wide. At one time, most of Europe was under the influence of the Celts. To celebrate over 2000 years of cultural heritage and Wales's long links with the rest of Europe, the Wales Tourist Board will be co-ordinating major events under the banner of Celtica 1991.

There will be festivals like Ewrosgol, held on the Llŷn Peninsula, for children who speak minority languages, a World Harp Festival in Cardiff, a Dylan Thomas Festival in Swansea, and a Celtic Literature Festival. New and exciting exhibitions on the Celts will be held at Cardiff's National Museum of Wales and at the European Centre for Traditional and Regional Cultures, Llangollen.

Come and join us in celebrating an important part of Britain's heritage. For further information please write to Celtica 1991 at the Wales Tourist Board, Brunel House, 2 Fitzalan Road, Cardiff CF2 1UY.

One for you diary – Garden Festival Wales 1992

It's green, it's great, it's fun. Garden Festival Wales will be held at an imaginatively transformed site at Ebbw Vale, South Wales, from 1 May to 1 October 1992. The festival promises to be fun for all and the biggest green event of the year. Be there!

Cutty Sark Tall Ships Race

The magnificent spectacle of some of the world's most elegant sailing ships sailing into one of the world's finest natural harbours is one event not to be missed in 1991. From 7 July onwards, around 60 tall-masted sailing vessels will start arriving in the Milford Haven Waterway, described by Admiral Lord Nelson as one of the world's best harbours.

The big day for spectators is 14 July, when the fleet will assemble before the race start to stage a spectacular Parade of Sail. The parade will sail up the great waterway towards the heart of Pembrokeshire before turning around and heading for the mouth of the Haven where the 'Tall Ships' race begins on 15 July.

The Spectacle of Sail

The sight of this fleet of sailing ships cruising along the banks of the Haven promises to be unforgettable. It is expected that some of the biggest square-rigged ships afloat will be present. Already Russia and Poland have indicated that such vast vessels as the *Kruzenshtern* and the *Sedov* will participate. These are 3000-tonners with an acre of combined sail and decks longer than football pitches! North American ships and Britain's own *Winston Churchill* are also expected.

The Haven will be buzzing with activity in the days leading up to the race. A colourful week of events is planned for the dockside at Milford Haven starting on 7 July, including massed bands, concerts and traditional music. The race itself, an annual event, will take the ships to Cork, Belfast and Aberdeen before finishing at Delfzjil in Holland.

Cutty Sark central accommodation booking

The race organisers have appointed Pembrokeshire Cottages as the official accommodation agents for the exciting build-up period to the race. Pembrokeshire Cottages can, subject to availability, arrange accommodation of any kind – hotel, guest house, B&B, self-catering, or caravan – for the week during which the fleet will be in port or for just a couple of nights based around the magnificent Parade of Sail.

But hurry! Accommodation during race week may be limited. Book now – Pembrokeshire Cottages' trained staff are there to help you. Call 0437-781764 or Fax 0437-781080 today! Or write to Pembrokeshire Cottages, Park House, Tiers Cross, Haverfordwest, Pembrokeshire, Dyfed SA62 4DB.

Milford Haven

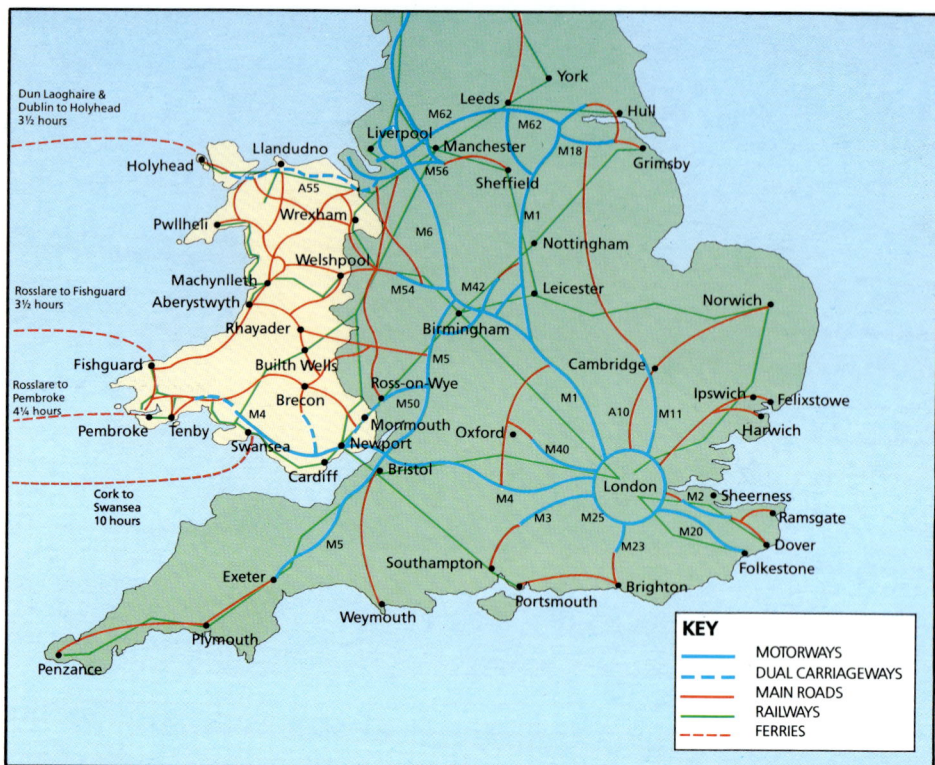

KEY

———	MOTORWAYS
– – –	DUAL CARRIAGEWAYS
———	MAIN ROADS
———	RAILWAYS
– – –	FERRIES

Dun Laoghaire &
Dublin to Holyhead
3½ hours

Rosslare to Fishguard
3½ hours

Rosslare to
Pembroke
4¼ hours

Cork to
Swansea
10 hours

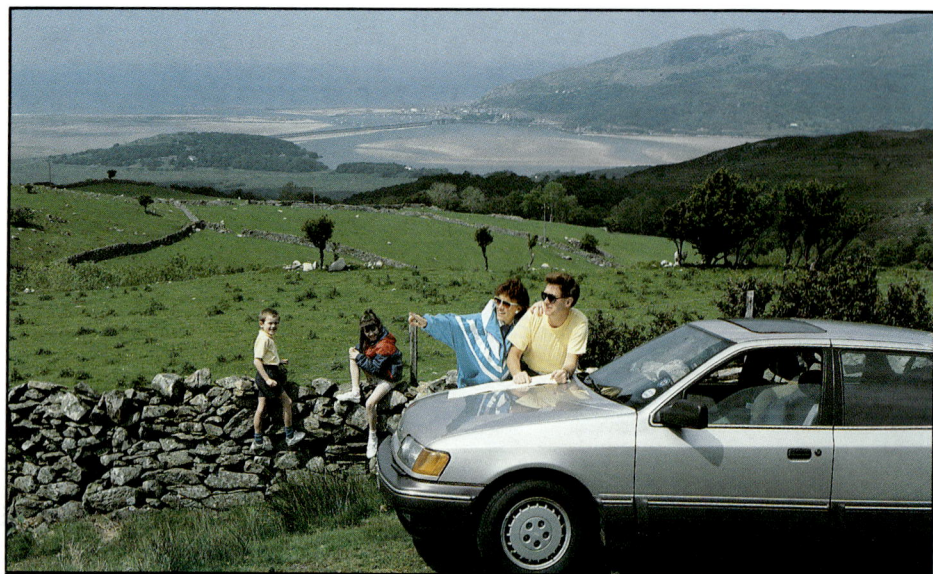

MOTORING ABOVE THE MAWDDACH ESTUARY, MID WALES

By Car	Miles	Journey Time
London to Cardiff	155	3 hours
Leicester to Swansea	188	$3^1/_2$ hours
Birmingham to Aberystwyth	122	3 hours
Manchester to Llandudno	86	2 hours
Bristol to Llandudno	214	4 hours
York to Llangollen	135	$2^1/_2$ hours

'By Car' mileages, which have been kindly supplied by the AA, represent optimum routes.

By Express Coach	Journey Time
London to Cardiff	$2^3/_4$ hours
Birmingham to Swansea	$3^1/_4$ hours
Manchester to Llandudno	3 hours
Bristol to Carmarthen	$3^1/_2$ hours
Nottingham to Cardiff	$4^1/_2$ hours
Sheffield to Rhyl	4 hours

By Train	Journey Time
London to Cardiff	$1^3/_4$ hours
London to Llandudno	$3^3/_4$ hours
London to Fishguard	4 hours
Birmingham to Swansea	$3^1/_4$ hours
Wolverhampton to Aberystwyth	3 hours
Portsmouth to Swansea	$4^1/_2$ hours
York to Cardiff	$4^1/_2$ hours

By Sea	Sailings Daily (High Season)	Voyage Time
Dun Laoghaire to Holyhead	2	$3^1/_2$ hours
Dublin to Holyhead	2	$3^1/_2$ hours
Rosslare to Fishguard	3	$3^1/_2$ hours
Cork to Swansea	1	10 hours
Rosslare to Pembroke Dock	2	$4^1/_2$ hours

Getting to Wales is quick and easy, trouble-free and inexpensive. You'll enjoy your holiday right from the start, without the worries of airport delays and the seemingly inevitable frustrations of long-distance travel. And when you arrive, you'll find that Wales is a grand touring country.

By Car

No other UK holiday destination is so well connected. Motorways bring you into Wales quickly and easily. The M4 travels deep into South-west Wales, while the A55 coastal 'Expressway' whisks traffic past most of the old North Wales bottlenecks – and there are even more improvements taking place. Travellers to Mid Wales can take advantage of the M54 which links with the M6/M5/M1.

You can rediscover the pleasure in motoring along Wales's highways and byways. Arm yourself with a map and explore the hills and mountains on roads that remain blissfully traffic-free apart from a few peak summer weekends. You'll find scenic routes on major and minor roads – call in at Tourist Information Centres for suggestions.

By Coach

Coach travel has really improved in recent years. Services are quick and efficient, and the coaches themselves are equipped with all the extras – hostess service, refreshments, videos, on-board toilets, air-conditioning – that make travel a comfortable and pleasurable experience. Express services link Wales with almost all major towns in England and Scotland. Details from your local travel agent or National Express office.

Within Wales you can travel from north to south (or vice versa!) by the Traws Cambria service. It runs for over 200 miles on a daily schedule linking Bangor with Cardiff, calling at places such as Caernarfon, Aberystwyth and Carmarthen. A second Traws Cambria route operates on a daily summer schedule between Liverpool, Wrexham and Cardiff.

Towns and villages throughout Wales are connected, of course, by a whole range of services, which operate on a local and regional basis. And don't forget that one of the best ways to see the country is on a day or half-day local coach excursion. For details of coach travel within Wales, please contact Tourist Information Centres and local bus stations.

If you want to combine coach and rail travel within North and Mid Wales then ask about unlimited-travel Rover tickets (see 'By Rail' section for details).

Major operators serving Wales are:

National Welsh, 33 West Canal Wharf, Cardiff, South Glamorgan CF1 5DB. Tel: (0222) 371331.

Crossville Wales Ltd, Imperial Buildings, Glan y Môr Road, Llandudno Junction, Gwynedd LL31 9RH. Tel: (0492) 596969.

South Wales Transport, 1 Plymouth Street, Swansea, West Glamorgan SA1 3QF. Tel: (0792) 47511 (Mon-Sat 8.30–6.00; Sun & Bank Hols 10.00–6.00)

InterCity services also link South Wales with Birmingham, Sheffield, York and Newcastle. A speedy, regular service from London (Euston) calls in at the North Wales resorts. This coast is also served by direct services from Manchester and the West Midlands. Mid Wales resorts are linked by services via Shrewsbury and the Cambrian Coast line.

Travelling around Wales by train is a delight. Frequent services in fast, modern sprinter trains make it easy to take days out by train and BR's scenic branch lines are a wonderful travel experience. The beautiful Heart of Wales line cuts across country from Shrewsbury to Swansea via Craven Arms, while the Conwy Valley line runs into the mountains from Llandudno Junction to Blaenau Ffestiniog. And don't miss the superb Cambrian Coast service, which operates along a mountain-backed shoreline from Pwllheli to Machynlleth and Aberystwyth. Ask about the money-saving unlimited-travel Rover and Ranger fares, some of which include the use of bus services. Your local Rail Travel Centre will have all the details.

Great Little Trains

You can't visit Wales without taking a ride on one of its famous narrow-gauge railways. Most are members of the Great Little Trains of Wales – contact them c/o Wharf Station, Tywyn, Gwynedd LL36 9EY. Tel: (0654) 710472.

By Rail

Journey times by rail really are impressive – a fastest time of just $1\frac{3}{4}$ hours from London (Paddington) to Cardiff, and just over $2\frac{1}{2}$ hours to Swansea from where the West Wales line connects Carmarthen with branch lines to Milford Haven, Pembroke and Fishguard. Fast

By Sea

No less than five services operate across the Irish Sea: Dublin to Holyhead, Rosslare to Pembroke Dock (both B&I), Dun Laoghaire to Holyhead, and Rosslare to Fishguard (both Sealink Stena Line) and Cork to Swansea which operates during March–September (Swansea-Cork Ferries).

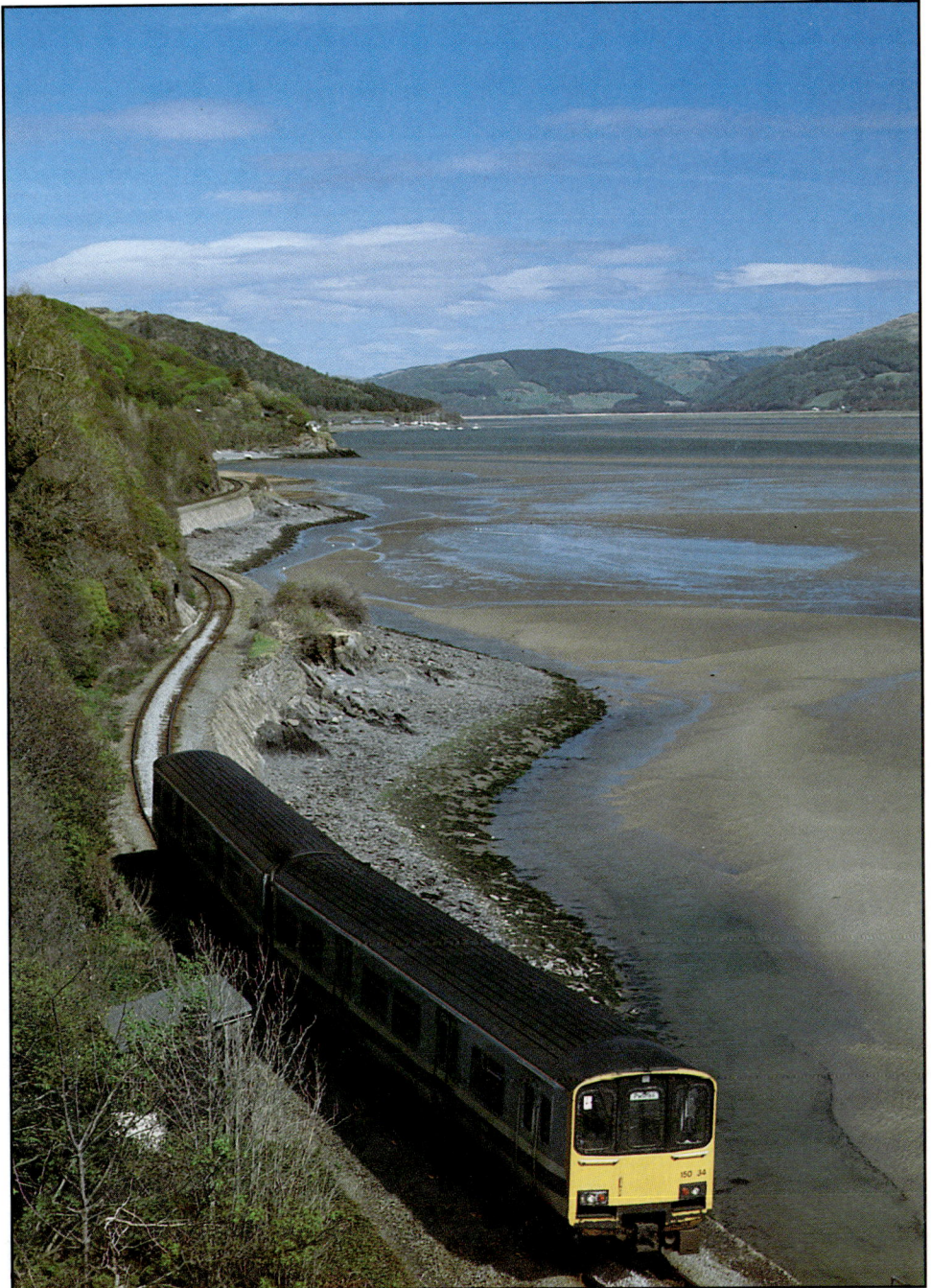

CAMBRIAN COAST RAILWAY

This guide contains a great choice of places to stay. There's something for all tastes and pockets. Take a look at the tempting range of luxury resort and country house hotels featured. Then there's friendly farmhouse accommodation for those wishing to sample the rural way of life. If you're on business, Wales has first-class hotels in its cities and towns which provide all the expected comforts and amenities. And if you're on a budget, then choose a great-value guest house.

A wide choice is just part of the Welsh formula. We've taken extra-special measures to make sure that you find the place that's just right for you. Everything is explained on the following pages, so it's worth taking a few minutes to study the information on the classification, grading and award schemes. You'll end up with a clear idea of the way in which the accommodation is presented in this guide – and, what's more important, you'll know that you can make your booking in complete confidence.

All checked out . . . to help you choose

For a start, every single establishment in this guide has been thoroughly checked by the Wales Tourist Board – so there's no uncertainty about standards. We then classify them into different categories so that you can choose the place best suited to your tastes and budget. *Please note, though, that the descriptive wording and symbols in the accommodation advertisements have been provided by the proprietor.* It should also be noted that our classifications, awards and gradings were correct at the time of publication. Inspections are on-going and improvements made by establishments could have resulted in revised classification since publication.

Crowns spell out the facilities and service

The nationwide Crown classification system, applicable to hotels, guest houses and farmhouses, help pinpoint the facilities on offer. Every establishment has been inspected and classified on one of six levels. Quite simply, the higher the number of Crowns, the greater the range of facilities, equipment and services on offer.

Please bear in mind that the Crown classification scheme is structured in such a way that an establishment in a lower category may well provide some of the facilities found at a higher level. But – most important of all – please remember that Crowns are not a guide to quality. A lower classification does not imply lower standards in comparison to an establishment with more Crowns.

L

'Listed'. Clean and comfortable accommodation, though the range of facilities and services may be limited.

Better-equipped accommodation, with a wider range of facilities, including washbasins in all bedrooms and a lounge area.

Accommodation offering a more extensive range of facilities and services (the latter in particular), including early morning tea/coffee and calls.

The range of facilities increases, with at least one-third of bedrooms with en-suite WC and bath or shower, plus easy chair and full-length mirror in all bedrooms.

👑👑👑👑

An even wider range of facilities and services, Colour TV, radio and telephone in all bedrooms. At least three-quarters of bedrooms with en-suite WC and bath or shower.

👑👑👑👑👑

The highest classification, with an extensive range of facilities and services, including room service, night porter and laundry service. All bedrooms with en-suite facilities.

Making the Grade

For 1991, we have introduced a new quality grading scheme for hotels, guest houses and farmhouses. The scheme – which, unlike the Crown classification, is voluntary – gives the establishment a quality grade. The grading, which represents an opinion taken by Wales Tourist Board-appointed inspectors, is an overall appraisal of quality based on such considerations as standards of furniture, decor, comfort, service and food.

Highly Commended

Exceptional standards of comfort and service. This is a very special accolade representing exceptional quality standards.

Commended

Excellent standards of comfort and service.

Merit

Very good standards of comfort and service.

Please remember that high quality can be found everywhere. Size, or a lack of crowns, are no barriers to a top-quality rating. A small hotel with limited facilities, for example, might win a high-quality grading based on its exceptional standards.

The establishments which have not yet chosen to be quality assessed are nevertheless still inspected to ensure that they provide an acceptable standard of comfort and service. These establishments come under the Crown classification scheme only.

Award-winning Guest Houses and Farmhouses

Good guest houses and farmhouses can now hold their own against many a hotel. Standards have improved beyond recognition since the old days of simple bed and breakfast and basic accommodation.

The coveted Wales Tourist Board Award recognises and rewards the best. Award winners have superior standards of furnishing, facilities, comfort and surroundings and have completed a tourism training course. Look out for the distinctive award symbol on the following pages. It's the hallmark of something extra special.

Key to Symbols

🛏	Total number of bedrooms
🛁	Number of bedrooms with en-suite bathrooms
AWARD	Recipient of the Wales Tourist Board Guest House and Farmhouse Award
HW	Bookable through the Holidays Wales central reservations service
T	Bookable through Travel Agents
🐕	Dogs accepted by arrangement
C	Children under 12 accommodated free if sharing parents' room (meals charged extra).
SP	Special weekend/midweek or short-break holidays.
🚭	Facilities provided for non-smokers arrangement
TW	Taste of Wales member
🚆	Railway Station

How to book

Enquiries

Just a reminder to make things easier all round. When booking a room – or simply making an enquiry – always state:

* ★ the dates you wish to stay, with any alternatives;
* ★ how many people are in your party;
* ★ whether you have any special requirements, such as vegetarian or other diets, terms for children, facilities for pets and so on.

Booking Direct

Telephone or write to the place of your choice. If you 'phone, remember to send a follow-up letter of confirmation.

Booking Forms and Central Reservations

You can, if you wish, use the booking forms provided at the back of this guide, where you'll also find details of 'Holidays Wales' reservations. Simply complete the appropriate form and send it direct to the accommodation of your choice or, where applicable, to Holidays Wales reservations.

CALL *Holidays* **(0792) 645555**

Holidays Wales provides a free reservations and help service on behalf of the Wales Tourist Board.

All accommodation in this brochure displaying the HW *symbol can be booked through this central Agency.*

If you need advice before making your final choice it may be helpful to telephone first. The 'Holidays Wales' friendly booking team, supported by a fully computerised reservations system will be pleased to help you. They can also arrange insurance or book tickets for coach or train. An agreement with a national car hire company means they can also hire you a car from your home town.

Whether you are thinking of Wales for your annual holiday or just a short break, call (0792) 645555 any day of the week between 9.00am and 7.00pm or just write to:–

Holidays Wales Ltd
P.O Box 40
Swansea
West Glamorgan
SA1 1PX

(There is a 'Holiday Wales' booking form at the back of this brochure).

Prices

Rates are per person based on two people sharing a double or twin room. There may be supplements for a single room and private bath/shower. Daily rates are for bed and breakfast. Weekly rates are for dinner, B&B. Prices quoted in this guide were supplied to the Wales Tourist Board during June–September 1990. So do check all prices and facilities before confirming your booking. All prices include VAT at the current rate.

Deposits

Most places will ask for a deposit when a telephone or written reservation is being made. Some establishments may request payment in advance from clients, particularly at hotels when there is no written and confirmed reservation.

Late arrivals

If you are arriving late, telephone the establishment to let the proprietor know and indicate what time you expect to arrive.

Cancellations and Insurance

When you confirm a holiday booking, bear in mind that you are entering a legally binding contract which entitles the proprietor to compensation if you fail to take up the accommodation. It's always wise to arrange holiday insurance to cover you for cancellation and other unforeseen eventualities.

If you do have to alter your travel plans, always advise the holiday operator or proprietor immediately.

Further Information

Please get in touch with us if you need any further advice or information, including more details on minimum standards and the Crown and award schemes, as well as the new grading scheme. Contact Wales Tourist Board, Dept. TCAM, Davis Street, Cardiff, CF1 2FU.

Wales in the West End

If you're in London, visit the Wales Information Bureau at the British Travel Centre, 12 Regent Street. Wales Tourist Board staff will provide all the information you need to plan your visit to Wales and you may book your holiday through the Room Centre. Tel: (071) 409 0969.

A Taste of Wales

Many hotels, farmhouses, guest houses, restaurants and inns throughout Wales are members of the *Blas ar Gymru* – Taste of Wales scheme. Taste of Wales makes the most of fresh local ingredients. It's all about traditional and modern recipes, a pride in preparation and high standards of cuisine.

Chefs in Wales have a wonderful range of foods to work with. Succulent Welsh lamb, delicious Pembrokeshire potatoes and fresh produce of all kinds provide them with a bountiful larder. There are superb seafoods, quality cheese (which experts have compared with the finest in France) and tasty treats such as *sewin* (sea-trout) from Wales's rivers and lakes.

These foods are the basis of a creative Welsh cuisine. Lighter, more modern dishes co-exist with old favourites such as *cawl* (a hearty soup). Today's menus feature dishes such as shellfish pancake in lobster sauce as well as traditionally prepared Welsh lamb.

Give yourself a Taste of Wales treat when you're on holiday. Look out for the distinctive Taste of Wales sign on your travels. All members are listed in *Taste of Wales – Restaurant, Food and Travel Guide* – published by Jarrold with support from the Wales Tourist Board and available from Tourist Information Centres and good bookshops. Taste of Wales members featured in this brochure have the **TW** symbol in their entries.

Using this Guide

It's easy to find your way around this book. The remainder of the guide is filled with 'where to stay' information – hotels, guest houses and farmhouses. First, we divide the accommodation up into three main regions – North, Mid and South Wales – which are colour coded. Each region is then divided into smaller areas so that you can turn immediately to the specific part of Wales that interests you. It's all explained here on the map and index.

Within each small area, the resorts, towns and villages are listed alphabetically with their accommodation. Each place has a map reference enabling you to pinpoint its location on the detailed gridded maps at the back of the book.

North Wales

1. Isle of Anglesey
2. North Wales Coast Resorts
3. Llŷn – Snowdon's Peninsula
4. Snowdonia Mountains & Coastline
5. Clwyd Countryside & Heritage

Mid Wales

6. Meirionnydd
7. Ceredigion
8. Montgomeryshire
9. Heart of Wales

South Wales

10. Pembrokeshire
11. The Coastline and Vales of Dyfed
12. Brecon & the Beacons
13. Swansea, Mumbles & Gower
14. Cardiff & the South Wales Coast
15. Vale of Usk & Wye Valley
16. South Wales Valleys

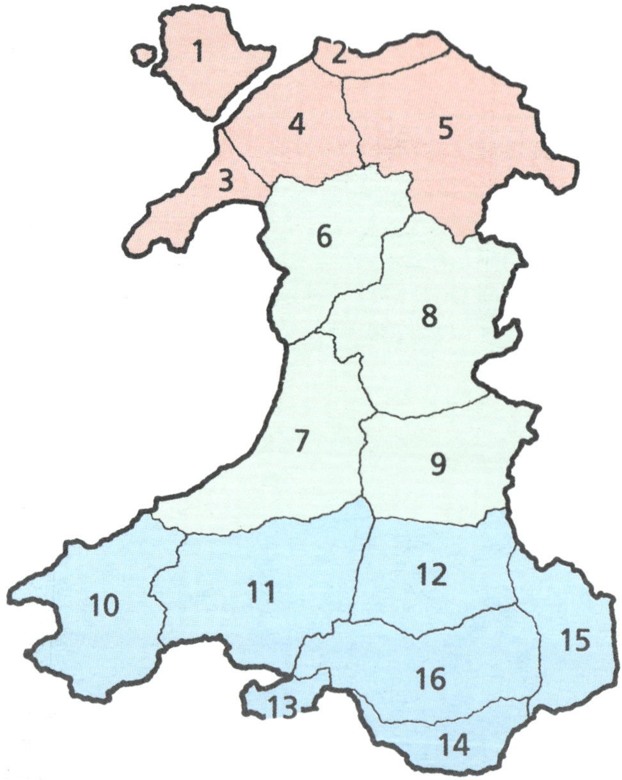

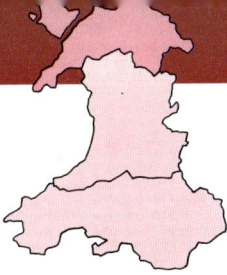

The view from the Great Orme headland, overlooking the hotel-lined promenade at Llandudno to the foothills of Snowdonia, encapsulates the character of this part of Wales. North Wales is a region where visitors enjoy the very best of coast and country. Snowdonia's towering mountains are only a stone's throw from a sparkling, sandy coastline, allowing North Wales's seaside resorts to double up as superbly located touring centres.

Stay at any of the popular coast resorts – Llandudno, Colwyn Bay, Rhyl or Prestatyn – and spend the morning on the beach, the afternoon in the hills and mountains. These resorts have an excellent selection of places to stay (Llandudno, for example, boasts the biggest choice of hotels in Wales). There's something for all tastes and pockets – everything from luxury hotels to attractive, well-equipped guest houses.

Those in search of the quieter coasts will make for the Isle of Anglesey or the Llŷn Peninsula. With the opening and further extension of the A55 Expressway, a road which avoids many of the old coastal bottlenecks, these parts of North Wales are so much easier to get to. But the picture along Anglesey's sandy shoreline and Llŷn's spectacular cliff-backed coast is still peaceful.

Both coasts are designated as being of 'Outstanding Natural Beauty'. The places to stay here are mostly small and friendly – make for charming, castle-crowned Criccieth, for example, or the pretty sailing centre of Beaumaris.

North Wales is famous for its mountains. Snowdon, the jagged 3,560 ft. peak, is the highest point in Southern Britain. It gives its name to the Snowdonia National Park, an upland area of dramatic, boulder-strewn landscape, cool mountain lakes, rushing rivers and densely wooded valleys. Charming old country towns, with a good selection of comfortable hotels, dot the landscape. Stay at Llanrwst in the lovely Vale of Conwy, or the popular mountain resort of Betws-y-Coed, or tiny Beddgelert tucked away beneath Snowdon.

Further east, the countryside becomes softer, greener and gentler. Clwyd's rolling hills (another 'Area of Outstanding Natural Beauty'), windy moors and sheltered vales can be explored from places such as Denbigh, Ruthin (two characterful medieval towns) and Llangollen, the home of the colourful International Musical Eisteddfod, held each July.

RIVER DEE AT LLANGOLLEN

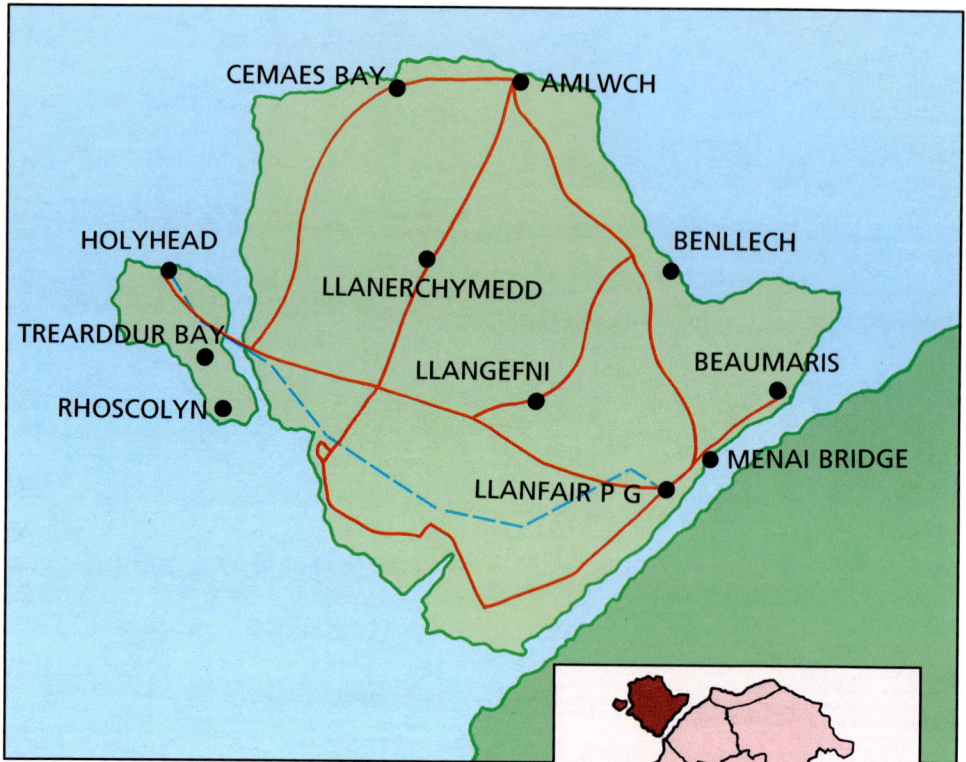

It's always possible to find a quiet stretch of sands away from it all on this lovely island. Anglesey's 125-mile shoreline represents the unhurried face of the North Wales coast. Its resorts and sailing centres are small – stay at handsome Beaumaris or pretty little Moelfre – but there's nothing diminutive about the island's many attractions.

Take to the beach in a big way along Newborough Warren's vast sands and dunes. At Beaumaris, visit the last – and some say greatest – of North Wales's chain of mighty medieval castles or the magical Museum of Childhood. The National Trust's magnificent Plas Newydd mansion is full of treasures, while Pili Palas is filled with exotic butterflies from all over the world and at the award-winning Anglesey Sea Zoo at Brynsiencyn, you can walk through a shipwreck without getting wet.

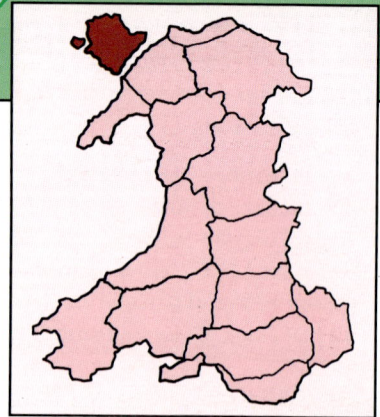

The biggest thing of all on Anglesey is the longest place name in the world (here shortened to a humble Llanfair P.G.), where you'll find a correspondingly large, high-quality craft shop specialising in woollens and tweeds.

AMLWCH   Map Ref Ac1

Quaint Anglesey port, market town and holiday resort. Superb coastal scenery and excellent boating. Golf course, heated indoor swiming pool.

Hotels

Lastra Farm Hotel

Penrhyd, Amlwch,
Isle of Anglesey
Gwynedd LL68 9TF
Tel: (0407) 830906

Traditional Welsh farmhouse converted into a comfortable homely hotel. All bedrooms with private facilities, separate television lounge also tea and coffee making facilities. Restaurant open to general public with a reputation for serving only the finest cuisine. Lovely coastal walks, golfing, fishing, pony trekking nearby. Visa and Access accepted. Please write or phone for brochure.

		NIGHTLY B&B PER PERSON		WEEKLY D,B&B PER PERSON			
SP TW		MIN £	MAX £	MIN £	MAX £		5
		16.00	17.00	170.00	180.00	OPEN 1-12	5

AMLWCH HARBOUR

BEAUMARIS Map Ref Ae3

Beautifully sited Anglesey coastal resort with splendid 13th century castle. 15th century Tudor house, Victorian goal, enchanting Museum of Childhood, interesting museum of craft and trade tools and the "Beaumaris Experience". Yachting Centre with golf course and excellent fishing; 6th century Penmon Priory nearby. Ideal touring centre for Snowdonia with superb views of mountains across Menai Strait. Lovely Beaumaris Festival in early summer.

Hotels

Bishopsgate House Hotel and Restaurant

54 Castle Street,
Beaumaris, Isle of Anglesey,
Gwynedd LL58 8AB
Tel: (0248) 810302

COMMENDED

This elegant Georgian town house is surely one of the finest small hotels in the area. Public rooms and bedrooms are all individually furnished to a high standard. All bedrooms have en-suite facilities, television, radio and hot beverages. The restaurant enjoys a reputation for providing quality and value. At Bishopsgate, comfort, hospitality and good food are paramount. We hope that your first visit to our home will not be your last.

		NIGHTLY B&B PER PERSON		WEEKLY D,B&B PER PERSON			
T SP		MIN £	MAX £	MIN £	MAX £		10
		21.00	24.00	202.00	221.00	OPEN 2-12	10

WALES
It's magic

Guest Houses

Ty'n Pystyll

Beach Road, Llanddona,
Beaumaris,
Isle of Anglesey,
Gwynedd LL58 8UN
Tel: (0248) 811224
Fax: (0535) 723818

COMMENDED

A beautiful executive residence situated in 2 acres of carefully landscaped gardens offering country seclusion and stunning views over Red Wharf Bay and the open sea. Llanddona Beach ½ mile, Beaumaris 4 miles. All rooms have superb sea views and are tastefully furnished and fully equipped with remote control TV sets, hairdryers, electric blankets, tea/coffee facilities, shaver points. Two suites have en-suite bathrooms, one being our four poster luxury suite.

HW T C		NIGHTLY B&B PER PERSON		WEEKLY D,B&B PER PERSON			4
		MIN £	MAX £	MIN £	MAX £		2
		17.00	20.00	000.00	000.00	OPEN 1-12	

Farmhouses

Plas Cichle

Beaumaris,
Isle of Angelsey,
Gwynedd LL58 8PS
Tel: (0248) 810488

AWARD

COMMENDED

This beautiful period farmhouse, set in 200 acres, close to the historic town of Beaumaris and the Menai Strait, offers accommodation in spacious double or family rooms with private bathrooms, TV and beverage facilities. All enjoy panoramic views. Sandy beaches, sailing and golf nearby. Ideal touring base. Emphasis on home cooked, local produce. Enjoy the freedom of the farm. Mae croeso cynnes i chi yma. Brochure available from Mrs Eirwen Roberts.

HW T SP		NIGHTLY B&B PER PERSON		WEEKLY D,B&B PER PERSON			3
		MIN £	MAX £	MIN £	MAX £		3
		14.50	16.00	135.00	150.00	OPEN 2-11	

BENLLECH

Map Ref Ad2

Popular holiday village above a sweeping bay on Anglesey's east coast. 4 miles of good sands, safe bathing, sailing, bowls, walking. Nearby cliffs are rich in fossils. Visit the Rhuddlan Fawr Open Farm at nearby Brynteg.

Hotels

Glanrafon Hotel

Bangor Road, Benllech,
Isle of Anglesey,
Gwynedd LL74 8TF
Tel: (0248) 852364

Hot and cold water and shaver points in all bedrooms, double and family rooms. Special rates for children. Lounge with colour TV, central heating. Full fire certificate. Golden sands, delightful coves. Ideally situated for golf, fishing, horse riding and touring Snowdonia National Park.

		NIGHTLY B&B PER PERSON		WEEKLY D,B&B PER PERSON			17
							12
		MIN £	MAX £	MIN £	MAX £	OPEN 5-10	
		18.00	23.00	173.00	209.00		

BENLLECH BEACH

The Golden Sands Hotel

Benllech Bay, Isle of Anglesey,
Gwynedd LL74 8SP
Tel: (0248) 852384

The Golden Sands hotel aptly named as it overlooks the beach just 60yds away. Luxury accommodation with family, twin, double and single bedrooms all en-suite with colour TV and tea making. Conservatory lounge with panoramic views of the beach. Cocktail bar adjacent to dining room where excellent cuisine is served. Sea food menu, 'a la carte and table d'hôte. Olde worlde bar downstairs. Children adored. Reduced rates OAP's. Great welcome to honeymooners. Complimentary breaks and mini weekends. Write or phone for colour brochure.

		NIGHTLY B&B PER PERSON		WEEKLY D,B&B PER PERSON			12
							11
		MIN £	MAX £	MIN £	MAX £	OPEN 1-12	
		34.00	38.00	235.00	260.00		

Wilma Lodge Private Hotel

Bay View Road, Benllech,
Isle of Anglesey, Gwynedd
LL74 8TW
Tel: (0248) 852367

Licensed modern private hotel providing comfortable accommodation and friendly service. 450yds from Benllech beach and convenient for exploring the island and Snowdonia. Most rooms en-suite, all with tea/coffee facilities. Reductions for under 12's sharing parents room. Bar, TV, and quiet lounges. Excellent cuisine with 4 course breakfast and 5 course dinner. Open all year (except Xmas). Bookings for any period, autumn, winter and spring breaks at special rates. Access/Visa facilities.

		NIGHTLY B&B PER PERSON		WEEKLY D,B&B PER PERSON			13
							8
		MIN £	MAX £	MIN £	MAX £	OPEN 1-12	
		15.75	18.00	164.50	182.00		

CEMAES BAY

Map Ref Ac1

Quaint, unspoilt village with stone quay, boating, fishing and swimming on rugged northern shores of Anglesey. Wylfa Nuclear Power Station open to the public.

Hotels

Harbour Hotel & Restaurant

Harbour View, Cemaes Bay,
Isle of Anglesey, Gwynedd
LL67 0NN
Tel: (0407) 710273
Fax: (0407) 711277
Central Reservations: (0407) 710977

MERIT

The Harbour Hotel is enviably situated overlooking the quaint picturesque harbour and sandy coved beach which is 30 yards away. Children are always welcome. Many of the rooms are family rooms. All have colour TV, own bathrooms and tea making facilities. The restaurant overlooks the beach. Table d'hôte and full 'a la carte menu and bar snacks menu. 18 hole golf course and pony trekking nearby and everything possible for your comfort and relaxation. Ring for brochure and details. Ideal base for exploring Anglesey. Resident proprietors.

		NIGHTLY B&B PER PERSON		WEEKLY D,B&B PER PERSON			18
							18
		MIN £	MAX £	MIN £	MAX £	OPEN 1-12	
		16.00	20.00	149.00	–		

HERITAGE OF A NATION (VHS/BETA)

Narrated by Richard Burton, this 25-minute video presents the heritage of Wales from prehistoric to modern times. Wale's natural beauty is also depicted within some memorable sequences.

Guest Houses

Hafod Country House

Cemaes Bay,
Isle of Anglesey,
Gwynedd LL67 ODS
Tel: (0407) 710500

AWARD — COMMENDED

We welcome you to share our spacious Edwardian house peacefully situated in an acre of gardens close to the village and beach. Superb sea and mountain views. Elegant lounge, separate dining room. Comfortable bedrooms, two en-suite, beverage facilities. Renowned for excellent food using fresh garden produce. Winner North Wales Golden Supercook Award. Residential licence.

HW T SP ⅅ✕	NIGHTLY B&B PER PERSON		WEEKLY D,B&B PER PERSON		🛏 3 🛏 2
	MIN £	MAX £	MIN £	MAX £	OPEN
	13.50	15.00	150.50	161.00	3-10

Treddolphin Guest House

Beach Road, Penrhyn,
Cemaes Bay, Isle of Anglesey,
Gwynedd LL67 0ET
Tel: (0407) 710388

Situated in an elevated position overlooking bay and coast presenting good home cooking. All bedrooms have private shower and H&C. There is free babysitting and courtesy tea and biscuits in lounge in the evening. Ideal for relaxing holiday. Abundant unspoilt coastal scenery and beaches. Near 18 hole golf course. Ample parking. Village minutes walk away. Competative rates. Children half price up to 16 years old sharing parents room. For a welcoming service ring Roberta and Harold Williams.

HW T SP ⅅ✕	NIGHTLY B&B PER PERSON		WEEKLY D,B&B PER PERSON		🛏 8 🛏 –
	MIN £	MAX £	MIN £	MAX £	OPEN
	9.50	9.50	77.00	77.00	1-12

HOLYHEAD Map Ref Aa2

Stands on Holy Island, linked by causeway to Anglesey. Port for Irish Ferries. roman remains and maritime museum in town. Sailing centre and sailing school. Sea angling, cliff and hill walking. RSPB centre; enjoy the sight of sea birds and coastal flora and the view from the cliffs to the South Stack Lighthouse.

Hotels

Trearddur Bay Hotel

Lôn Isallt, Trearddur Bay,
Isle of Anglesey, Gwynedd
LL65 2UN
Tel: (0407) 860301
Telex: 61609 Fax: (0407) 861181

Indoor heated swimming pool, adjacent to sandy beach. Ideally situated for golf, country pursuits and water sports All bedrooms superbly furnished and euipped with colour television, hairdryer, trouser press, telephone, beverages, 24 hour service. Excellent restaurant and bars. All set in beautiful gardens. A perfect setting for coast or country holidays.

HW T 🐕 SP	NIGHTLY B&B PER PERSON		WEEKLY D,B&B PER PERSON		🛏 27 🛏 27
	MIN £	MAX £	MIN £	MAX £	OPEN
	38.00	70.00	285.00	345.00	1-12

LLANERCHYMEDD
Map Ref Ac2

Central Anglesey village with easy access to island's beaches. Visit Din Llugwy, prehistoric remains of fortified village, the working windmill at Llandeusant and the Llyn Alaw Visitor Centre.

Guest Houses

Drws y Coed

Llanerchymedd, Isle of
Anglesey Gwynedd
LL71 8AD
Tel: (0248) 470473

AWARD — COMMENDED

With wonderful panoramic views of Snowdonia, this extremely well appointed farmhouse is situated in beautiful wooded countryside in the centre of Anglesey. It is a 550 acre working farm, beef, sheep and arable. All bedrooms are en-suite with TV, radio and beverage facilities. Full central heating, lounge with log fire. Emphasis on good food and cleanliness. Games room. Free pony rides. WTB Farmhouse Award. Farm Holiday Guide Diploma Award. Warm Welsh welcome assured.

HW SP ⅅ✕	NIGHTLY B&B PER PERSON		WEEKLY D,B&B PER PERSON		🛏 4 🛏 4
	MIN £	MAX £	MIN £	MAX £	OPEN
	16.00	16.00	150.00	150.00	1-11

SOUTH STACK, NEAR HOLYHEAD

LLANFAIR P.G.
Map Ref Ad3

Famous for its full 58 letter mame of Llanfairpwllgwyn-gyllgogerychwyrndrobwll-llantysiliogogogoch, which means "St. Mary's Church by the white aspen near the violent whirlpool and St. Tysilio's Church by the red cave". Fine craft centre with extensive choice of products; Plas Newydd stately home nearby. Marvellous views from the 90ft Marquess of Angelsey column; Bryn Celli Ddu burial chamber. ≋

Hotels

Carreg Bran Hotel

Church Lane, Llanfair P.G., Isle of Anglesey, Gwynedd LL61 5YH
Tel: (0248) 714224
Telex: 61464 CABRANG
Fax: (0248) 715983

The Carreg Bran prides itself on the quality of service, comfort and cuisine offered to guests. Recently refurbished with great care and imagination. All en-suite bedrooms have satellite remote TV, telephone, hairdryer, trouser press, tea and coffee facilities, central heating. Function/ conference room up to 150 people. A popular venue for weddings. Nestling on the banks of the Menai Strait with plentiful amenities such as sailing, golfing, beautiful coastline, impressive castles. Brochure available on request.

HW	T	NIGHTLY B&B PER PERSON		WEEKLY D,B&B PER PERSON		🚗 33
🐾	SP					🛏 33
		MIN £	MAX £	MIN £	MAX £	OPEN
		31.25	39.90			1-12

22

LLANGEFNI   Map Ref Ad3

Market town and shopping centre, Anglesey's administrative "capital". Fine touring base; almost all the island's coastline is within 10-15 mile radius. Many prehistoric sites and attractions nearby. Theatre ans sports centre. Trout fishing in nearby Cefni reservoir.

Hotels

Tre-Ysgawen Hall

Capel Coch, Nr Llangefni, Isle of Anglesey, Gwynedd LL77 7UR
Tel: (0248) 750750
Fax: (0248) 750035

HIGHLY COMMENDED

A 19th century manor house recently restored. Now open as a deluxe country house hotel, surrounded by woodland and landscaped gardens. Views over Snowdonia. 19 individually furnished and decorated en-suite bedrooms, each with every facility expected. 24 hour service. Fine dining. Menus change daily and prepared by master chefs. Extensive list of wines. 3,000 acre shoot. Comfortable lounge and cocktail bar. For total relaxation Tre-Ysgawen Hall.

HW	T	NIGHTLY B&B PER PERSON		WEEKLY D,B&B PER PERSON		🛏 19
🐾						🚗 19
		MIN £	MAX £	MIN £	MAX £	OPEN
		53.35	75.35	340.75	479.35	1-12

THE MENAI SUSPENSION BRIDGE

MENAI BRIDGE
Map Ref Ad3

The first town motorists enter on Anglesey after crossing Telford's graceful suspension bridge (built 1826) over the Menai Strait. Grand views of Snowdonia on mainland. Tegfryn Gallery has work by contemporary Welsh artists; Pili Palas butterfly world and Anglesey Column nearby.

Hotels

Anglesey Arms Hotel

Mona Road, Menai Bridge, Isle of Anglesey, Gwynedd LL59 5EA
Tel: (0248) 712305

Colour TV, radio, tea making facilities, shaver points in all bedrooms. Single, double and family rooms. Special rates for children. Lounge with colour TV, central heating, full fire certificate. Golden sands, delightful coves. Ideally situated for golf, fishing, horse riding and touring Snowdonia National Park.

🐾	C	NIGHTLY B&B PER PERSON		WEEKLY D,B&B PER PERSON		🚗 17
SP						🛏 16
		MIN £	MAX £	MIN £	MAX £	OPEN
		25.00	32.00	183.00	239.00	1-12

RHOSCOLYN
Map Ref Ab3

Picturesque sandy bay on Holy Island (road access) near Holyhead. Coastal walks, safe swimming, excellent sailing facilities in nearby Trearddur Bay.

Hotels

The Old Rectory

Rhoscolyn,
Nr Holyhead,
Isle of Anglesey,
Gwynedd LL65 2DQ
Tel: (0407) 860214

AWARD

COMMENDED

A fine Georgian country house within a mile of Rhoscolyn's delightful sandy bay. Outstanding country and sea views. Ideal for sailing, bird-watching and family holidays. Lovely coastal walks. Excellent accommodation, food and service. All guest rooms have en-suite bathrooms, colour television and tea/coffee making facilities. Licensed. Children very welcome. Write or phone for brochure to Edna Aldred. Access/Visa payment facilities.

	NIGHTLY B&B PER PERSON		WEEKLY D,B&B PER PERSON		🛏 5 🛏 5
	MIN £	MAX £	MIN £	MAX £	OPEN
	20.50	20.50	195.00	195.00	2-11

TREARDDUR BAY
Map Ref Aa2

Most attractive holiday spot set amongst low cliffs on Holy Island, near Holyhead. Ample accommodation, golden sands, golf, sailing, fishing, swimming.

Hotels

Beach Hotel

Lôn St Ffraid,
Trearddur Bay,
Isle of Anglesey,
Gwynedd LL65 2YT
Tel: (0407) 860332 Telex: 61529
Fax: (0407) 861140

COMMENDED

Prime position on Britain's treasure island. 26 bedrooms all en-suite, TV/radio, award winning restaurant, leisure complex includes swim spa, sauna, sunbeds, fitness room, squash courts, 10 table snooker hall. Old worlde pub and bistro, Raffles night club, family diner and wine bar. Ideally situated for ferries to Dublin with late check in facilities and night porter.

HW T 🐕 C SP	NIGHTLY B&B PER PERSON		WEEKLY D,B&B PER PERSON		🛏 26 🛏 26
	MIN £	MAX £	MIN £	MAX £	OPEN
	55.00	70.00	300.00		1-12

Highground Hotel

Off Ravenspoint Road,
Trearddur Bay, Isle of
Anglesey, Gwynedd LL65 2YY
Tel: (0407) 860078

Magnificent panoramic coastal views are a feature of Highground, a small family-run licensed hotel where the personal touch counts. A haven for family holidays and the perfect centre for walking, bird watching, water sports, crafts and castles. Golden beaches, rocky coves, with the sea at the bottom of our garden! All bedrooms have colour television and coffee/tea facilities. Elegant en-suite rooms with period furnishings also available. Access/Visa payment welcomed.

T SP	NIGHTLY B&B PER PERSON		WEEKLY D,B&B PER PERSON		🛏 6 🛏 3
	MIN £	MAX £	MIN £	MAX £	OPEN
	14.50	19.00	168.00	189.00	1-12

WALES: SELF-CATERING GUIDE 1991

A wide selection of self-catering accommodation is featured between the covers of this guide. Over 250 properties are described, including cottages, flats, chalets, caravan holiday home parks and touring caravan/camping parks. General travel information is also included.

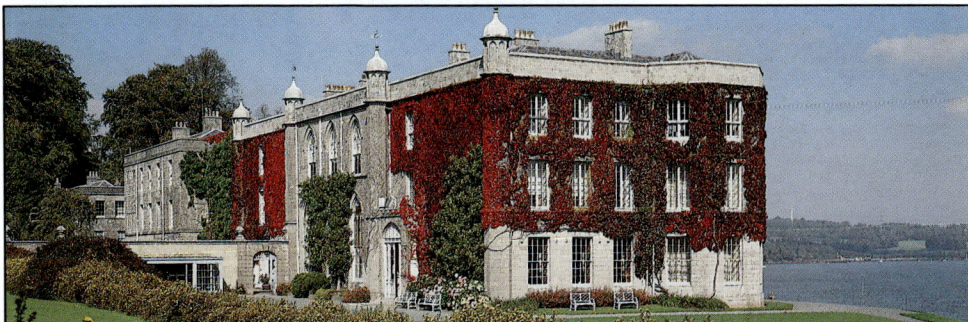

PLAS NEWYDD, NR. LLANFAIR P.G.

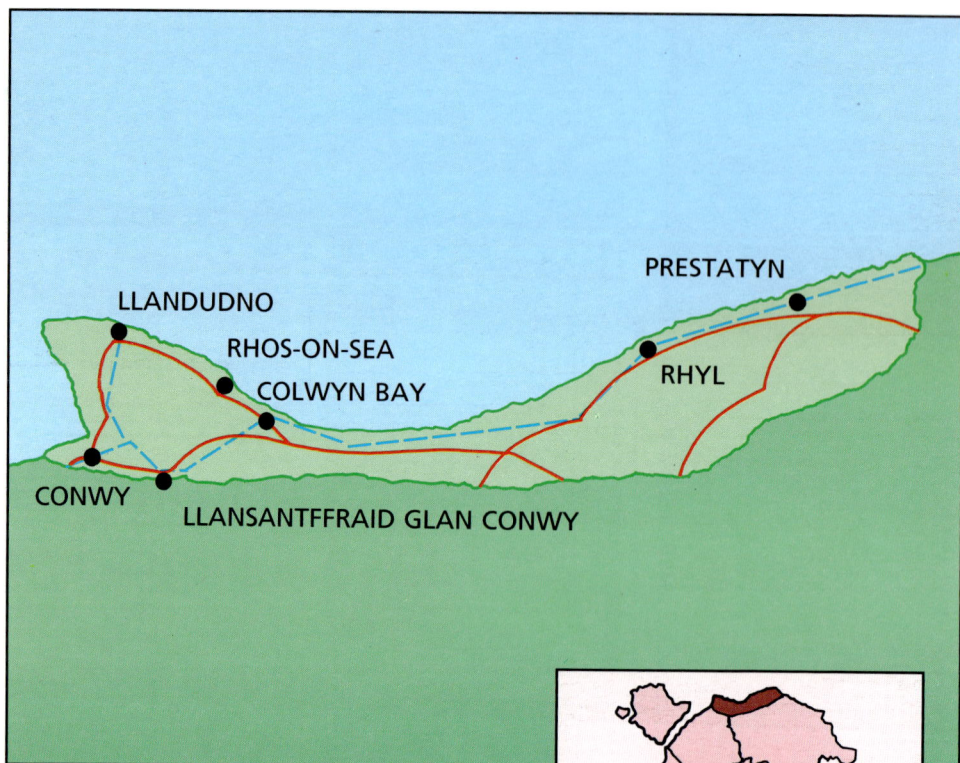

This ever popular coast stretches from Conwy at one end to Prestatyn at the other. At medieval Conwy, it's difficult to pick the most impressive sight – is it the towering castle or the craggy backcloth of mountains behind? Elegant Llandudno, with its memories of *Alice in Wonderland,* is a resort of rare character. It's a place where period charm (the resort's ornate Victorian architecture is a delight) goes hand-in-hand with up-to-the-minute appeal.

Colourful Colwyn Bay and lively Rhyl are two ever-popular family resorts. The sands are great, the entertainments endless and, like Llandudno, the resorts are ideally located for touring Snowdonia. Don't miss the Welsh Mountain Zoo at Colwyn Bay with its new Chimpanzee World, or Rhyl's latest attraction, the 240 ft. high Sky Tower built for the Glasgow Garden Festival and, while in Rhyl make the most of the guaranteed good climate at the imaginative Sun Centre on the seafront. Sandy Prestatyn also has an action-packed entertainments scene, enhanced even further by the excellent Nova Centre.

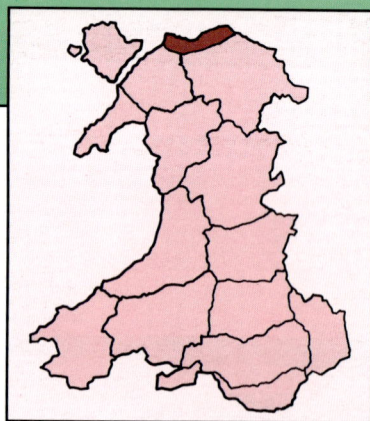

COLWYN BAY
Map Ref Bb4

Attractive bustling seaside resort. Promenade amusements. Good touring centre for Snowdonia. Leisure centre, Eirias Park, Dinosaur World, famous Mountain Zoo with new Chimpanzee World, Puppet theatre. Golf, tennis, riding and other sports. Wide range of hotels and guest houses. Quieter Rhos on Sea at western end of bay.

Hotels

Ashmount Hotel

College Avenue, Rhos On Sea,
Colwyn Bay, Clwyd LL28 4NT
Tel: (0492) 44582   COMMENDED

Ashmount is a quality 2 star hotel family run offering service of a very high standard. Superbly appointed throughout with all 18 bedrooms having bathroom en-suite. Colour TV, radio, video channel, direct dial telephone, tea and coffee making facilities. Ground floor rooms, wheelchair access. Pets welcome. Situated in a lovely peaceful area just off promenade.

HW T SP C	NIGHTLY B&B PER PERSON		WEEKLY D,B&B PER PERSON		18 18
	MIN £ 18.80	MAX £ 27.00	MIN £ 182.52	MAX £ 225.00	OPEN 1-12

Edelweiss Hotel

Off Lawson Road,
Colwyn Bay, Clwyd LL29 8HD
Tel: (0492) 532314
Fax: (0492) 534707

A slice of countryside in the heart of a charming coastal resort, this friendly Four Crown hotel in its own wooded gardens has footpaths to promenade, Eirias Park and leisure centre. En-suite rooms, colour TVs, tea/coffee makers, direct dial phone. Sauna, solarium. Cosy bar. Lounge and games room.

HW C TW	NIGHTLY B&B PER PERSON		WEEKLY D,B&B PER PERSON		26 26
	MIN £ 21.00	MAX £	MIN £ 195.00	MAX £	OPEN 1-12

Holcombe Hotel

9 Grosvenor Road,
Colwyn Bay, Clwyd
LL29 7YF
Tel: (0492) 530423   COMMENDED

We are a small family run detached hotel situated on the level in a delightful residential area yet close to all amenities. All bedrooms have private bath/shower room, colour TVs, tea making facilities, central heating, two en-suite ground floor bedrooms. Reduction for children. Cosy bar, TV lounge. Private parking. Ideal for touring North Wales. Bed and breakfast from £13 p p, dinner, bed and breakfast from £17. Sorry no dogs.

HW T C SP	NIGHTLY B&B PER PERSON		WEEKLY D,B&B PER PERSON		8 8
	MIN £ 13.00	MAX £ 15.00	MIN £ 112.00	MAX £ 135.00	OPEN 1-12

Lyndale Hotel & Restaurant

Abergele Road, Colwyn
Bay, Clwyd LL29 9AB
Tel: (0492) 515429

Superior coastal hotel overlooking Beautiful Bay of Colwyn. Ideal for Snowdonia. Superb restaurant, table d'hôte and full 'a la carte menus prepared by full time professional chef. All rooms en-suite, colour TVs and full facilities. Quality, cleanliness, value for money and service of paramount importance. Special weekly rates, 2 & 3 day breaks from £59.50 P P, D B & B available all year. Numerous activities available including 6 Golf courses within easy reach. Colour brochure available.

HW T C SP	NIGHTLY B&B PER PERSON		WEEKLY D,B&B PER PERSON		14 14
	MIN £ 26.00	MAX £ 32.00	MIN £ 235.00	MAX £ 198.50	OPEN 1-12

St. Margarets Hotel

Princes Drive, Colwyn Bay,
Clwyd LL29 8RP
Tel: (0492) 532718   MERIT

Edwardian hotel recently refurbished and upgraded. Most rooms en-suite. Renowned for excellent value and warm hospitality. Two minutes from promenade. Licensed. Car park. Central heating. TV and tea making facilities all bedrooms. High standard of cuisine and service guaranteed. Special diets by arrangement. Full Christmas and New Year programme. RAC. Les Routiers.*

T C	NIGHTLY B&B PER PERSON		WEEKLY D,B&B PER PERSON		13 10
SP	MIN £ 16.00	MAX £ 18.00	MIN £ 125.00	MAX £ 155.00	OPEN 1-12

COLWYN BAY

WALES *It's magic*

Guest Houses

Crossroads Guest House

Coed Pella Road, Colwyn
Bay, Clwyd LL29 7AT
Tel: (0492) 530736

Victorian house with considerable charm and relaxing atmosphere. Although in the town centre there are scenic views of the woods and mountains from all rooms. All bedrooms have heating, television, tea making facilities, solarium available. Guests returning is our recommendation. An ideal centre for exploring the outstanding scenic and historical areas of North Wales. Proprietors Barry and Margaret Owens.

		NIGHTLY B&B PER PERSON		WEEKLY D,B&B PER PERSON			4
		MIN £	MAX £	MIN £	MAX £		–
		10.0500	11.50	95.00	103.00	OPEN 1-12	

THE WONDER OF WALES (VHS)

The beauty of Wales and its many attractions are the stars of this 24-minute video. The film features Wales's rich cultural and architectural heritage, and includes coverage of the most recent attractions. Narrated by Sian Phillips.

CASTLES AND HISTORIC PLACES IN WALES

A superb full-colour book produced by the Wales Tourist Board and Cadw: Welsh Historic Monuments. Describes over 140 historic sites, including Wales's great medieval castles, Roman remains, elegant country houses and mysterious preshistoric sites. A historic introduction sets the scene and 12 pages of maps help visitors to plan their routes.

CONWY   Map Ref Bb4

Historic town with mighty castle and complete medieval town walls on river bank. Dramatic estuary setting. Many ancient buildings including Aberconwy House and Plas Mawr. Telford suspension Bridge, popular fish quay, spectacular wall walks. Golf, pony trekking, Butterfly House, aquarium, pleasure cruisers. Tiny "smallest house" on quay. Touring centre for Snowdonia with good range of accommodation.

Hotels

Berthlwyd Hall Hotel

Llechwedd, Conwy
Gwynedd LL32 8DQ
Tel: (0492) 592409

AA RAC, Ashley Courtenay and Derek Johannsen recommended. Beautiful Victorian manor hotel of unique charm and character, situated in picturesque Snowdonia National Park. Only 1 mile Conwy Castle, 45 minutes Chester. Residents dining room, Truffles French restaurant, bar, games room, heated outdoor pool. Nine luxurious bedrooms, four poster. Special breaks available. Ideally located golf, horse riding, beaches, Bodnant Garden.

		NIGHTLY B&B PER PERSON		WEEKLY D,B&B PER PERSON			9
		MIN £	MAX £	MIN £	MAX £		8
		35.00	53.00	221.00	334.00	OPEN 1-12	

Castle Bank Hotel

Mount Pleasant, Conwy,
Gwynedd LL32 8NY
Tel: (0492) 593888   MERIT

Family owned hotel in own grounds close to Conwy town walls. All rooms have shower and toilet, colour TV, tea maker and hairdryer. We pride ourselves on our extensive menus and carefully prepared food, which earn us praise for our consistently high standard from our regular cumstomers. We aim to make your holiday a memorable one and look forward to welcoming you to Castle Bank. Write or phone now for brochure and menu.

T	SP	NIGHTLY B&B PER PERSON		WEEKLY D,B&B PER PERSON			9
		MIN £	MAX £	MIN £	MAX £		8
		23.00	23.00	210.00	210.00	OPEN 2-12	

The Lodge

Tal-y-Bont, Conwy,
Gwynedd LL32 8YX
Tel: (0492) 69766   HIGHLY COMMENDED

*Situated in a tranquil rural setting in the peaceful Conwy Valley, you'll find our hotel a perfect spot to explore the spectacular scenery of North Wales. Our restaurant is known for its high standard and uses own grown produce. All rooms en-suite, tea and coffee making, heating, colour TV. AA/RAC**, Ashley Courtenay Recommended. Ideal for walking riding, golf, fishing and sightseeing. Please write or telephone for colour brochure. Open Christmas.*

HW	T	NIGHTLY B&B PER PERSON		WEEKLY D,B&B PER PERSON			10
	C	MIN £	MAX £	MIN £	MAX £		10
SP TW		17.50	25.00	190.00	230.00	OPEN 1-12	

The Old Rectory

Llanrwst Rd., Llansantffraid,
Glan Conwy, Nr Conwy,
Gwynedd LL28 5LF
Tel: (0492) 580611
Fax: (0492) 584555

HIGHLY COMMENDED

Dramatic Snowdonian vistas, breathtaking sunsets and floodlit Conwy Castle are enjoyed from this elegant Georgian country house, idyllically set in 2½ acres of beautiful gardens. Three miles from historic Conwy, Bodnant Garden and Llandudno. Gourmet food, Egon Ronay recommended, served in country house style. Luxury en-suite bedrooms with draped beds. Antiques, paintings for guests to enjoy. BTA Commended. A beautiful haven of peace where a harpist plays on some summer evenings.

HW	T	NIGHTLY B&B PER PERSON		WEEKLY D,B&B PER PERSON		🛏 4
🐕✕						🛁 4
TW		MIN £	MAX £	MIN £	MAX £	OPEN
		30.00	40.00	345.00	395.00	2-11

Tir-y-Coed Country House Hotel

Ro-wen, Conwy, Gwynedd
LL32 8TP
Tel: (0492) 650219

COMMENDED

Set in landscaped gardens in one of Snowdonia's most picturesque villages, Tir-y-Coed combines a peaceful, relaxing atmosphere with high standards of comfort and cuisine. The hotel is situated some four miles inland from Conwy off the B5106 and is ideally placed amidst beautiful scenery for walking, riding, fishing, golfing and sightseeing. All bedrooms have en-suite shower/bathroom, tea/coffee tray, heating and colour television. Licensed. RAC**AA*, Ashley Courteney Recommended. Ample parking.

HW	T	NIGHTLY B&B PER PERSON		WEEKLY D,B&B PER PERSON		🛏 7
🐕	SP					🛁 7
		MIN £	MAX £	MIN £	MAX £	OPEN
		18.00	20.75	177.50	197.00	1-12

The White House Hotel

Bangor Road, Conwy,
Gwynedd LL32 8DP
Tel: (0492) 592420/572236
Fax: (0492) 592420

Situated within walking distance of medieval walled town of Conwy. We have 9 twin/double rooms, 7 en-suite. All have TV, phone, tea/coffee making facilities. Special rates for children. Short breaks available at attractive rates. Plenty of parking space. Close to golfing, hiking, fishing, trekking, skiing. All major credit cards taken.

HW	T	NIGHTLY B&B PER PERSON		WEEKLY D,B&B PER PERSON		🛏 9
🐕	SP					🛁 7
		MIN £	MAX £	MIN £	MAX £	OPEN
		23.00	25.00	184.45	196.35	1-12

Guest Houses

The Old Ship Guest House

28 High Street, Lancaster
Square, Conwy, Gwynedd
LL32 8DE
Tel: (0492) 596445

MERIT

Welcome to our unique 16th century guest house, situated within the historic castle walls, close to all amenities. All our bedrooms are cosy, full of character with colour television, central heating, hand-basin, hairdryer and beverage facilities. Some rooms have en suite facilities. Sample our much talked about Captain's or Admiral's breakfast. Residential licence.

T	🐕	NIGHTLY B&B PER PERSON		WEEKLY D,B&B PER PERSON		🛏 6
SP	🐕✕					🛁 2
		MIN £	MAX £	MIN £	MAX £	OPEN
		13.50	19.00			1-12

CONWY CASTLE

WALES
It's magic

LLANDUDNO
Map Ref Bb3

Premier coastal resort of North Wales with everything the holidaymaker needs. Two beaches, spacious prom, Victorian pier, excellent shops, wide selection of hotels and guest houses. Donkey rides, Punch and Judy, ski slope, Alice in Wonderland exhibition, museums (one featuring old motorcycles) and art gallery. Visit the Great Orme headland above the resort and ride the Cabin Lift and tramway. Conference centre. Many daily coach excursions. ≈

Hotels

Ashby Hotel

31 Church Walks, Llandudno,
Gwynedd LL30 2HL
Tel: (0492) 75608

Attractive Victorian detached house now a comfortable family run licensed hotel. Located between both shores in quiet tree lined road close to Orme, Haulfre Gardens and all amenities. Excellent home cooked food and varied menu. Spacious rooms with en-suite facilities, colour TV, and beverage makers. Twin, double and family rooms available. Pleasant gardens for guests use. Parking space. A very warm welcome awaits you here.

HW T ⃰	NIGHTLY B&B PER PERSON		WEEKLY D,B&B PER PERSON		🛏 7
	MIN £	MAX £	MIN £	MAX £	🛏 7
	13.50		129.50		OPEN 1-12

Ashfields Hotel

32 Deganwy Avenue,
Llandudno, Gwynedd
LL30 2YB
Tel: (0492) 879220

👑👑

Ashfields is a friendly family run hotel offering high standard of comfort, service, home cooking. We aim to please. Situated on the level, close to shops, beaches. Colour TV lounge, licensed, private parking, modern bedrooms with colour TV, teasmade. Access to hotel at all times. Telephone or write for brochure Bob, Val, Carl Cox.

HW T 🐕 SP	NIGHTLY B&B PER PERSON		WEEKLY D,B&B PER PERSON		🛏 11
	MIN £	MAX £	MIN £	MAX £	🛏 2
	11.00	11.00	112.00	112.00	OPEN 1-12

Beach House Hotel

82 Church Walks, Llandudno,
Gwynedd LL30 2HD
Tel: (0492) 77933

👑

Beach House Hotel 40 yards from promenade adjacent to pier, main shopping areas and ski slope. All rooms colour TV, radio, hairdryer, tea/coffee tray. Choice en-suite shower or bath. Home cooked meals with a choice of menu.

HW T 🐕 C SP ➡	NIGHTLY B&B PER PERSON		WEEKLY D,B&B PER PERSON		🛏 8
	MIN £	MAX £	MIN £	MAX £	🛏 4
	13.00	15.00	120.00	130.00	OPEN 1-12

CABLE CAR, LLANDUDNO

Belle Vue Hotel

26 North Parade, Llandudno,
Gwynedd LL30 2LP
Tel: (0492) 879547

👑👑
COMMENDED

Comfortable family run hotel ideally situated on the sea front facing south with lovely views of the bay. AA**RAC**. All rooms en-suite with video, colour television, radio, telephone, hairdryer, tea/coffee tray. Bar. Lift to all floors. Car park. Sun terrace. Snooker and table tennis. Excellent food. A la carte and table d'hôte menu.

HW T 🐕 SP	NIGHTLY B&B PER PERSON		WEEKLY D,B&B PER PERSON		🛏 17
	MIN £	MAX £	MIN £	MAX £	🛏 17
	22.00	26.00	189.00	214.00	OPEN 3-11

The Hatfield Hotel

12 St. David's Road,
Llandudno, Gwynedd
LL30 2UL
Tel: (0492) 76518

👑👑

Here at the Hatfield, we offer you a homely, friendly atmosphere in comfortable centrally heated surroundings, where we pride ourselves on wholesome cooking. All double rooms have en-suite bath or shower. Tea making facilities in all bedrooms. Situated on level ground in a select residential area known as the garden centre of LLandudno.

SP	NIGHTLY B&B PER PERSON		WEEKLY D,B&B PER PERSON		🛏 10
	MIN £	MAX £	MIN £	MAX £	🛏 7
	13.50	15.50	120.00	136.00	OPEN 1-12

WALES *It's magic*

Headlands Hotel

Hill Terrace, Llandudno,
Gwynedd LL30 2LS
Tel: (0492) 77485   MERIT

The only star rated hotel with panoramic views of Llandudno Bay, Conwy Estuary and the mountains of Snowdonia. All bedrooms have sea or country views, some with four poster beds. Headlands' renowned cuisine and quiet elegance ensure a relaxing break from work-a-day routine.

HW T / SP	NIGHTLY B&B PER PERSON		WEEKLY D,B&B PER PERSON		🛏 17 🛌 15
	MIN £ 21.00	MAX £ 23.00	MIN £ 160.00	MAX £ 220.00	OPEN 3-12

Kensington Hotel

Central Promenade,
Llandudno, Gwynedd
LL30 1AT
Tel: (0492) 76784   COMMENDED

A family run hotel situated on the central promenade with views of Snowdonia from the rear. All rooms are en-suite with television and tea and coffee making facilities. Lift to all floors. Daily choice of menu. In-hotel entertainment provided in the bar and ballroom. Large residents car park. The town's amenities are within easy walking distance. Close to conference and leisure centre, theatre and swimming pool. Party rates available. Open Christmas.

HW T	NIGHTLY B&B PER PERSON		WEEKLY D,B&B PER PERSON		🛏 36 🛌 26
	MIN £ 16.50	MAX £ 19.00	MIN £ 147.00	MAX £ 168.00	OPEN 2-12

Ormescliffe Hotel

Promenade, Llandudno,
Gwynedd LL30 1BE
Tel: (0492) 77191   MERIT
Fax: (0492) 860311

An outstanding seafront hotel with an enviable reputation for high standards and friendly, efficient service. All sixty bedrooms have private facilities, colour television, radio and tea and coffee tray. During the summer months dancing and cabaret is featured on several evenings per week. An ideal venue for either business or pleasure.

HW T C	NIGHTLY B&B PER PERSON		WEEKLY D,B&B PER PERSON		🛏 60 🛌 60
	MIN £ 22.00	MAX £ 26.00	MIN £ 215.00	MAX £ 230.00	OPEN 1-12

Hollybank

9 St. David's Place, Llandudno,
Gwynedd LL30 2UG
Tel: (0492) 78521   COMMENDED

Sunny, spacious, tastefully furnished private family hotel, close to all amenities, including station, shops, beaches. Ideally situated for skiing, golf, water sports. Noted by guests for its friendly atmosphere and personal service. Bright pleasant dining room and lounge. Residential licence, lockable off street car park, payphone, CH, fire certificate. All bedrooms spacious and comfortable with colour TVs and drinks facilities, many with en-suites. Children's reductions to 13.

HW	NIGHTLY B&B PER PERSON		WEEKLY D,B&B PER PERSON		🛏 7 🛌 4
	MIN £ 12.00	MAX £ 16.00	MIN £ 112.00	MAX £ 140.00	OPEN 3-11

Lynton House Hotel

80 Church Walks, Llandudno,
Gwynedd LL30 2HD
Tel: (0492) 75057   COMMENDED

A small homely hotel fifty yards from the pier. Close to shops, ski slope and all amenities. All rooms are decorated to a high standard with bathroom en-suite, colour TV, tea/coffee tray and telephone. Highly recommended home cooking with choice of menu. 4 poster room available. Special diets catered for.

HW T C / SP	NIGHTLY B&B PER PERSON		WEEKLY D,B&B PER PERSON		🛏 8 🛌 8
	MIN £ 14.00	MAX £ 17.50	MIN £ 130.00	MAX £ 160.00	OPEN 1-12

Ravenhurst Hotel

West Shore, Llandudno,
Gwynedd LL30 2BB
Tel: (0492) 75525   COMMENDED

Superb situation on lovely West Shore. Wonderful views of sea and mountains. Choice of menu. Diets catered for. Ground floor bedrooms, heated throughout. All rooms en-suite with colour TV. Games room. Golf, riding, swimming, sailing all nearby. Residential licence. Ideal for touring Snowdonia and North Wales. Return bookings are our recommendation. Phone now for brochure.

HW T / SP	NIGHTLY B&B PER PERSON		WEEKLY D,B&B PER PERSON		🛏 24 🛌 24
	MIN £ 21.00	MAX £ 23.00	MIN £ 193.00	MAX £ 202.50	OPEN 3-11

WALES: BED AND BREAKFAST GUIDE 1991

Wales offers great-value budget B&B accommodation — and this guide proves it, by featuring over 500 hotels, guest houses and farmhouses where you can stay for just £16 or under per person per night. The Guide also contains detailed maps and comprehensive holiday information.

Sunnydowns Hotel

66 Abbey Road,
Rhos On Sea, Clwyd
LL28 4NU
Tel: (0492) 44256
Central Reservations: (0492) 530010

MERIT

You are assured of a warm and friendly welcome at the Sunnydowns with every bedroom having a private bathroom, colour TV, in house video, clock radio and tea/coffee making facilities. 2 minutes walk to beach, shops, bowling, squash, tennis, water sports, 5 minutes drive to Llandudno and Colwyn Bay. TV lounge. Licensed bar and restaurant. Games room with pool table etc. Children and pets welcome. Special Xmas breaks.

HW T	NIGHTLY B&B PER PERSON		WEEKLY D,B&B PER PERSON		🛏 15
	MIN £	MAX £	MIN £	MAX £	🛏 15
	17.00	17.00	160.00	160.00	OPEN 1-12

Tan Lan Hotel

Great Orme's Road,
West Shore, Llandudno,
Gwynedd LL30 2AR
Tel: (0492) 860221

COMMENDED

*Elegant RAC/AA ** licensed hotel situated on quieter West Shore at foot of Great Orme, yet close to all amenities. Excellent cuisine prepared by chef/proprietor with full choice of menu. All rooms at ground or first floor level with en-suite facilities, colour TV, tea/coffee maker, clock radio. R.A.C. Hospitality "H". Hotel fully centrally heated with two relaxing lounges. Ideal for touring Snowdonia. Private car park. Mini breaks, midweek bookings accepted. Highly recommended.*

SP	NIGHTLY B&B PER PERSON		WEEKLY D,B&B PER PERSON		🛏 18
	MIN £	MAX £	MIN £	MAX £	🛏 18
	20.00	22.00	175.00	184.00	OPEN 3-11

Waverley Hotel

North Parade, Llandudno,
Gwynedd LL30 2LP
Tel: (0492) 76933

MERIT

Superb seafront position only yards from pier and shops. This family run hotel provides good service and pleasing choice of menu. All bedrooms are spacious and have tea making, clock/radios, colour TV and most have sea views. Enjoy our private sun terrace, sauna, central heating and beautiful sea and mountain views.

SP	NIGHTLY B&B PER PERSON		WEEKLY D,B&B PER PERSON		🛏 15
	MIN £	MAX £	MIN £	MAX £	🛏 10
	13.00	15.00	120.00	135.00	OPEN 3-10

Westbourne Hotel

8 Arvon Avenue, Llandudno,
Gwynedd LL30 2DY
Tel: (0492) 77450

Very central and on flat ground. chef proprietor. All bedrooms contain colour TV, tea mkaing facilities, full central heating, some also en-suite including one on the ground floor. First class food and service. Pensioner reductions. Near to sea and shops. R.A.C.and Les Routiers. Licenced. Open Christmas. SAE for brochure or phone Doris.

SP	NIGHTLY B&B PER PERSON		WEEKLY D,B&B PER PERSON		🛏 13
	MIN £	MAX £	MIN £	MAX £	🛏 4
	13.00	14.50	115.50	122.50	OPEN 3-12

Guest Houses

Stoneleigh Guest House

10 St. David's Road,
Llandudno, Gwynedd
LL30 2UL
Tel: (0492) 75056

Homely run family guest house situated in quiet residential area on level. Few minutes from town, railway, bus and all facilities. Comfortable TV lounge, dining room with separate tables. High standard cuisine. Personal attention guaranteed. Tea making facilities in all rooms. Access to rooms at all times. Central heating throughout. Car park.

HW T SP	NIGHTLY B&B PER PERSON		WEEKLY D,B&B PER PERSON		🛏 7
	MIN £	MAX £	MIN £	MAX £	
	12.50	14.00	122.50	133.00	OPEN 1-12

CASTLES AND HISTORIC PLACES IN WALES

A superb full-colour book produced jointly by the Wales Tourist Board and Cadw: Welsh Historic Monuments. Describes over 140 historic sites, including Wales's great medieval castles, Roman remains, elegant country houses and mysterious prehistoric sites. A historic introduction sets the scene and 12 pages of maps help visitors to plan their routes.

WALES *It's magic*

RHOS-ON-SEA

RHOS-ON-SEA
Map Ref Bc4

Attractive seaside village linking Llandudno and Colwyn Bay with promenade, beach, golf, water skiing, puppet theatre. Colwyn Bay Mountain Zoo nearby.

Guest Houses

The Cedar Tree

27 Whitehall Rd., Rhos-on-Sea
Colwyn Bay, Clwyd
LL28 4HU
Tel: (0492) 45867

MERIT

Comfortable friendly guest house 300 yards promenade. Convenient Snowdonia National Park, North Wales castles, Bodnant Gardens, Conwy, railway/coach stations within 1 mile. Private parking. En-suite facilities all bedrooms. Central heating. Tea/coffee making facilities, family room available. Special rates for children sharing parents' room. Excellent cuisine, separate tables. Attractive lounge with colour television. Fire certificate. Weekly terms available. Excellent value.

	NIGHTLY B&B PER PERSON		WEEKLY D,B&B PER PERSON		7
					7
	MIN £	MAX £	MIN £	MAX £	OPEN
	13.00	16.00	123.00	137.00	1-11

RHYL
Map Ref Bd4

Fun-packed coast resort offering all-round entertainment. The Sun Centre "indoor beach" with swimming pool, surfing pool and slides together with 240ft Sky Tower are two major attractions; others include Ocean World, Knights Cavern, Big Funfair, Marine Lake, Superbowl, Botanical Gardens. Safe swimming, sailing. Extensive holiday caravan parks. Ideal seaside resort for the whole family.

Hotels

Pier Hotel

23 East Parade, Rhyl,
Clwyd LL18 3AL
Tel: (0745) 350280

Give yourself a treat. Come and stay at the Pier Hotel. Seafront, en-suite, colour television in all rooms, teasmade facilities, bar. Warm welcome. Personal attention at all times. 5 minutes from sea. 5 minutes from town.

T SP	NIGHTLY B&B PER PERSON		WEEKLY D,B&B PER PERSON		9
					6
	MIN £	MAX £	MIN £	MAX £	OPEN
	11.00	13.00	70.00	90.00	1-12

SLIDE PACKS

The following slide packs are available for purchase from the Wales Tourist Board:

North Wales Scenery	£2.00	(4 slides)
Mid Wales Scenery	£2.00	(4 slides)
South Wales Scenery	£2.00	(4 slides)
Historic Sites	£3.00	(6 slides)

Contact: Photo Librarian, WTB, Brunel House, 2 Fitzalan Road, Cardiff CF2 1UY

RHYL HARBOUR

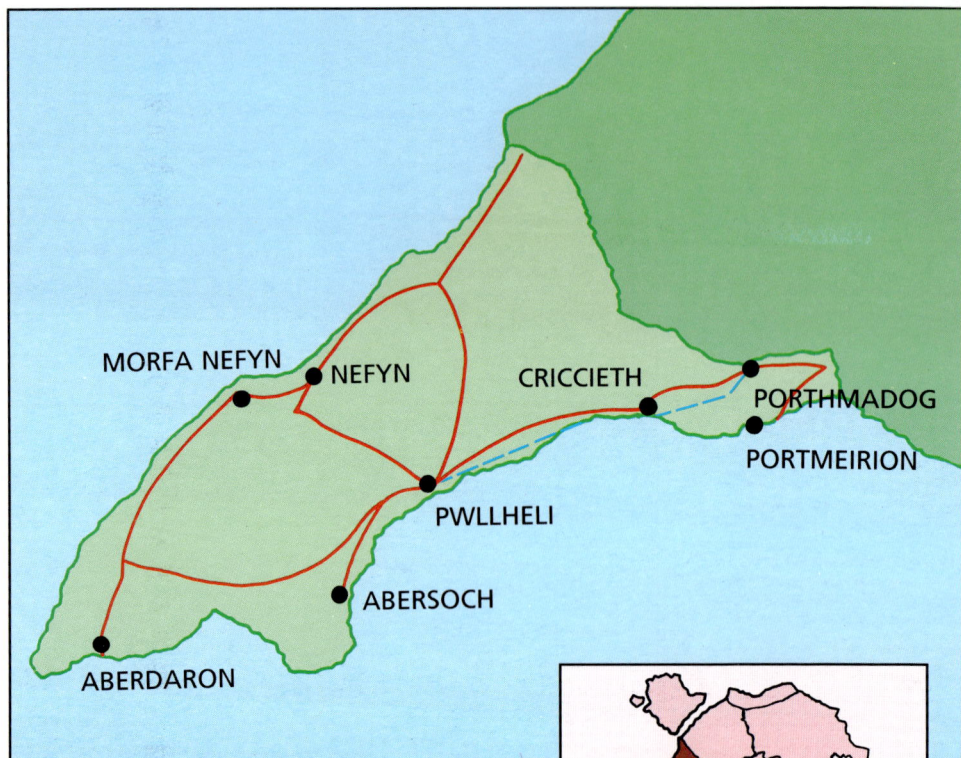

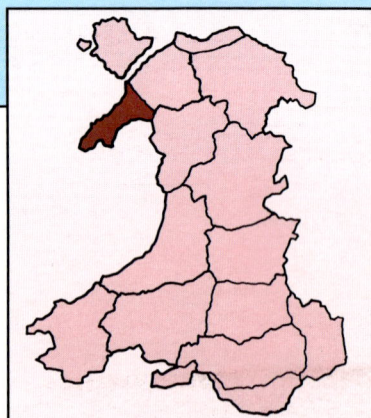

The Llŷn Peninsula is another of North Wales's 'Areas of Outstanding Natural Beauty'. The accolade applies to the spectacular coastline fringing this narrow finger of land that points straight into the sea from Snowdonia. At times – around the charming little resorts of Criccieth, Pwllheli and Nefyn – the coast has a gentle, sandy character. But along other parts of this peaceful peninsula, mountains take a shuddering plunge into the sea as land meets water along a curtain of cliffs.

Llŷn is a peninsula of storm-tossed headlands and sheltered bays. It is a resilient, remote part of Wales where traditional ways live on, and where the old ports of Porthmadog and Abersoch have found new life as busy sailing centres.

Starcoast World at Pwllheli offers a fun-packed day out for the whole family.

ABERDARON
Map Ref Aa5

Small picturesque village on tip of Llŷn Peniinsula. Pilgrims making for Bardsey Island, clearly seen across Bardsey Sound, used to rest at Y Gegin Fawr, now a cafe and souvenir shop.

Guest Houses

Carreg Plas Guest House

Aberdaron, Pwllheli,
Gwynedd LL53 8LH
Tel: (075886) 308

👑👑
MERIT

17th century manor house of historic interest in secluded wooded grounds, two miles from Aberdaron, close to the Whistling Sands beach, surrounded by stretches of magnificent coastline largely National Trust owned. Range of room sizes, most having own facilities. Home cooking of high standard. Special reductions for children. Cots and highchairs provided. No Smoking in the house.

🐕 SP 🍴	NIGHTLY B&B PER PERSON		WEEKLY D,B&B PER PERSON		🛏 7
	MIN £	MAX £	MIN £	MAX £	🛏 4
	13.00	17.00	135.00	160.00	OPEN 1-12

ABERSOCH
Map Ref Ac5

Dinghy sailing and windsurfing centre with safe sandy beaches. Superb coastal scenery with easy walks. Pony trekking, golf, fishing and sea trips. Llanengan's historic church nearby.

Hotels

Belmont Private Hotel

Lôn Sarn Bach, Abersoch,
Gwynedd LL53 7EE
Tel: (075881) 2121

👑👑
MERIT

Licensed private hotel near beach and village. Family rooms with special rates for children, cot, highchair available, also single, double rooms all with heating and vanity units, beverage trays. Guest TV/ video lounge, well stocked bar, patio, dining room with separate tables, car park. Fresh home cooked evening meals or bar food available with vegetarian and specialist diets catered for. Riding, sailing, golf, walking, fishing nearby. Low season breaks. Brochure on request.

HW T 🐕 SP 🍴	NIGHTLY B&B PER PERSON		WEEKLY D,B&B PER PERSON		🛏 6
	MIN £	MAX £	MIN £	MAX £	🛏 –
	13.00	15.00	130.00	147.00	OPEN 1-12

Egryn Hotel

Lôn Sarn Bach, Abersoch,
Gwynedd LL53 7EE
Tel: (075881) 2332

👑
👑👑

Situated within easy walking distance of beach, village, golf course and other amenities. Egryn is a licensed hotel and restaurant offering superb accommodation, friendly atmosphere and good varied catering. Since beginning in 1981 we have established a reputation for quality and value and have now been awarded RAC** status having met all the stringent requirements this level now demands.

HW T 🐕	NIGHTLY B&B PER PERSON		WEEKLY D,B&B PER PERSON		🛏 7
	MIN £	MAX £	MIN £	MAX £	🛏 5
	14.50	25.00			OPEN 1-12

Tudor Court Hotel and Restaurant

Lôn Sarn Bach, Abersoch,
Gwynedd LL53 7EB
Tel: (075881) 3354

👑
👑👑
COMMENDED

Situated in the ideal position, just 3 minutes from the village and the beach. Also convenient for the golf course, horse riding, sailing and touring the beautiful Llŷn Peninsula. All rooms have their own facilities and colour TV. Weekend or mid-week breaks arranged. Bar lounge. Assuring you of a warm welcome at all times. Open all year including Christmas and New Year. Ashley Courtenay recommend R.A.C. **.

HW T 🐕 SP	NIGHTLY B&B PER PERSON		WEEKLY D,B&B PER PERSON		🛏 7
	MIN £	MAX £	MIN £	MAX £	🛏 6
	19.50	28.50	200.00	270.00	OPEN 1-12

ABERSOCH BEACH

Guest Houses

Berwyn Guest House

Lôn Golff, Abersoch,
Gwynedd LL53 7EF
Tel: (075881) 2392

One minute from beach and golf course, Berwyn is ideally situated, central yet a peaceful location. Comfortable heated rooms (some en-suite), have colour television, tea/ coffee facilities. Fresh home cooked evening meals available, with comfortable lounge in which to relax. Ample parking. A warm welcome awaits at Berwyn.

HW	T	NIGHTLY B&B PER PERSON		WEEKLY D,B&B PER PERSON		🛏 5
🐕	SP	MIN £	MAX £	MIN £	MAX £	🛏 2
		11.00		125.00		OPEN 1-12

Tŷ Draw Guest House

Lôn Sarn Bach, Abersoch,
Gwynedd LL53 7EL
Tel: (075881) 2647

COMMENDED

Beautiful guest house with sea and mountain views, set in large attractive gardens in a quieter part of the village yet only 5 minutes walk to the beach and shops. Ideal centre for walking and all water sports. Single, double and family rooms with reduced rates for children. All rooms have vanitory units. Comfortable lounge with TV, tea and coffee facilities. Large and secure car/boat park.

HW	T	NIGHTLY B&B PER PERSON		WEEKLY D,B&B PER PERSON		🛏 7
🐕		MIN £	MAX £	MIN £	MAX £	🛏 –
		11.00				OPEN 4-9

CRICCIETH   Map Ref Ad7

Ideal family resort, with safe beach and seafront hotels. Romantic ruined castle overlooking sea. Salmon and sea trout in nearby rivers and lakes. Festival of Music and the Arts in June

Hotels

Glyn y Coed Hotel

Porthmadog Road, Criccieth,
Gwynedd LL52 0HL
Tel: (0766) 522870
Fax: (0766) 523341

MERIT

Lovely Victorian house overlooking sea, mountains and Criccieth Castle. AA/RAC Listed. Cosy bar, highly recommended home cooking. En-suite bedrooms with colour TV, tea making facilities, central heating, parking in grounds. Children welcome, moderate rates. Special parties catered for at reduced rates. Brochure with pleasure. Send SAE please.

HW	T	NIGHTLY B&B PER PERSON		WEEKLY D,B&B PER PERSON		🛏 9
🐕	SP	MIN £	MAX £	MIN £	MAX £	🛏 8
		16.00		150.00		OPEN 1-11

CASTLES AND HISTORIC PLACES IN WALES

A superb full-colour book produced by the Wales Tourist Board and Cadw: Welsh Historic Monuments. Describes over 140 historic sites, including Wales's great medieval castles, Roman remains, elegant country houses and mysterious preshitoric sites. A historic introduction sets the scene and 12 pages of maps help visitors to plan their notes.

Min-y-Gaer Hotel

Porthmadog Road, Criccieth,
Gwynedd LL52 0HP
Tel: (0766) 522151

MERIT

A pleasant, licensed hotel, conveniently situated near the beach, with delightful views of the Cardigan Bay coastline. 10 comfortable rooms (9 en-suite) are all centrally heated and have a colour TV and tea/coffee making facilities. An Ideal base for touring Snowdonia. Reduced rates for children. Car park. AA/RAC Listed. Brochure on request.

HW	T	NIGHTLY B&B PER PERSON		WEEKLY D,B&B PER PERSON		🛏 10
🐕	C					
SP		MIN £	MAX £	MIN £	MAX £	🛏 9
		13.50	17.00	136.00	156.00	OPEN 3-10

Guest Houses

Craig-y-Môr Guest House

West Parade, Criccieth,
Gwynedd LL52 0EN
Tel: (0766) 522830

COMMENDED

Having decided on North Wales, now contact us. Top value. We are on the west front of Criccieth, ideally situated for touring Snowdonia, Meirionnydd and Llŷn Peninsula. We offer home cooking (including vegetarian), comfortable, single to family size bedrooms with en-suite facilities, radio and television, parking, full central heating. Children very welcome. Do come and join us - a warm welcome awaits you. A. & B. Williamson.

HW	T	NIGHTLY B&B PER PERSON		WEEKLY D,B&B PER PERSON		🛏 7
🐕	SP	MIN £	MAX £	MIN £	MAX £	🛏 7
		14.00	16.00	140.00	153.00	OPEN 2-10

WALES It's magic

MORFA NEFYN
Map Ref Ab6

Popular Llŷn Peninsula seaside village, with extensive sandy beaches, between little harbour at Porthdinllaen and resort of Nefyn. Set against mountainous backdrop of Garn Boduan. Historical and Maritime Museum at Nefyn.

Hotels

Erw Goch Hotel

Morfa Nefyn Pwllheli
Gwynedd LL53 6BW
Tel: (0758) 720539

Family hotel in own grounds with large car park. Ideally situated to take full advantage of the many sandy beaches, fine picturesque golf courses, recreational persuits and places of historic interest nearby. Family holidays or short breaks all year round. Licensed bar ¼ snooker table, table tennis.

HW T SP	NIGHTLY B&B PER PERSON		WEEKLY D,B&B PER PERSON		🛏 15
	MIN £	MAX £	MIN £	MAX £	🛏 0
	16.00	17.50	160.00	180.00	OPEN 1-12

NEFYN
Map Ref Ab6

Old fishing village on Llŷn Peninsula perched above sweeping bay. Two miles of sand, safe swimming, sailing and fishing. Visit the Llŷn Historical and Maritime Museum.

Hotels

Caeau Capel Hotel

Rhodfa'r Môr, Nefyn,
Pwllheli Gwynedd
LL53 6EB
Tel: (0758) 720240

COMMENDED

Family run hotel in own grounds with tennis, putting green and gardens. Ideally situated for beach, golf, sailing and fishing. Children and dogs welcome. Short breaks at special terms. Excellent home cooking. Golf breaks arranged. Resident proprietors Ron and Sylvia Beard. RAC and AA*.

HW T SP	NIGHTLY B&B PER PERSON		WEEKLY D,B&B PER PERSON		🛏 19
	MIN £	MAX £	MIN £	MAX £	🛏 12
	18.95	24.84	159.00	211.15	OPEN 3-10

Dolwen House

Ffordd Dewi Sant, Nefyn,
Gwynedd LL53 6EA
Tel: (0758) 720667

MERIT

Charming detached house, near centre of Nefyn assuring peace and quiet with ample parking. Ideally situated for touring or exploring the Llŷn and Snowdonia. Well furnished heated bedrooms, tea/coffee making facilities. Licensed residents bar, comfortable TV lounge. Evening meal or bar/restaurant and vegetarian menu available. Recommended for fine food and warm atmosphere.

🐕 SP	NIGHTLY B&B PER PERSON		WEEKLY D,B&B PER PERSON		🛏 6
	MIN £	MAX £	MIN £	MAX £	🛏 0
	14.00	15.50	132.00	142.00	OPEN 1-12

Nanhoron Arms Hotel

Fford Dewi Sant, Nefyn,
Pwllheli, Gwynedd LL53 6EA
Tel: (0758) 720203

COMMENDED

The Nanhoron Arms Hotel is situated in Nefyn, on the Llŷn Peninsula, 500 yards from the beautiful Horseshoe Bay with cliff top walks, close to Caernarfon, Pwllheli and Abersoch. Children welcome with their own special menu and safe fully equipped play area. We have 19 fully fitted en-suite bedrooms with beverage facilities, hairdryer, direct dial telephone, including family rooms. Relax and dine in our exclusive St. David's Restaurant. Golfing, shooting. Breaks available.

🐕 SP TW	NIGHTLY B&B PER PERSON		WEEKLY D,B&B PER PERSON		🛏 19
	MIN £	MAX £	MIN £	MAX £	🛏 19
	21.50	30.00	225.00	295.00	OPEN 1-12

CRICCIETH BEACH AND CASTLE

PORTHMADOG
Map Ref Ae7

Harbour town and shopping centre named after William Madocks, who built mile-long Cob embankment. Steam narrow-gauge Ffestiniog Railway runs to Blaenau Ffestiniog, with its slate caverns. Also Welsh Highland Railway. Pottery, maritime museum, car museum. Portmeirion Italianate village and good beaches nearby.

Hotels

Tan yr Onnen Hotel

Penamser Road, Porthmadog, Gwynedd LL49 9NY
Tel: (0766) 512443

MERIT

Tony and Betty Dady, resident proprietors, offer you friendly hospitality at their attractive private hotel situated in its own gardens at the edge of town. Within easy reach of beautiful sandy beaches and spectacular Snowdonia. Twelve rooms, single, double, twin and family (some en-suite) plus breakfast. Hot and cold water, heating, shaver points, beverage making facilities and colour TV in all bedrooms. Ample car parking. Les Routiers recommended.

HW T ⌘✕	NIGHTLY B&B PER PERSON		WEEKLY D,B&B PER PERSON		🛏 12
	MIN £	MAX £	MIN £	MAX £	🛁 3
	15.00	18.75			OPEN 3-12

Guest Houses

35 Madoc Street

Porthmadog,
Gwynedd LL49 9BU
Tel: (0765) 512843

L

Friendly welcome for all. Good home cooking, heating in all rooms, TV lounge, tea/coffee making facilities, keys supplied. Special rates for children. Shops, buses, trains, cinema nearby. Ideally situated for visiting Portmeirion Italianate Village, the mountains of Snowdonia, the Ffestiniog Railway steam trains, the lovely sandy beaches are near. Open all year. Proprietor Mrs R. Skellern.

HW T 🐕	NIGHTLY B&B PER PERSON		WEEKLY D,B&B PER PERSON		🛏 3
	MIN £	MAX £	MIN £	MAX £	🛁 0
	9.00	11.00	98.00	105.00	OPEN 1-12

The Oakleys Guest House

The Harbour, Porthmadog,
Gwynedd LL49 9AS
Tel: (0766) 512482

L

Situated on the harbour in Porthmadog. Licensed. An excellent base for visiting Snowdonia, Portmeirion and the beaches of Llŷn Peninsula, taking in Pwllheli, Abersoch and Criccieth. Fishing, sea trout, salmon, golf course nearby. Spacious free car park. Comfortable lounge. Informal holiday atmosphere. Two bedrooms with showers, one bedroom en-suite. Electric blankets. Contact Mr & Mrs A. H. Biddle proprietors.

HW	NIGHTLY B&B PER PERSON		WEEKLY D,B&B PER PERSON		🛏 8
	MIN £	MAX £	MIN £	MAX £	👍 1
	12.00	13.00	110.00	120.00	OPEN 3-10

Farmhouses

Cefn Uchaf Guest House

Garndolbenmaen,
Porthmadog, Gwynedd
LL51 9PJ
Tel: (076675) 239

COMMENDED

Secluded modernised farmhouse in 12½ acres. Central heating, log fires. Comfortable bedrooms with H&C, colour TV, tea/coffee making facilities. Lounge, games room. Fire certificate. Excellent home cooking with interesting varied menu. Vegetarian meals a speciality. Packed lunches. Railways, castles, beaches, mountains very close. Fishing, riding, golf nearby. Play area and donkey rides for children. Friendly farm animals. Pets welcome. Special rates for children. For brochure please contact Anne or Chris Easton.

T 🐕 ⌘✕	NIGHTLY B&B PER PERSON		WEEKLY D,B&B PER PERSON		🛏 9
	MIN £	MAX £	MIN £	MAX £	🛁 2
	12.75	15.00	127.00	149.00	OPEN 1-12

PORTMEIRION BEACH

PWLLHELI   Map Ref Ac7

Small resort big in appeal to sailors; 200 craft are moored in its Outer Harbour. Promenade with excellent, spacious beach, shopping, golf, Leisure Centre. River and sea fishing. Exciting Starcoast World, a major attraction, nearby.

Nantcol Saddlery & Welsh Pony Stud

Ty'n-y-Mynydd Farm, Boduan, Pwllheli, Gwynedd LL53 8PZ
Tel: (0758) 720311

L

Set on the glorious Llŷn Peninsula. The farm is an ideal base for holidays, near to all amenities, beaches, 18 hole golf course. 10 minutes from Pwllheli. Traditional 200 year old farmhouse offers B&B, home cooking, self catering in charming cottage or 6 berth caravan. All bed linen free. Ample space for touring caravans, tents. Pets welcome. Situated at home of world famous champion Nantcol Welsh Pony Stud.

	NIGHTLY B&B PER PERSON		WEEKLY D,B&B PER PERSON			2
HW T						0
SP	MIN £	MAX £	MIN £	MAX £	OPEN 1-12	
	12.00	15.00				

PORTHMADOG BEACH

LET A GUIDE SHOW YOU THE WAY

Why not book a Wales Official Tourist Guide for your next visit to Wales. Fees are very reasonable and a driver/guide can take the strain out of navigation and map reading whilst you sit back and enjoy your tour. Members of the Wales Official Tourist Guide Association are the only qualified tourist guides in Wales and the association is registered with the Wales Tourist Board. Any kind of guided tours are undertaken – from hourly tours by car or coach from a designated centre, to extended tours of any duration throughout Wales. For more information contact Gwennie Johnson, W.O.T.G.A., Cae'r Felin, Chwilog, Criccieth, Gwynedd LL53 6SW. Tel: (0766) 810889.

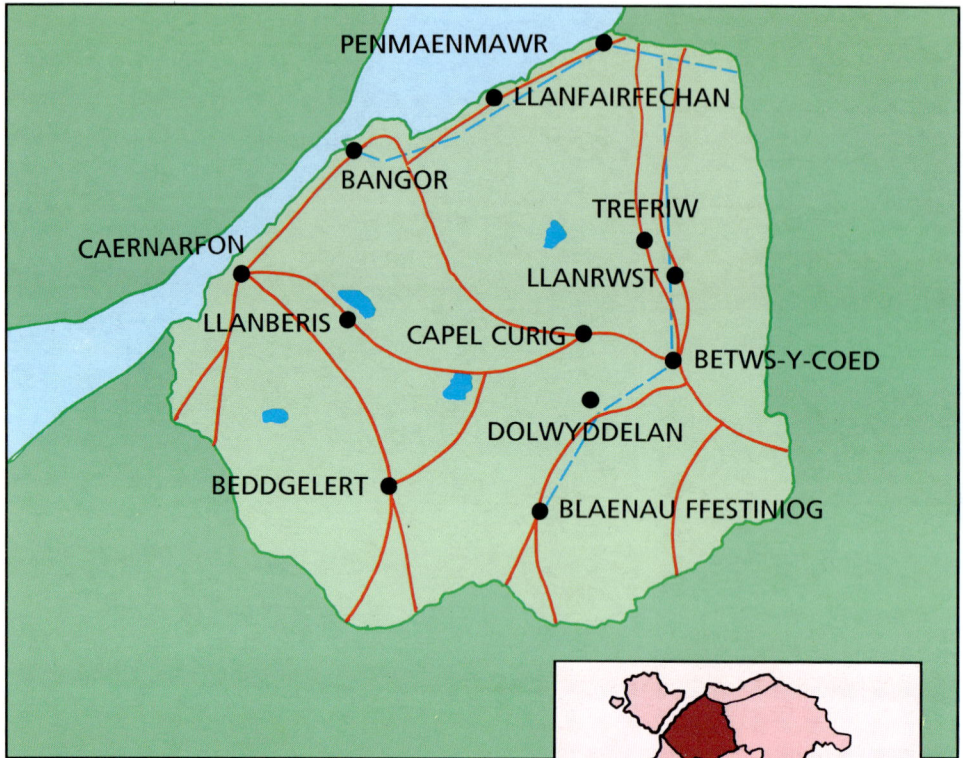

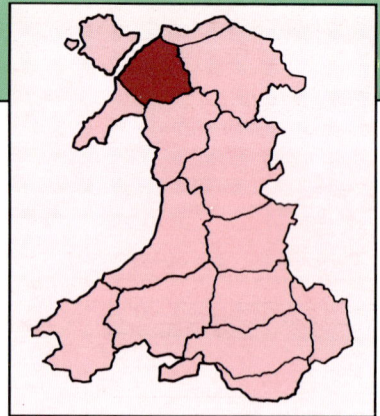

The highest peaks in England and Wales are to be found here – not that you'll have to look far to find them. Mount Snowdon, the rugged heart of the Snowdonia National Park, dominates the horizon.

Llanberis, always popular as a base for walkers and climbers, is also a centre of great attractions. Visit the National Slate Museum, Padarn Country Park, Dolbadarn Castle and the 'Power of Wales' for an underground trip through the tunnels of the Dinorwig hydro-electric scheme. Or take a ride on the Llanberis Lake Railway or the famous Snowdon Mountain Railway.

Pretty Beddgelert, like everything else in this area, is dwarfed by the ever-present mountains. Even mighty Caernarfon Castle, Wales's most famous fortress, seems subdued by its surroundings. Bangor's Penrhyn Castle is a fabulous re-creation, built by a 19th-century slate baron (take a look at charming Bangor Pier, restored to its original splendour, while you're there). At Blaenau Ffestiniog you can go underground at Llechwedd Slate Caverns and Gloddfa Ganol Slate Mine. And if you want a bird's-eye view of those mountains, then hop on a flight from the new Caernarfon Air World.

BEDDGELERT
Map Ref Ae6

Village romantically set amid glorious mountain scenery, with Nant Gwynant to the east and rocky Aberglaslyn Pass to the south. Snowdonia's grandeur all around; Wordsworth made a famous dawn ascent of Mount Snowdon from here. Marvellous walks; links with legendery dog named Gelert. Visit the Sygun Copper Mine and Cae Du Farm Park, two nearby attractions.

Hotels

Bryn Eglwys Country House Hotel

Beddgelert,
Gwynedd LL55 4NB
Tel: (076686) 210

COMMENDED

Bryn Eglwys has a glorious setting in the heart of Snowdonia close to the River Glaslyn. Off the main road in its own grounds with fabulous views, the hotel overlooks the picturesque village of Beddgelert and places priority on fine facilities, including full en-suite bathrooms, excellent cuisine and relaxing atmosphere.

	NIGHTLY B&B PER PERSON		WEEKLY D,B&B PER PERSON		🛏 16
HW T SP 🐾 ♿	MIN £	MAX £	MIN £	MAX £	🛁 12
	27.00	32.00			OPEN 1-12

Sygun Fawr Country Hotel

Beddgelert,
Gwynedd LL55 4NE
Tel: (076686) 258

MERIT

In the heart of Snowdonia, secluded 17th century Welsh manor house commaning magnificent views of the Gwynant Valley and Snowdon range. Open all year. Licensed. Ideal base for walking. Sauna available. En-suite bedrooms, tea/coffee facilities. Home cooking, vegetarian menu. Proprietors N. & M. Wilson and S. & C. Crick.

	NIGHTLY B&B PER PERSON		WEEKLY D,B&B PER PERSON		🛏 7
🐾 SP	MIN £	MAX £	MIN £	MAX £	🛁 6
	15.00	19.00	159.00	183.00	OPEN 1-12

Tanronen Hotel

Beddgelert,
Gwynedd LL55 4YB
Tel: (076686) 347

Situated at the head of the magnificent Glaslyn Pass amidst grandeur of mountains, rushing streams, placid lakes, deep forests, all are here in abundance. Excellent cuisine. Fully centrally heated. Colour TV available in bedrooms. Two intimate little bars. Access and Barclaycard accepted. Robinsons Traditional Draught Beers.

	NIGHTLY B&B PER PERSON		WEEKLY D,B&B PER PERSON		🛏 8
HW T SP	MIN £	MAX £	MIN £	MAX £	🛁 0
	17.50	17.50	170.00	170.00	OPEN 1-12

Guest House

Ael y Bryn

Caernarfon Road,
Beddgelert, Gwynedd LL55 4UY
Tel: (076686) 310

A detached house with beautiful views across the River Colwyn and Moel Hebog Mountain. All rooms have vanity units, shaver points and tea/coffee making facilities. Guests own lounge with TV. Good home cooked evening meals available. Vegetarians welcome. Ample free parking. A well situated guest house, ideal for holidays in the Snowdonia National Park, yet only a short drive from beautiful beaches.

	NIGHTLY B&B PER PERSON		WEEKLY D,B&B PER PERSON		🛏 3
SP ♿	MIN £	MAX £	MIN £	MAX £	🛁 0
	12.00		133.00		OPEN 1-12

Colwyn Guest House

Beddgelert
Gwynedd LL55
Tel: (076686) 276

18th century cottage guest house. Small, warm and friendly. Beamed lounge, log fire in original stone fireplace. Overlooking river in centre of picturesque village surrounded by mountains. Spectacular scenery winter and summer. Perfect base for touring Snowdonia's valleys, lakes and forests. Little shops/inns/cafes in village. Central heating. Small bar. Real food to prior order. 3 day discount. Walkers welcome, group rates.

	NIGHTLY B&B PER PERSON		WEEKLY D,B&B PER PERSON		🛏 6
HW T C SP	MIN £	MAX £	MIN £	MAX £	🛁 2
	11.00	15.00	133.00		OPEN 1-12

BEDDGELERT VILLAGE

WALES
It's magic

Plas Colwyn Guest House

Beddgelert,
Gwynedd LL55 4UY
Tel: (076686) 458

Lynda and John Osmond invite you to explore the beauty of Snowdonia then come back to a warm welcome, in this idyllic village. We offer delicious home cooked meals, and are licensed. Vegetarians welcome. All rooms are centrally heated, bedrooms have H&C, tea and coffee facilities. Guests private lounge and private off road parking. It's just the place to relax in comfort, and we are non smoking throughout.

HW T	NIGHTLY B&B		WEEKLY D,B&B		🛏 6
🐕 C	PER PERSON		PER PERSON		
SP 🍴	MIN £	MAX £	MIN £	MAX £	🛏 2
	12.00	15.00	131.60	150.50	OPEN 1-12

BETWS-Y-COED
Map Ref Bb6

Wooded village and popular mountain resort in picturesque setting where three rivers meet. Good hotels and guest houses, close to best mountain area of Snowdonia. Tumbling rivers and waterfalls emerge from a tangle of treetops. Trout fishing, craft shops, golf course, railway and motor museums, Snowdonia National Park Visitor Centre. Nature trails very popular hikers. Swallow Falls a "must". 🚆

SWALLOW FALLS

Hotels

Cae'r Berllan Restaurant with rooms

Betws Road, Nr Llanrwst,
Gwynedd LL26 0PP
Tel: (0492) 640027

Complete tranquility reigns in this magnificent 16th century country house built in 1570. Full of massive oak beams and family antiques. Perfectly situated for exploring the Snowdonia/North Wales area between Betws-y-Coed and Llanrwst. Luxurious beamed bedrooms, private facilities TV etc Wonderful views from every window. Renowned for high standards of cuisine served in the relaxed atmosphere of our inglenook dining room.

HW T	NIGHTLY B&B		WEEKLY D,B&B		🛏 2
🐕 SP	PER PERSON		PER PERSON		
🍴	MIN £	MAX £	MIN £	MAX £	🛏 2
	20.00	25.00	–	–	OPEN 1-12

Craig Dinas Country Hotel

Dinas Hill, Betws-y-Coed,
Gwynedd LL24 0HF
Tel: (0690) 710254

Magnificent view, best in Wales. Very friendly atmosphere. Home cooking. A la carte restaurant. Licensed. Easy access to Snowdon mountains, forts and castles. Ample walking tracks through forest of Snowdonia National Park. Hotel set in 5 acres of wooded private ground. Log fires, CH all rooms. Pony trekking, climbing, fishing, golf. Forty minutes to beach. We overlook Lledr Valley, the most beautiful valley in Britain, mountains beyond. Ideal centre to see North Wales.

HW 🐕	NIGHTLY B&B		WEEKLY D,B&B		🛏 8
SP	PER PERSON		PER PERSON		
	MIN £	MAX £	MIN £	MAX £	🛏 5
	16.50	20.00	175.00	190.00	OPEN 1-12

Craig y Dderwen Country House Hotel

Betws-y-Coed,
Gwynedd LL24 0AS
Tel: (06902) 293 / 362
Fax: 06902 362

Welcome to our elegant 3 star comfy house hotel in a dramatic alpine setting in 5 acres of secluded gardens on the banks of the River Conwy only minutes walk from the heart of Betws-y-Coed. Recently refurbished, 18 luxurious bedrooms, four poster suites, log fires, fine wines and exciting cuisine, including vegetarian from the repertoire of the chef proprietor. Gourmet breaks, honeymoon hushaways and activity holidays arranged locally. Children welcome.

🐕 SP	NIGHTLY B&B		WEEKLY D,B&B		🛏 18
	PER PERSON		PER PERSON		
	MIN £	MAX £	MIN £	MAX £	🛏 18
	27.00	37.50	240.00	299.00	OPEN 1-12

Cross Keys Hotel & Restaurant

Betws-y-Coed,
Gwynedd LL24 0BN
Tel: (0690) 710334

14th century hotel of character with golf, pony trekking and fishing in close proximity. Ideally situated for walking and climbing in Snowdonia. Comfortable and friendly family run hotel. Some bedrooms private facilities, others own vanity units plus ample shower facilities. Superb restaurant, full 'a la carte or table d'hôte menus, bar menus available. Also available - riding, two day breaks.

SP	NIGHTLY B&B		WEEKLY D,B&B		🛏 16
	PER PERSON		PER PERSON		
	MIN £	MAX £	MIN £	MAX £	🛏 12
	12.50	18.50	140.00	171.50	OPEN 1-12

Fairy Glen Hotel

Dolwyddelan Road,
Betws-y-Coed
Gwynedd LL24 0SH
Tel: (06902) 269

MERIT

A warm and friendly welcome awaits you at our 17th century family run hotel, quietly situated overlooking the River Conwy amongst some of the most magnificent scenery in North Wales. Only one mile from Betws-y-Coed village. All our rooms are fully centrally heated with tea/coffee facilities, colour television and most are en-suite. Family rooms available. Our kitchen offers you freshly prepared home cooked food in a relaxing atmosphere. We are ideally situated for all the tourist attractions or the lakes and mountains of Snowdonia. Cosy residents cocktail bar. AA*RAC* Brochure from resident proprietors Jean and Graham Ball.

T		NIGHTLY B&B PER PERSON		WEEKLY D,B&B PER PERSON		🛏 10
SP						🛁 7
		MIN £	MAX £	MIN £	MAX £	OPEN 2-11
		15.00	19.00	161.00	190.00	

Glan Aber

Holyhead Road,
Betws-y-Coed, Gwynedd
LL24 0AB
Tel: (06902) 325

Located in the middle of the beautiful village of Betws-y-Coed. Close to golf course, railway, craft shops. Recently refurbished to a high standard by the new owners who aim to please their guests by offering all en-suite bedrooms with TV, tea makers, cocktail bar, games room, drying facilities for walkers equipment. Guests private lounge. Elegant decor throughout the hotel and dining room to complement the excellent cuisine provided by our chef. Car parking.

HW	T	NIGHTLY B&B PER PERSON		WEEKLY D,B&B PER PERSON		🛏 17
	SP					🛁 17
		MIN £	MAX £	MIN £	MAX £	OPEN 1-12
		15.00	20.00			

Pont-y-Pair Hotel

Betws-y-Coed,
Gwynedd LL24 0BN
Tel: (06902) 407

L

Set in the heart of Snowdonia, Betws-y-Coed is situated at the at the meeting of five valleys. A tourist haven of rugged beach. Friendly, family run hotel with full public bar facilities, boasting Tetly and Ansells real ales, pool room. Excellent food served 11am -11pm. Packed lunches on request. Colour TV, Central heating in all rooms. Warm welcome awaits you.

HW	T	NIGHTLY B&B PER PERSON		WEEKLY D,B&B PER PERSON		🛏 14
C	SP					🛁 0
		MIN £	MAX £	MIN £	MAX £	OPEN 1-12
		14.00	14.00	196.00	196.00	

Royal Oak Hotel

Holyhead Road, Betws-y-Coed,
Gwynedd LL24 0AY
Tel: (0690) 710219
Fax: (0690) 710433

AA/RAC*** former coaching inn overlooking River Llugwy. Enchanting riverside resort, ideal for touring North Wales. Luxury en-suite bedrooms with telephone and television. Grill open all day and elegant restaurant offering extensive menus using only freshest produce available, prepared by our chef a member of La Chaine Des Rotisseurs. Midweek and weekend breaks available.

HW	T	NIGHTLY B&B PER PERSON		WEEKLY D,B&B PER PERSON		🛏 27
	SP					🛁 27
TW						
		MIN £	MAX £	MIN £	MAX £	OPEN 1-12
		25.00	34.00	245.00	315.00	

WALES *It's magic*

Ty Gwyn Hotel

London Road, Betws-y-Coed,
Gwynedd LL24 0SG
Tel: (06902) 383 / 787

COMMENDED

AA** with hospitality award, RAC**. Friendly warm, cosy and inviting has described this family run centuries old coaching inn with its beamed ceilings, antique furniture and inglenooks. Each pretty bedroom has been individually designed. Some with four poster beds and a honeymoon suite with four poster bed and health spa tub. Award winner Family Welcome Guide and voted Newcomer of the Year by Les Routiers.

T		NIGHTLY B&B PER PERSON		WEEKLY D,B&B PER PERSON		🛏 13
SP						🛁 9
		MIN £	MAX £	MIN £	MAX £	OPEN 1-12
		17.00	35.00	209.65	335.65	

Waterloo Hotel

Betws-y-Coed,
Gwynedd LL24 0AR
Tel: (06902) 411

COMMENDED

The leading hotel in Snowdonia with hotel and motel rooms plus 4 cottages. Ideal location for touring mountains and coastlines. All rooms en-suite with colour TV, telephone, tea and coffee tray. Garden room restaurant. Excellent cuisine and wine list. Choice of bars with real ale. Snooker, pool and darts. Fitness and leisure complex, indoor heated swimming pool, sauna, solarium, jacuzzi, steam, multigym, exercise machines, coffee shop. AA***RAC.

HW	T	NIGHTLY B&B PER PERSON		WEEKLY D,B&B PER PERSON		🛏 39
	SP					🛁 39
		MIN £	MAX £	MIN £	MAX £	OPEN 1-12
		31.00	37.00	316.75	360.50	

Guest Houses

Bron Celyn Guest House

Llanrwst Road, Betws-y-Coed,
Gwynedd LL24 0HD
Tel: (06902) 333 changing
to (0690) 710333

A warm welcome is assured at this delightful homely guest house just ½ mile outside the main village of Betws-y- Coed set in a beautiful elevated position overlooking the village, Gwydyr Forest and Llugwy and Conwy valleys in Snowdonia National Park. Ideal centre for touring, walking, climbing, fishing, golf. Most rooms en-suite. All with beverage makers. Central heating, lounge, garden, car park. Full English breakfast, packed meals, snacks, 3 course evening meals. Special diets by arrangement.

	NIGHTLY B&B PER PERSON		WEEKLY D,B&B PER PERSON		
	MIN £	MAX £	MIN £	MAX £	OPEN
	13.00	15.00	136.50	150.50	1-12

Bryn Bella Guest House

Llanrwst Road,
Betws-y-Coed, Gwynedd   COMMENDED
LL24 0HD
Tel: (06902) 627

Small friendly Victorian guest house situated in a quiet elevated position in the Snowdonia National Park overlooking the picturesque village of Betws-y-Coed. All rooms have been recently refurbished and have washbasin, beverage facilities and colour TV. Some rooms have shower and toilet en-suite. Ideal centre for touring, climbing, riding, fishing and golf. Ample parking.

NIGHTLY B&B PER PERSON		WEEKLY D,B&B PER PERSON		
MIN £	MAX £	MIN £	MAX £	OPEN
13.00	16.00	–	–	1-12

Tan Dinas

Coed Cynhelier Road,
Betws-y-Coed,
Gwynedd LL24 0BL
Tel: (06902) 710635

MERIT

A welcome awaits you at this lovely Victorian house. Situated in 3 acres of woodland offering peace, seclusion, forest walks, only 500 yards from village centre. Spacious centrally heated rooms, tea/coffee facilities. Three en-suite, TV and video library available for rooms. Comfortable lounges, log fire, satellite TV. Splendid views. Ample parking. Dinner available. Home cooking. Licenced.

	NIGHTLY B&B PER PERSON		WEEKLY D,B&B PER PERSON		
SP	MIN £	MAX £	MIN £	MAX £	OPEN
	14.00	16.00	–	–	1-12

Ty'n-y-Celyn House

Llanrwst Road, Betws-y-Coed,
Gwynedd LL24 0HD
Tel: (06902) 202   HIGHLY COMMENDED

Ty'n-y-Celyn is nestling in a quiet position overlooking the picturesque village of Betws-y-Coed. Beautiful views of the Llugwy Valley, mountains and Conwy river. Situated in Snowdonia National Park, an ideal centre for walking, touring, sea sports, golf, riding, fishing and canoeing. All rooms tastefully and completely refurbished, very comfortable, robust breakfast and warm welcome.

	NIGHTLY B&B PER PERSON		WEEKLY D,B&B PER PERSON		
	MIN £	MAX £	MIN £	MAX £	OPEN
	16.00	20.00	–	–	3-12

Farmhouse

Tyddyn Gethin Farm

Penmachno,
Betws-y-Coed, Gwynedd
LL24 0PS
Tel: (06903) 392

Always a welcome at Tyddyn Gethin, clean and comfortable, good home cooking, near to Conwy Falls and woollen mill, very central for touring. Dining room, sitting room, bathroom with shower and bath, separate shower room, three bedrooms, hot/cold in bedrooms. 200 yards off B-4406. ½ mile from village Penmachno, 3½ miles from Betws-y-Coed. Two sitting rooms one non smoking offering lovely views of mountains and woodland.

	NIGHTLY B&B PER PERSON		WEEKLY D,B&B PER PERSON		
	MIN £	MAX £	MIN £	MAX £	OPEN
	21.00	23.00	224.00	231.00	1-12

LET A GUIDE SHOW YOU THE WAY

Why not book a Wales Official Tourist Guide for your next visit to Wales. Fees are very reasonable and a driver/guide can take the strain out of navigation and map reading whilst you sit back and enjoy your tour. Members of the Wales Official Tourist Guide Association are the only qualified tourist guides in Wales and the association is registered with the Wales Tourist Board. Any kind of guided tours are undertaken — from hourly tours by car or coach from a designated centre, to extended tours of any duration throughout Wales.
For more information contact Gwennie Johnson, W.O.T.G.A., Cae'r Felin, Chwilog, Criccieth, Gwynedd LL53 6SW.
Tel: (0766) 810889.

WALES
It's magic

CAERNARFON
Map Ref Ad4

Dominated by magnificent 13-th-century castle, most famous of Wales's medieval fortresses. Many museums – museums in castle, maritime and "Shops of Old" museums in town, Caernarfon Air Museum at Dinas Dinlle, Segontium Roman Fort and Museum on hill above town. Popular sailing, old harbour, market square, Lloyd George statue. Holiday centre at gateway of Snowdonia. Parc Glynllifon nearby.

Hotels

Bryn Eisteddfod Hotel

Clynnog Fawr, Caernarfon,
Gwynedd LL54 5DA
Tel: (028686) 431

COMMENDED

Situated 10 miles south of Caernarfon (A499) on the outskirts of the village of Clynnogfawr. Bryn Eisteddfod is ideally positioned for touring the Llŷn Peninsula and Snowdonia. All rooms are en-suite with colour TV, tea/coffee making facilities and afford beautiful sea or mountain views. 1 acre landscaped gardens in a quiet location make this an ideal hotel for your holiday. Vegetarian meals always available. Family rooms. Brochure on request.

HW T	NIGHTLY B&B PER PERSON		WEEKLY D,B&B PER PERSON		🛏 8
	MIN £	MAX £	MIN £	MAX £	🛏 6
	20.00	22.00	189.00	203.00	OPEN 1-12

Chocolate House

Plas Treflan, Caeathro,
Caernarfon
Gwynedd LL55 2SE
Tel: (0286) 672542

MERIT

Your own en-suite "cottage" in our picture book courtyard designed for couples touring Snowdonia. Choose from our extensive 'a la carte menu, simple or gourmet or vegetarian, delicious chocolate desserts. Bar restaurant, snooker, solarium, videos. Superb malts, cognacs. A high proportion of visitors return or recommend friends. Children 12+. Visa/Access. Brochure available.

T SP	NIGHTLY B&B PER PERSON		WEEKLY D,B&B PER PERSON		🛏 9
	MIN £	MAX £	MIN £	MAX £	🛏 9
	17.00	19.00	155.00	185.00	OPEN 1-12

Gorffwysfa Hotel

St. David's Road,
Caernarfon, Gwynedd LL55 1BH
Tel: (0286) 2647

Elegant Victorian licensed hotel in quiet leafy area enjoying panoramic sea and country views. Comfortable, spacious accommodation includes CH, colour TV, radio, drinks facilities in all rooms, some en-suite with sea views. Enjoy watching superb sunsets over Anglesey. Wide choice of menu. Gorffwysfa is an ideal base from which to explore the many delights of this beautiful part of Wales. Off season breaks, parties/children welcome. Parking.

HW T SP	NIGHTLY B&B PER PERSON		WEEKLY D,B&B PER PERSON		🛏 7
	MIN £	MAX £	MIN £	MAX £	🛏 4
	12.00	16.00	125.00	150.00	OPEN 1-12

Menai Bank Hotel

North Road, Caernarfon,
Gwynedd LL55 1BD
Tel: (0286) 673297
Fax: (0286) 673297

MERIT

Family owned AA*RAC* hotel with extensive views over the Menai Strait to Anglesey. Easy walking distance to town centre and castle. Explore Snowdonia, Llŷn Peninsula and Anglesey. Comfortable bedrooms with tea/coffee facilities, colour television, many en-suite. Restaurant, varied menu, well stocked bar, bar food, lounge, pool table, pay phone, hotel car park, lawned flower gardens. Bargain breaks early and late season. Golf concessions. Write or telephone for colour brochure/tariff.

T SP	NIGHTLY B&B PER PERSON		WEEKLY D,B&B PER PERSON		🛏 15
	MIN £	MAX £	MIN £	MAX £	🛏 9
	14.00	20.00	150.00	168.00	OPEN 1-11

Seiont Manor Hotel

Llanrug, Caernarfon,
Gwynedd LL55 2AQ
Tel: (0286) 673366
Fax: (0286) 2840

Once in a while you discover an hotel which is rather special. Seiont Manor is just that. Secluded in 150 acres of parkland, the Manor boasts 28 individually designed bedrooms with mini bar, colour TV, tea/coffee making facilities, gourmet restaurant, wood panelled library lounge, indoor heated pool and sauna. Salmon fishing in grounds.

HW T SP	NIGHTLY B&B PER PERSON		WEEKLY D,B&B PER PERSON		🛏 28
	MIN £	MAX £	MIN £	MAX £	🛏 28
	42.50	45.00	300.00	360.00	OPEN 1-12

St Beuno Coach Inn

Clynnog Fawr, Caernarfon,
Gwynedd LL54 5PB
Tel: (0286) 86212

Old coach inn on the A499 overlooking Caernarfon Bay. Ideal for family holidays, golf, fishing, shooting breaks, gym, snooker t/tennis, skittles, pool, videos. The Inn is open all day 12-11 for good food/ real ale. Low cost winter breaks. Open all year including Christmas and New Year. A friendly family run Coach Inn.

HW T SP	NIGHTLY B&B PER PERSON		WEEKLY D,B&B PER PERSON		🛏 8
	MIN £	MAX £	MIN £	MAX £	🛏 2
	7.50	15.00	150.00	240.00	OPEN 1-12

Guest Houses

Caer Siddi

Llanddeiniolen,
Caernarfon,
Gwynedd LL55 3AD
Tel: (0248) 670462

AWARD — COMMENDED

Former Georgian vicarage in peaceful rural setting with glorious views to Snowdon, Caernarfon Bay and the Rivals. Ideally located for all Gwynedd attractions, 4 miles to Caernarfon. Fully modernised, warm spacious accommodation. Colour TV lounge, children's price reductions, farmhouse breakfast, 3 course evening meals, home cooking and baking, tea making facilities, fire certificate. WTB Farmhouse and Guest House Award.

🐕	NIGHTLY B&B PER PERSON		WEEKLY D,B&B PER PERSON		🛏 2
	MIN £	MAX £	MIN £	MAX £	🛏 0
	12.00	12.00	140.00	140.00	OPEN 1-12

The White House

Llanfaglan,
Caernarfon,
Gwynedd LL54 5RA
Tel: (0286) 673003

AWARD — COMMENDED

The White House is a large detached house in its own grounds overlooking Foryd Bay with the Snowdonia mountains behind. There are five tastefully decorated bedrooms, with three bathrooms en-suite and two with private bath or shower. All rooms have tea making facilities and colour TV. Guest are welcome to use the resident's lounge, outdoor pool and gardens. Ideally situated for bird-watching, walking, boating, golf and visiting the historic welsh castles.

HW T C	NIGHTLY B&B PER PERSON		WEEKLY D,B&B PER PERSON		🛏 5
	MIN £	MAX £	MIN £	MAX £	🛏 3
	15.50	17.00	–	–	OPEN 1-12

Farmhouses

Bronant

Bontnewydd, Caernarfon,
Gwynedd LL54 7UF
Tel: (0286) 830451

Architect designed stone house of character overlooking Caernarfon Bay and Menai Strait. 2 miles from Royal Borough Caernarfon. Beautiful views sea, mountains, superb beaches. Lounge, colour TV, 2 dining rooms, separate tables. Children welcome. Pets by arrangement. Good wholesome food. Traditional farmhouse breakfast also Welsh cream teas. Central heating.

🐕	NIGHTLY B&B PER PERSON		WEEKLY D,B&B PER PERSON		🛏 3
	MIN £	MAX £	MIN £	MAX £	🛏 0
	12.00	–	125.00	–	OPEN 1-12

CAERNARFON CASTLE

Rhyddallt Ganol

Caeathro, Caernarfon,
Gwynedd LL55 2TH
Tel: (0286) 2085

L

MERIT

Caernarfon 2½ miles. A warm welcome awaits you at Rhyddallt Ganol amidst the peace and quietness of a beautiful garden. 2 double, 1 twin room available, hot and cold all rooms. Evening meal optional.

🐕	NIGHTLY B&B PER PERSON		WEEKLY D,B&B PER PERSON		🛏 3 🛏 0
	MIN £	MAX £	MIN £	MAX £	OPEN
	18.00	20.00	196.00	210.00	1-12

DOLWYDDELAN
Map Ref Bb6

Village on the A470 at the foot of Moel Siabod in the Snowdonia National Park. Convenient for exploring Gwydyr Forest and North Wales coast resorts. Excellent walking countryside. Imposing 12th century stone castle, birthplace of Llywelyn the Great, Prince of Wales. 12th-century church. 🚂

DOLWYDDELAN CASTLE

Hotels

Elen's Castle Hotel

Dolwyddelan,
Gwynedd LL25 0EJ
Tel: (06906) 207

👑👑

COMMENDED

*A commended small family run hotel in the beautiful Lledr valley in the heart of Snowdonia National Park. 10 comfortable bedrooms, 8 en-suite, clock/radio, tea/coffee making facilities. Four poster and family rooms. Friendly service. Residential bar. Free parking. Free fishing, course and game. 2½ acres grounds. Excellent touring. "Guestaccom" Accommodation, Goodroom Award. RAC**AA.*

HW T 🐕 SP ✕	NIGHTLY B&B PER PERSON		WEEKLY D,B&B PER PERSON		🛏 10 🛏 8
	MIN £	MAX £	MIN £	MAX £	OPEN
	16.00	19.00	149.00	163.00	1-12

LLANBERIS   Map Ref Ae4

Popular centre for walkers and climbers; least difficult (5 miles) walk to Snowdon summit starts here. For easy ride up take Snowdon Mountain Railway. Many things to see and do in this lively mountain town – Llanberis Lake Railway, slate industry museum, Power of Wales interpretive centre with unforgettable trip into the awesome tunnels of the Dinorwig Hydro-Electric Scheme, activity-packed Padarn Country Park, ancient Dolbadarn Castle, Bryn Bras Castle at nearby Llanrug.

Hotels

Dolafon Hotel

High Street, Llanberis,
Gwynedd LL55 4SU
Tel: (0286) 870993

👑👑

MERIT

Enjoy an away from it all holiday in Snowdonia National Park. Dolafon is a residential licensed hotel in its own grounds with ample parking and all amenities to make your stay pleasurable. An ideal base for touring and exploring our lakes and local amenities including lakeside and mountain railways. Six en-suites, two family rooms all with colour TV, tea/coffee facilities all rooms. Groups welcome. A satisfying breakfast is assured.

SP 🐕 ✕	NIGHTLY B&B PER PERSON		WEEKLY D,B&B PER PERSON		🛏 10 🛏 6
	MIN £	MAX £	MIN £	MAX £	OPEN
	12.50	14.50	150.00	164.00	2-11

Dolbadarn Hotel and Trekking Centre

High Street,
Llanberis, Gwynedd LL55 4SU
Tel: (0286) 870277

👑👑

Dolbadarn Hotel and Trekking Centre is a friendly family run hotel under the personal supervision of Aneuryn and Jeanette Jones. The hotel is centrally heated with H&C in all bedrooms, several have private facilities. The restaurant serves good wholesome food while bar snacks are always available during lunch hours from both bars.

HW T 🐕 SP	NIGHTLY B&B PER PERSON		WEEKLY D,B&B PER PERSON		🛏 26 🛏 3
	MIN £	MAX £	MIN £	MAX £	OPEN
	18.00	20.00	188.00	230.00	1-12

WALES
It's magic

45

Gwynedd Hotel & Restaurant

High Street, Llanberis,
Gwynedd LL55 4SU
Tel: (0286) 870203

A warm welcome at our family run hotel, in the centre of Llanberis. Situated near the foot of Snowdon, it is a perfect location for touring and walking in Snowdonia. We offer extensive bar and restaurant menus and comfortable accommodation. Families and groups are very welcome. Out door activities can be arranged for you. Special weekend breaks available throughout the year.

HW T	NIGHTLY B&B PER PERSON		WEEKLY D,B&B PER PERSON			10
SP	MIN £	MAX £	MIN £	MAX £		5
	13.50	18.50	98.00	126.00		OPEN 1-12

Pen-y-Gwryd Hotel

Nantgwynant,
Gwynedd LL55 4NT
Tel: (0286) 870211

Home of British mountaineering situated in the heart of Snowdonia where the successful 1953 Everest Expedition come for their reunions. Fishing, canoeing, climbing nearby. Outdoor swimming pool. Games room. Open weekends only in January and February.

	NIGHTLY B&B PER PERSON		WEEKLY D,B&B PER PERSON			22
	MIN £	MAX £	MIN £	MAX £		1
	32.00	40.00	178.50	000.00		OPEN 3-11

Rainbow Court

Pentir, Nr. Bangor,
Gwynedd LL57 4UY
Tel: (0248) 353099

Delightful quiet village setting three miles A5/55 between Caernarfon, Llanberis and Bangor. Walking, water sports,lakes, mountains, sea, riding, golf, flying, castles. Superb en-suite accommodation. Child reductions when sharing parents room. A la carte, breakfast/dinner plus superb vegetarian menu. Delightful coffee shop with fantastic gateux and pastries. You are welcome to bring your own wine to lunch or dinner. Par excellence service, accommodation and food. Totally non smoking establishment.

SP	NIGHTLY B&B PER PERSON		WEEKLY D,B&B PER PERSON			3
	MIN £	MAX £	MIN £	MAX £		2
	12.50	17.50	145.00	180.00		OPEN 1-12

Guest Houses

Crochendy Guest House

Mur Mawr, Llanberis,
Caernarfon, Gwynedd LL55 4TG
Tel: (0286) 870700

Small guest house within Snowdonia National Park enjoys spectacular views from its delightful grounds just one mile above Llanberis and offers exceptional food and excellent accommodation. Terms from £12.50 nightly bed and breakfast. Dinner and packed lunches also available. Residential licence. Special rates during November and February. Enquiries to Jane and Peter Richards.

SP	NIGHTLY B&B PER PERSON		WEEKLY D,B&B PER PERSON			3
	MIN £	MAX £	MIN £	MAX £		1
	12.50	16.50	-	-		OPEN 2-11

SLIDE PACKS

The following slide packs are available for purchase from the Wales Tourist Board:

North Wales Scenery	£2.00	(4 slides)
Mid Wales Scenery	£2.00	(4 slides)
South Wales Scenery	£2.00	(4 slides)
Historic Sites	£3.00	(6 slides)

Contact: Photo Librarian, WTB, Brunel House, 2 Fitzalan Road, Cardiff CF2 1UY

LLYN CRAFNANT NEAR LLANRWST

TREFRIW
Map Ref Bb5

Woollen mill village on west side of Conwy Valley, with Trefriw Wells Spa. Lakes at Llyn Crafnant and Llyn Geirionnydd, both local beauty spots. Good walking country.

Hotels

The Fairy Falls Hotel

Trefriw,
Gwynedd LL27 0JH
Tel: (0492) 640250

Ideally placed in the heart of the Conwy Valley in the immediate vicinity of an abundance of beauty spots and places of interest. All beaches and major attractions within easy driving distance. Motel type accommodation in our new Geirionnyd Lodge. All rooms being spacious and well appointed with en-suite facilities, colour TV, coffee and tea making facilities. Beautiful character inn and restaurant. Vast range of excellent cuisine from bar snacks in our characterful village inn, to 'a la carte in our beautiful olde worlde restaurant.

HW T C SP	NIGHTLY B&B PER PERSON		WEEKLY D,B&B PER PERSON		🛏 6 🛁 6
	MIN £	MAX £	MIN £	MAX £	OPEN 1-12
	16.50	20.00	165.00	183.00	

Ty Newydd Guest House

Ty Newydd, Trefriw,
Gwynedd LL27 0JH
Tel: (0492) 641210

Small family run guest house in the village centre offering clean comfortable accommodation with a friendly atmosphere. All rooms tea/coffee facilities, wash-basins, razor points, TV lounge. English breakfast. Free parking 100 yds. Child reductions. Central heating. Ideally situated for all North Wales attractions. Close to scenic mountains and lakes or livelier coastal towns. Choice of village inns for relaxing evenings. Experience the beautiful Conwy Valley.

HW T	NIGHTLY B&B PER PERSON		WEEKLY D,B&B PER PERSON		🛏 3 🛁 0
	MIN £	MAX £	MIN £	MAX £	OPEN 1-12
	10.00	15.00	112.00	126.00	

WALES It's magic

SNOWDON MOUNTAIN RAILWAY

Clwyd Countryside and Heritage

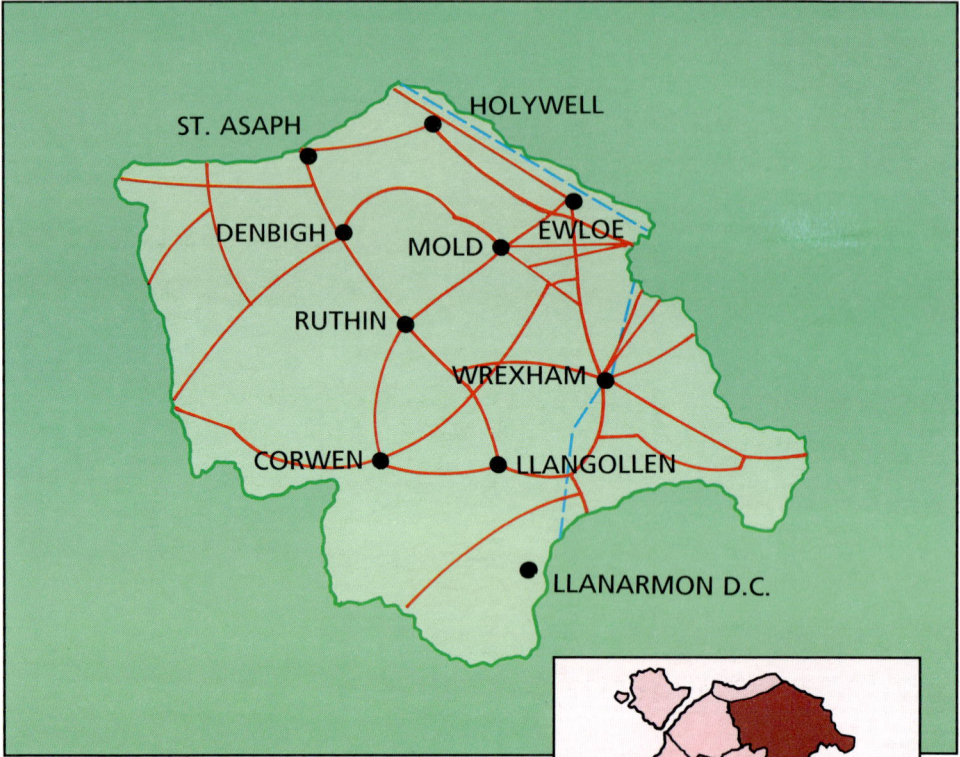

Clwyd's green hills and vales are steeped in history. Ruthin is renowned for its medieval buildings (not to mention its medieval banquets). The shell of a spectacularly located castle guards Llangollen, the pretty riverside home of the International Musical Eisteddfod, held annually in early July. Denbigh still has reminders of its days as a fortresss town, while Holywell's name comes from its ancient well, one of the traditional 'Seven Wonders of Wales'.

Bodelwyddan Castle, winner of the 'Museum of the Year' award in 1989, is home to a superb collection of 19th-century works of art from the National Portrait Gallery. Erddig Hall, near Wrexham, is the National Trust's supreme example of 'upstairs, downstairs'

living. Clwyd's wealth of history and heritage spreads itself across a lovely landscape. Take time off to explore the Clwydian Hills, the heather-covered Hiraethog moorlands and the undiscovered Berwyn Mountains.

The Royal National Eisteddfod, Wales's most important cultural gathering, takes place this August at Mold.

DENBIGH — Map Ref Be5

Castled town in Vale of Clwyd, with much historic interest. Friary and Museum. Pony trekking, riding, fishing, golf, tennis and bowls. Indoor heated swimming pool. Centrally located for enjoying the rolling hills of Clwyd, a rich farming area full of small, attractive villages.

Guest Houses

Cayo Guest House

74 Vale Street, Denbigh, Clwyd
LL16 3BW
Tel: (0745) 812686

Ideally situated for touring North Wales with most outdoor activities available nearby. Guests have access at all times. Licensed, TV lounge, central heating and fire certificate. Family rooms available - 50% reduction for children sharing parents' room. Well behaved dogs very welcome. Local produce bought daily. Home-made preserves available.

	NIGHTLY B&B PER PERSON		WEEKLY D,B&B PER PERSON			
	MIN £	MAX £	MIN £	MAX £		5
	11.00	12.50	77.00	87.50	OPEN 1-12	0

EWLOE — Map Ref Cc5

Settlement close to the Wales/England border near Hawarden. Remains of a medieval castle built by Welsh princes. Deeside Leisure Centre close by.

Hotels

St. David's Park Hotel

St. David's Park, Ewloe, Clwyd
CH5 3PW
Tel: (0244) 520800
Fax: (0244) 520580

Due to open in April 1991, St. David's Park Hotel will offer visitors to Wales new standards of food and accommodation. Designed in landscaped gardens around an inner courtyard, to "5 Crown brief", the hotel has rooms specifically designed for families and disabled. Superb leisure facilities round off a total experience beyond comparison.

	NIGHTLY B&B PER PERSON		WEEKLY D,B&B PER PERSON			
	MIN £	MAX £	MIN £	MAX £		121
	35.00	60.00	—	—	OPEN 1-12	121

HOLYWELL — Map Ref Cb4

Place of pilgrimage for centuries, the "Lourdes of Wales" with St. Winifred's Holy Well. Remains of Sasingwerk Abbey (1131) nearby. Leisure Centre with swimming pools. Greenfield Valley Heritage Park.

Farmhouses

Greenhill Farm

Holywell, Clwyd
CH8 7QF
Tel: (0352) 713270

AWARD   MERIT

Greenhill is a 15th century timber framed farmhouse on a working farm. Modernised to include 2 family rooms (one en-suite), twin and double bedrooms all with tea making facilities. We have an oak beamed lounge and panelled dining room. Also games/utility room with washing facilities and snooker table. Children are especially welcome.

	NIGHTLY B&B PER PERSON		WEEKLY D,B&B PER PERSON			
	MIN £	MAX £	MIN £	MAX £		4
	11.50	—	122.50	—	OPEN 3 11	1

AUTUMN IN CLWYD

LLANARMON DYFFRYN CEIRIOG
Map Ref Eb2

Delightful little village locked away in Berwyn Mountains, with good fishing, walking and excellent inns. Home of the bard Ceiriog (John Hughes) — the church has a memorial to him. 240ft Pistyll Rhaeadr waterfall, the highest in Wales, in the mountains to the south-west.

Hotels

Hand Hotel

Llanarmon Dyffryn Ceiriog,
Nr.Llangollen,
Clwyd LL20 7LD
Tel: (069176) 666 / 264
Fax: (069176) 262

COMMENDED

Small country hotel in idyllic surroundings at head of Ceiriog Valley. Offering relaxing holdays for all age groups. Dramatic and beautiful scenery. 14 en-suite bedrooms comfortably furnished. Full central heating and log fires. Excellent and varied cuisine. Traditional Welsh hospitality. Children, pets welcome.

HW T SP	NIGHTLY B&B PER PERSON		WEEKLY D,B&B PER PERSON		🛏 14
	MIN £	MAX £	MIN £	MAX £	🛁 14
	32.00	32.00	280.00	280.00	OPEN 1-12

LLANGOLLEN
Map Ref Ec1

Romantic town on Dee, famous for its International Musical Eisteddfod; singers and dancers from all over the world come here every July. The town's many attractions include a canal museum, pottery, weavers, ECTARC European Centre for Tradition and Regional Cultures and a standard gauge steam railway. Plas Newydd home (of Ladies of Llangollen fame) is nearby. Valle Crucis Abbey, in a superb setting, is 2 miles away and ruined Castell Dinas Bran overlooks the town. Browse through the town's little shops; stand on its 14th century stonebridge; cruise along the canal. Golf course and wonderful walking in the surrounding countryside.

Hotels

Abbey Grange Hotel

Horseshoe Pass Road,
Llangollen, Clwyd LL20 8NN
Tel: (0978) 860753
Fax: (0978) 860753

Just 1½ miles from the charming country town of Llangollen. All rooms are en-suite with TV, tea/coffee facilities and telephone. Full central heating throughout. Family roooms available with special prices for children. Bar and restaurant meals available. Large private car park. Golf, fishing, rambling and indoor sports within easy travelling distance.

HW T SP	NIGHTLY B&B PER PERSON		WEEKLY D,B&B PER PERSON		🛏 8
	MIN £	MAX £	MIN £	MAX £	🛁 8
	21.00	23.00	175.00	189.00	OPEN 1-12

Gales of Llangollen

18 Bridge Street, Llangollen,
Clwyd LL20 8PF
Tel: (0978) 860089
Fax: (0978) 861313

An 18th century building situated in the lovely Vale of Llangollen, housing Gales Wine and Food Bar which has luxury en-suite bedrooms with colour TV, telephone, tea/coffee facilities. Family rooms available. Meals are available in the wine bar which is listed in Good Food Guide, Good Hotel Guide and has won the Prix D'Elite Award for its excellent wines.

T	NIGHTLY B&B PER PERSON		WEEKLY D,B&B PER PERSON		🛏 8
	MIN £	MAX £	MIN £	MAX £	🛁 8
	20.00	—	—	—	OPEN 1-12

Hendy Isa

Llangollen, Clwyd
LL20 8DE
Tel: (0978) 861232

Two miles from the world famous town of Llangollen home of the International Eisteddfod and central for touring North Wales. This beautiful small hotel formerly a slate quarry stables, set in a magnificent location with a backdrop of mountains offering a high standard of en-suite accommodation, with all facilities, quiet and peaceful. Ideal for outdoor activities. Comes highly recommended by all visitors. Ideal for short breaks and perfect for Christmas.

HW T 🐕 SP 🚭	NIGHTLY B&B PER PERSON		WEEKLY D,B&B PER PERSON		🛏 5
	MIN £	MAX £	MIN £	MAX £	🛁 5
	12.50	20.00	120.00	170.00	OPEN 1-12

RIVER DEE AT LLANGOLLEN

Guest Houses

Dinbren House

Dinbren Road, Llangollen,
Clwyd LL20 8TF
Tel: (0978) 860593

*Lovely old house set in 2½ acre gardens.
Beautiful views and easy walking distance
to picturesque Llangollen, with golf, riding,
fishing, canoeing. Large comfortable
bedrooms all with central heating, wash-
basins, tea, coffee and television. Guests
own bathroom and shower rooms.
Reduced rates for children. Family room
available. Short drive to Chester and
Snowdonia.*

HW T	NIGHTLY B&B PER PERSON		WEEKLY D,B&B PER PERSON		🛏 4
SP					🍴 0
	MIN £	MAX £	MIN £	MAX £	OPEN
	12.00	13.00	—	—	1-12

Farmhouses

Ty'n Celyn Farmhouse

Tyndwr, Llangollen, Clwyd
LL20 8AR
Tel: (0978) 861117

*Spacious oak beamed farmhouse with
beautiful views. Comfortable guests
lounge with log fire. Each bedroom has
bathroom en-suite and tea/coffee facilities.
Colour TV, cot available. Just 1½ miles
from centre of Llangollen. Reduced rates
for children. Ideally situated for golf,
fishing, horse riding, canoeing, walking or
for a touring base. Ample parking space.*

HW T	NIGHTLY B&B PER PERSON		WEEKLY D,B&B PER PERSON		🛏 3
C SP					🍴 3
	MIN £	MAX £	MIN £	MAX £	OPEN
	13.00	15.00	—	—	1-12

MOLD
Map Ref Cb5

County town of Clwyd, on
edge of Clwydian Hills.
Theatre Clwyd offers wide
range of entertainment. Visit
Daniel Owen Centre,
memorial to "the Dickens of
Wales". Golf course.
Loggerheads Country Park in
wooded setting to the south-
west. Home of the 1991
National Eisteddfod of Wales

Guest Houses

The Old Mill Guest Lodge

Melin-y-Wern, Denbigh Road,
Nannerch, Mold, Clwyd
CH7 5RH
Tel: (0352) 741542   COMMENDED

*Family owned converted water mill stables
set within a rural conservation area. Single,
double and family accommodation. All
bedrooms en-suite with beverage tray,
trouser press, colour TV, radio, hairdryer,
shaver point. Pine furnishings and fixtures,
co-ordinated decor. Central heating. Fire
certificate. Gardens. Central for Roman
Chester, North Wales coast and mountains.
Local golf, fishing, horse riding and hill
walking. Private parking. Separate tables.
Open Christmas, New Year. Child
reductions. RAC Acclaimed.*

HW T	NIGHTLY B&B PER PERSON		WEEKLY D,B&B PER PERSON		🛏 7
					🍴 7
	MIN £	MAX £	MIN £	MAX £	OPEN
	18.25	18.25	176.75	176.75	1-12

RUTHIN
Map Ref Ca6

Attractive and historic market
town noted for its fine
architecture; curfew is still
rung nightly! Many captivating
old buildings. Hill-top town
square where medieval days
are held weekly in season.
Medieval banquets in Ruthin
Castle. Ancient St. Peter's
Church has beautiful gates
and carved panels. Good
range of small shops; carft
centre with workshops. Ideal
base for Vale of Clwyd.

Hotels

The Coach House Hotel & Restaurant

Park Road, Ruthin, Clwyd
LL15 1NB
Tel: (08242) 4223

*New family run hotel near the centre of
mediéval Ruthin, an excellent location for
daily excursions to the rest of North Wales.
Licensed restaurant, bar meals, lounge,
colour TV and coffee making facilities in all
rooms. Locked entrance gates ensure
secure private parking at night. Full fire
certificate, bar meals lunchtime and
evenings, 'a la carte restaurant evenings
only. CH, double, twin, single and family
rooms.*

HW C	NIGHTLY B&B PER PERSON		WEEKLY D,B&B PER PERSON		🛏 7
					🍴 7
	MIN £	MAX £	MIN £	MAX £	OPEN
	17.50	17.50	—	—	1-12

VALLE CRUCIS ABBEY, LLANGOLLEN

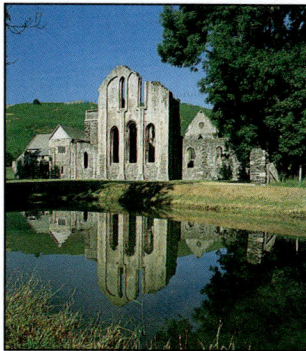

Guest Houses

Argoed Guest House

Off Mwrog Street, Llanfwrog,
Ruthin, Clwyd LL15 1LG
Tel: (08242) 3407
Fax: (08242) 4924

L

*An attractive timbered house with full
central heating, standing in private
grounds. Ample parking facilities. Single,
double, twin bedded and en-suite rooms
available. Lounge with TV, shower and
baths available. Beautiful garden with own
stream. Commanding superb views of
Clwydian Hills. Argoed is situated within
easy walking distance of Ruthin. Brittany
Ferries Recommended. Member of award
winning BB (GB) organisation. Convenient
for world famous Medieval Banquets.*

HW T	NIGHTLY B&B PER PERSON		WEEKLY D,B&B PER PERSON		🍴 3
	MIN £	MAX £	MIN £	MAX £	🛏 1
	15.00	15.00	–	–	OPEN 1-12

Guest Houses

Llanbenwch Farm

Llanfair Duffryn Clwyd,
Ruthin,
Clwyd LL15 2SH
Tel: (08242) 2340

AWARD   COMMENDED

*Mixed working farm conveniently situated
amidst and within easy reach most beauty
spots. AA Listed, Wales Farmhouse Award.
3 miles south of medieval Ruthin on A525.
Centrally heated, modernised 12th century
farmhouse with H&C, TV, tea making
facilities in bedrooms, dining room with
separate tables. Sorry no children under 5.
SAE for reply.*

T	NIGHTLY B&B PER PERSON		WEEKLY D,B&B PER PERSON		🍴 3
	MIN £	MAX £	MIN £	MAX £	🛏 0
	–	9.50	–	90.00	OPEN 3-10

VIDEOS

THE WONDER OF WALES (VHS)

The beauty of Wales and its many
attractions are the stars of this
24-minute video. The film features
Wales's rich cultural and architectural
heritage, and includes coverage of the
most recent attractions. Narrated by
Sian Phillips.

ST. ASAPH   Map Ref Be4

City with the smallest
cathedral in Britain, scene of
the annual North Wales Music
Festival. Prehistoric Cefn Caves
nearby. Pleasantly sited on
River Elwy in verdant Vale of
Clwyd. Three important
historic sites on door step —
medieval Rhuddlan Castle,
Bodelwyddan Castle (with
noted art collection) and
Bodrhyddan Hall.

WALES
It's magic

Guest Houses

Plas Penucha

Caerwys, Mold, Clwyd
CH7 5BH
Tel: (0352) 720210   COMMENDED

*Welcome to this 16th century farmhouse
altered over succeeding generations but
retaining sense of history and serenity in
comfortable surroundings. Extensive
gardens overlooking Clwydian Hills. Twin
bedroom (en-suite), double and single
rooms (wash-basins). Spacious lounge
with Elizabethan panelling and library
(grand piano). Full central heating. 2 miles
A55. Ideal touring centre for all North
Wales. Brochure from Nest Price.*

HW T	NIGHTLY B&B PER PERSON		WEEKLY D,B&B PER PERSON		🍴 4
	MIN £	MAX £	MIN £	MAX £	🛏 1
	12.50	12.50	110.00	110.00	OPEN 1-12

RHUDDLAN CASTLE

This is a relaxing region of wide, open spaces – a description that applies both to Mid Wales's coast and countryside. Nothing disturbs this region's timeless tranquillity and traditional composure. The busiest time of the week in most country towns, for example, is market day, when the streets are invaded by the local farming community intent on buying and selling – and catching up on the week's gossip.

The Mid Wales coast takes its shape from the great arc of Cardigan Bay, a sometimes sandy, sometimes cliff backed shoreline which stretches from Snowdonia right the way down to Pembrokeshire. The resorts along the bay complement their peaceful surroundings perfectly. The largest is modestly sized Aberystwyth, a charming seaside resort with a well-preserved Victorian seafront.

Other places to stay along the coast include Barmouth on the mouth of the beautiful Mawddach Estuary, Tywyn, Aberaeron (its Georgian harbour is a gem) and New Quay. All are ideal for an unhurried style of seaside holiday – and all are close to Mid Wales's unexplored hills, moors and mountains.

It's a little-known fact that there's more of the Snowdonia National Park in Mid Wales than in the north. Although the park is named after Snowdon, its boundary extends many miles southwards deep into Mid Wales. Mighty Cader Idris guards the southern boundary of the park, which then stretches north-eastwards to Bala and the Arennig Mountains.

Stay at stone-built Dolgellau, sheltered beneath Cader Idris, or handsome Machynlleth, or lakeside Bala, and explore Snowdonia's upland wildernesses. Further east, the high mountains decline to rolling border country around Welshpool, a beguiling area dotted with remote villages hidden in the folds of peaceful valleys.

Mid Wales is full of such hidden places. The unchanging heartlands of Wales lie inland from Aberystwyth – the empty moors of Plynlimon and the Cambrian Mountains, haunt of the red kite and home of the hardy hill-sheep farmer. Follow in the tracks of the old drovers by driving along the spectacular mountain roads that lead upwards from attractive old market towns like Rhayader, Llanidloes and Tregaron. And at Llandrindod Wells, soak up the ambience of a perfectly preserved Victorian spa town where the waters are still flowing for those who care to sample them.

LLYNNAU CREGENNEN NEAR DOLGELLAU

Meirionnydd

The mountains sweep down to the sea all along Meirionnydd's coastline. The view from the ramparts of Harlech Castle captures the essence of this highly scenic slice of Wales – the fortress stands on a rocky outcrop between the Snowdonia National Park's peaks and the sands of Cardigan Bay.

There are more dramatic encounters between mountain and sea along the Mawddach and Dyfi Estuaries. To enjoy the best of Meirionnydd's coast and country, stay at places like Barmouth and Aberdovey. Or head inland for forests, lakes, and hills around dark-stoned Dolgellau and mountain-ringed Bala. Meirionnydd's many attractions include the Fairbourne and Talyllyn narrow-gauge lines (respectively the smallest and longest-serving of Wales's little railways). Try the new dry ski slope at Trawsfynydd, visit Fairbourne's 'Butterfly Safari', and call in at the Corris Crafts Centre where many different craftsmen work.

ABERDOVEY/ ABERDYFI Map Ref Db6

Picturesque little resort and dinghy sailors' paradise on the Dyfi Estuary. All watersports, thriving yacht club, good inns looking out over the bay and 18-hole golf club links. Superb views towards hills and mountains. ⇌

Hotels

Bodfor Hotel

Sea Front, Aberdovey,
Gwynedd LL35 OEA
👑👑
Tel: (0654) 767475
Fax: (0654) 767679

Comfortable licensed hotel centrally situated opposite beach and car park. Most rooms en-suite overlooking the Dovey Estuary. All rooms have TV, telephone, tea making facilities. First class restaurant offering table d'hote and 'a la carte menus. Family rooms available. Golfers welcome, concessionary green fees offered. The hotel is open all year round and offers special breaks midweek or weekends from November to March.

🐕 © SP	NIGHTLY B&B PER PERSON		WEEKLY D,B&B PER PERSON		🛏 16 🛏 10
	MIN £	MAX £	MIN £	MAX £	OPEN 1-12
	22.00	30.00	197.70	245.70	

WALES: BED AND BREAKFAST GUIDE 1991

Wales offers great-value budget B&B accommodation – and this guide proves it, by featuring over 500 hotels, guest houses and farmhouses where you can stay for just £16 or under per person per night. The Guide also contains detailed maps and comprehensive holiday information.

Maybank Hotel & Restaurant

4 Penhelig Road, Penhelig, Aberdovey, Gwynedd LL35 0PT
👑👑
Tel: (065472) 500
changing to (0654) 767500

A very individual hotel. Renowned for the fresh quality of its food in the hotel's à la carte restaurant, affording beautiful vistas in the quieter established area of Penhelig. Exceptional views of the Dovey Estuary, Cardigan Bay and Aberdovey. All rooms with en-suite shower or bathroom, WC, colour TV, tea/coffee making facilities. Special seasonal packages available including golf/bargain break week/ weekends. Reading lounge plus intimate comfortable bar, terraced gardens and patio. Enjoy sea and fresh water fishing, sailing, windsurfing and other water sports. Beautiful walks and scenery in Snowdonia and RSPB reserves. AA*, Michelin/Ashley Courtenay recommended. Food Hotel Guide recommended.

🐕 SP	NIGHTLY B&B PER PERSON		WEEKLY D,B&B PER PERSON		🛏 5 🛏 5
	MIN £	MAX £	MIN £	MAX £	OPEN 2-12
	18.00	26.00	238.00	299.00	

Trefeddian Hotel

Aberdovey, Gwynedd
LL35 0SB
👑👑👑
Tel: (065472) 213
Fax: (065472) 7777

Unrivalled situation, uninterrupted views over golf links, sandy beach, Cardigan Bay. 46 bedrooms en-suite, most facing seaward. Lift, indoor heated swimming pool, putting green, badminton and tennis court, games room, solarium. Excellent cuisine. Families welcome. In Snowdonia National Park. Our 8 page colour brochure, tariff sent with pleasure. We look forward to welcoming you.

🐕 SP ⚓	NIGHTLY B&B PER PERSON		WEEKLY D,B&B PER PERSON		🛏 46 🛏 46
	MIN £	MAX £	MIN £	MAX £	OPEN 3-12
	29.00	37.00	245.00	273.00	

ABERDOVEY BEACH

BALA
Map Ref Dd2

Tree-lined main street has interesting little shops and charming hotels. Narrow-gauge railway runs one side of Bala Lake, 4 miles long (the longest natural lake in Wales) and ringed with mountains. Golf, sailing, fishing — a natural touring centre for Snowdonia.

Hotels

Fronbbarw Private Hotel

Stryd-y-Fron, Bala,
Gwynedd LL23 7YD
Tel: (0678) 520301

MERIT

Charming period mansion quietly situated on the hillside overlooking Bala town and lake, with magnificent views of the Berwyn Mountains. All rooms have hot/cold, central heating, tea/coffee making facilities. Lounge, separate TV lounge with colour television. Ample free parking. Dinner optional. Vegetarians catered for. Licensed. Ideal centre for sightseeing, walking, water sports.

HW	T	NIGHTLY B&B PER PERSON		WEEKLY D,B&B PER PERSON		🛏 8
SP	♿					🛁 2
		MIN £	MAX £	MIN £	MAX £	OPEN 3-11
		10.00	13.00	112.50	130.50	

BALA LAKE

Plas Coch Hotel

High Street, Bala,
Gwynedd LL23 7AB
Tel: (0678) 520309

MERIT

AA*RAC**. Situated in the centre of the lakeside town of Bala. Private car park. All bedrooms en-suite with colour TV, radio, direct line telephones, tea/coffee facilities. Fully licensed restaurant and bar meals. Come and enjoy good food and wine. Concessionary golf at Bala Golf Club. Water sports holidays such as sailing, windsurfing and canoeing can be arranged nearby. A warm welcome awaits you from resident hosts.

HW	T	NIGHTLY B&B PER PERSON		WEEKLY D,B&B PER PERSON		🛏 10
🐕	C					🛁 10
SP	♿✈	MIN £	MAX £	MIN £	MAX £	OPEN 1-12
		23.50	23.50	170.00	170.00	

Guest Houses

Dewis Cyfarfod

Llandderfel, Bala, Gwynedd
LL23 7DR
Tel: (06783) 243

COMMENDED

Ideally situated for touring Snowdonia, this delightful old house faces south across the beautiful Dee Valley. The sitting room and bar are havens of comfort and each pretty bedroom has colour TV, radio, hairdryer and hot drinks tray. You will find food of the highest quality in our candlelit dining room. BTA Commended.

HW	T	NIGHTLY B&B PER PERSON		WEEKLY D,B&B PER PERSON		🛏 5
🐕	C					🛁 4
		MIN £	MAX £	MIN £	MAX £	OPEN 1-12
		18.00	22.00	175.00	225.00	

BARMOUTH
Map Ref Db4

Superbly located resort on mouth of lovely Mawddach Estuary. Golden sands and miles of wonderful mountain and estuary walks nearby. Promenade, funfair, pony rides on beach. Lifeboat house. "Shipwreck Centre" museum and HQ of Merioneth Yacht Club. A thriving holiday town with good shops and inns. Excellent parking on seafront. ⊀

Hotels

Bontddu Hall Country House Hotel

Bontddu, Barmouth,
Gwynedd LL40 2SU
Tel: (0341) 49661
Fax: (0341) 49284

COMMENDED

Experience the fascination of staying in an historic country house (built by antecedents of Neville Chamberlain), set in 3 acres of landscaped gardens with magical views across the Mawddach Estuary to Cader Idris Mountains. All bedrooms en-suite with colour TV, telephone, radio, tea/coffee tray, hairdryer. Superb restaurant. Central heating. Licensed. Private car park. AA***RAC***. Egon Ronay. Ashley Courtenay.

HW	T	NIGHTLY B&B PER PERSON		WEEKLY D,B&B PER PERSON		🛏 20
SP	C					🛁 20
	♿✈	MIN £	MAX £	MIN £	MAX £	OPEN 3-12
TW		35.00	55.00	297.50	397.50	

Crystal House Hotel

19 Marine Parade, Barmouth, 👑👑
Gwynedd LL42 1NA
Tel: (0341) 280603

Sea front location, five minutes to shops, H&C water, tea making, shaver points and colour TV's in all rooms. Access at all times, home comforts assured and friendly atmosphere. Separate tables, delicious home cooking. A perfect base for visitors exploring Mid Wales. Some rooms with sea views. Residential licence. Fire certificate. Special rates for parties. Sorry no pets. Write or phone for brochure, Gerald and Marjorie Warburton.

T	SP	NIGHTLY B&B PER PERSON		WEEKLY D,B&B PER PERSON		🛏	9
		MIN £	MAX £	MIN £	MAX £	🛏	0
		11.00	12.00	112.00	120.00	OPEN 3-10	

Lawrenny Lodge Hotel & Restaurant

Barmouth, Gwynedd 👑👑
LL42 1SU
Tel: (0341) 280466

Situated in quiet location overlooking harbour and estuary but only five minutes walk from town. Many rooms en-suite, all rooms have colour television, clock/radio alarms and tea/coffee making facilities. Charming restaurant with extensive menu including vegetarian dishes. Ideally situated for the surrounding Snowdonia National Park and close to many leisure activities such as tennis, bowls, horse riding, golf and fishing. Special rates for children and senior citizens.

🐕	SP	NIGHTLY B&B PER PERSON		WEEKLY D,B&B PER PERSON		🛏	9
		MIN £	MAX £	MIN £	MAX £	🛏	5
		13.00	19.00	138.00	174.00	OPEN 3-12	

WALES
It's magic

Guest Houses

Fronhyfryd Guest House (Non-Smoking)

Llanaber, Barmouth, 👑👑
Gwynedd LL42 1YY
Tel: (0341) 280345

Beautiful non smoking detached guest house. Uninterrupted sea and mountain views. Excellent food and service. All rooms have colour TV, tea/coffee facilities, shaver point, hairdryer, H&C central heating, large car park. Multi gym and trouser press available. Single, double, family rooms. Dining room overlooks sea. Licensed. Fire certificate held. Short walk down path brings you on to beach and promenade. Snacks, picnics and choice of menu.

HW	T	NIGHTLY B&B PER PERSON		WEEKLY D,B&B PER PERSON		🛏	6
SP	✖	MIN £	MAX £	MIN £	MAX £	🛏	0
		13.30	15.00	140.00	161.00	OPEN 1-11	

Farmhouse

Llwyndu Farmhouse

Llanaber, Barmouth,
Gwynedd LL42 1RR 👑👑
Tel: (0341) 280144

AWARD
COMMENDED

Enjoy a relaxed friendly stay in our 17th century farmhouse. Les Routiers, AA and leading guides. Marvellous views over Cardigan Bay and surrounding mountains. Near Barmouth yet nicely secluded. All bedrooms, including suites in barn conversion with en-suite bathroom, beverage facilities etc. Imaginative cuisine, including vegetarian, in superb atmosphere of oak beams, inglenooks, candlelight and music. Children very welcome. A beautiful and interesting region to explore. For further information contact Paula or Peter Thompson.

SP	✖	NIGHTLY B&B PER PERSON		WEEKLY D,B&B PER PERSON		🛏	7
		MIN £	MAX £	MIN £	MAX £	🛏	7
		15.00	17.00	154.00	168.00	OPEN 2-11	

CORRIS — Map Ref Dc5

Village in foothills of Cader Idris Range. Corris Crafts Centre features work of many craftspersons, small museum dedicated to the Corris Railway. Lovely mountain scenery. National centre for Alternative Technology close by.

Hotels

Dulas Valley Hotel

Corris, Machynlleth, Powys 👑👑
SY20 9RD
Tel: (065473) 688   MERIT

The hotel is set in a beautiful valley overlooked by forests. We have extensive car parking facilities and a waterfall that runs between the hotel and lawn. Inside we have children's area, bar, restaurant, pool room. All bedrooms are tastefully decorated. Full en-suite, centrally heated, tea making facilities, colour TV, hairdryers. Situated 5 miles from Machynlleth on the A487 towards Dolgellau. Within easy reach of many coastal villages. A warm friendly welcome assured at all times.

HW	🐕	NIGHTLY B&B PER PERSON		WEEKLY D,B&B PER PERSON		🛏	4
SP		MIN £	MAX £	MIN £	MAX £	🛏	4
		20.00	20.00	175.00	175.00	OPEN 1-12	

BARMOUTH HARBOUR

DINAS MAWDDWY
Map Ref Dd4

Mountain village famed for its salmon and trout fishing and marvellous walks. On fringe of Snowdonia National Park. Visit the extensive Meirion woollen mill and visitor centre with craft shop, tea shop, and drive over the spectacular Bwlch Y Groes mountain road to Bala.

Hotels

Dolbrodmaeth Inn

Dinas Mawddwy, Machynlleth, Powys SY20 9LP
Tel: (06504) 333

In National Park close to Aran peaks. Ideal centre for touring. Guided walks by arrangement. All bedrooms with bathroom, colour television, telephone and beverage facilities. Bar and restaurant open on gardens, lawn slopes to River Dovey with own fishing. Centrally heated with log fire in the lounge. Enjoy traditional hospitality in modern comfort.

HW ⚲ SP ✕	NIGHTLY B&B PER PERSON		WEEKLY D,B&B PER PERSON		🛏 0 🛆 0
	MIN £	MAX £	MIN £	MAX £	OPEN
	23.00	30.00	198.00	240.00	1-12

Farmhouses

Bryncelyn Farm

Dinas Mawddwy, Machynlleth, Powys SY20 9JA 👑👑
Tel: (06504) 289

Bryncelyn farm is in the peaceful valley of Cywarch at the foot of Aran Fawddwy, set amidst some of the finest scenery. An excellent centre for enjoying surrounding North Wales, within easy reach of coast and market town of Machynlleth. Log fire, generous home cooked meals, tea and coffee making facilities, also spacious en-suite bedrooms, with heating. The Edwards family offers you a homely holiday in a comfortable farmhouse. The farm is two miles from Dinas Mawddwy.

HW T 🐕 SP ✕	NIGHTLY B&B PER PERSON		WEEKLY D,B&B PER PERSON		🛏 2 🛆 2
	MIN £	MAX £	MIN £	MAX £	OPEN
	12.00	14.00	–	–	1-12

DOLGELLAU
Map Ref Dc4

Handsome stone-built market town which seems to have grown naturally out of the mountains. The heights of Cader Idris loom above the rooftops. Interesting shops, pubs, cafes. Excellent base for touring the coast and countryside.

Hotels

Clifton House Hotel

Smithfield Square, Dolgellau, 👑
Gwynedd LL40 1ES 👑
Tel: (0341) 422554   COMMENDED

Centrally situated in the unspoilt market town of Dolgellau. This small hotel built on the remains of the former county gaol, now converted to the hotel's restaurant, offers comfortable well proportioned accommodation. A combination of home comforts, personal attention from proprietors Rob and Pauline Dix, an excellent menu (including vegetarian dishes) and good wine in the cellar restaurant ensure your stay will be a happy one. Regular guided walking weekends. AA and RAC *.

T SP TW	NIGHTLY B&B PER PERSON		WEEKLY D,B&B PER PERSON		🛏 7 🛆 4
	MIN £	MAX £	MIN £	MAX £	OPEN
	16.00	24.00	168.00	245.00	2-12

FAIRBOURNE AND BARMOUTH STEAM RAILWAY

Dolserau Hall Hotel

Dolgellau, Gwynedd 👑👑
LL40 2AG 👑👑
Tel: (0341) 422522   COMMENDED

With 5 acre grounds set in the heart of the Welsh countryside, Dolserau Hall is ideally situated for exploring Snowdonia. Centrally heated with comfortable lounges, spacious bedrooms and excellent food it offers a perfect escape all year. Mawddach and Wnion fishing available. Marion and Peter Kaye look forward to meeting you! Ashley Courtenay. AA**RAC.

HW T 🐾 SP	NIGHTLY B&B PER PERSON		WEEKLY D,B&B PER PERSON		🛏 14 🛆 14
	MIN £	MAX £	MIN £	MAX £	OPEN
	32.50	32.50	245.00	265.00	1-12

Royal Ship Hotel

Queens Square, Dolgellau, 👑
Gwynedd LL40 1AR 👑👑
Tel: (0341) 422209

This extensively modernised hotel stands in the centre of Dolgellau with a fine view of Cader Idris. Most bedrooms en-suite. Family rooms available and the luxurious Cader en-suite room for that special occasion. Colour TV in bedrooms. Full colour brochure on request. AA**RAC**. Car park. Access and Barclaycard accepted. Robinsons Traditional Draught Beers.

HW T SP	NIGHTLY B&B PER PERSON		WEEKLY D,B&B PER PERSON		🛏 24 🛆 16
	MIN £	MAX £	MIN £	MAX £	OPEN
	17.00	33.00	170.00	260.00	1-12

Guest Houses

Dwy Olwyn

Coed y Fronallt, Dolgellau,
Gwynedd LL40 2YG
Tel: (0341) 422822

A comfortable guest house situated in an acre of landscaped gardens boasing magnificent views of the Cader Idris mountain range. In a peaceful position, yet only 10 minutes walk from the town within the Snowdonia National Park. Close to all amenities, numerous walks. Good home cooking, cleanliness and personal attention assured. Tea, coffee facilities all bedrooms. Parking. Lounge with colour TV. Evening meals optional.

HW	T	NIGHTLY B&B PER PERSON		WEEKLY D,B&B PER PERSON		🛏	3
		MIN £	MAX £	MIN £	MAX £		–
		11.00	112.00			OPEN 3-10	

Heulwen

Llanfachreth, Dolgellau,
Gwynedd LL40 2UT
Tel: (0341) 423085

Heulwen is situated outside the quaint village of Llanfachreth, surrounded by beautiful views. It is an ideal centre for exploring the Snowdonia National Park. Hearty breakfasts, warm and homely bedrooms, lounge with colour TV, and large patio to while away the long summer evenings, all help to make your stay a memorable one.

HW	T	NIGHTLY B&B PER PERSON		WEEKLY D,B&B PER PERSON		🛏	3
		MIN £	MAX £	MIN £	MAX £		–
		11.00	115.00			OPEN 3-10	

Ivy House

Finsbury Square, Dolgellau,
Gwynedd LL40 1RF
Tel: (0341) 422535   MERIT

Country town guest house and restaurant offering attractive accommodation, a welcoming atmosphere and good food. Cellar bar. Lounge, full central heating. All bedrooms TV, tea and coffee facilities. Extensive menu of freshly prepared food. Idyllic walking and climbing area, maps and information available. Perfect centre for touring, fishing, little railways. Sandy beaches 9 miles.

T		NIGHTLY B&B PER PERSON		WEEKLY D,B&B PER PERSON		🛏	6
		MIN £	MAX £	MIN £	MAX £		3
		14.00	20.00			OPEN 1-12	

Farmhouses

Gwanas Farmhouse

Cross Foxes, Dolgellau,
Gwynedd LL40 2SH
Tel: (0341) 422624

This charming spacious farmhouse built in 1838 is situated in a beautiful position surrounded by hills where Tom and Mair Evans farm sheep and cattle on 1000 acres. Twin, double, family rooms with H&C, two bathrooms with showers, tea making facilities, central heating, TV, parking. Situated off A470 between Dinas Mawddwy and Dolgellau (three miles away), 400 yards from Cross Foxes Inn. Ideal touring base for beaches, railways, pony trekking. SAE for brochure.

HW	T	NIGHTLY B&B PER PERSON		WEEKLY D,B&B PER PERSON		🛏	3
		MIN £	MAX £	MIN £	MAX £		–
		10.50	12.50			OPEN 3-11	

FAIRBOURNE
Map Ref Db4

Quiet resort with 2 miles of sand south of Mawddach Estuary. railway buffs travel far to go on its 1' 3" gauge railway. Shops and accommodation. Car Parks. Butterfly farm. 🚂

Hotels

The Fairbourne Hotel

Fairbourne, Gwynedd,
LL38 2HQ
Tel: (0341) 250203

The Fairbourne Hotel, renowned for its good food, comfort and friendly atmosphere, is situated opposite the Estuary from Barmouth with commanding views of Cardigan Bay. Tea making facilities, private bathrooms, colour TV, bowls green, play room. Fully licensed. Ideally situated for pony trekking, sailing, climbing, golf and many more. Send for brochure Mr & Mrs Hodson.

HW		NIGHTLY B&B PER PERSON		WEEKLY D,B&B PER PERSON		🛏	23
		MIN £	MAX £	MIN £	MAX £		19
		19.50	20.50	165.00	179.00	OPEN 1-12	

MOTORING THROUGH BWLCH Y GROES

Guest Houses

Einion House

Friog, Fairbourne,
Gwynedd LL38 2NX
Tel: (0341) 250644

COMMENDED

Comfortably furnished family run guest house with homely atmosphere. Restaurant and residential licence. Full central heating and log fires. All bedrooms clock/radio, hairdryer and free tea making facilities. TV's available. Evening meals optional, vegetarians catered for. Children welcome. Pets by arrangement. Set in an area of exceptional scenery close to beach. Ideal for walking, touring and Great Little Trains. Write or phone for brochure.

HW T SP	NIGHTLY B&B PER PERSON		WEEKLY D,B&B PER PERSON		🛏 8 🛌 2
	MIN £	MAX £	MIN £	MAX £	OPEN
	12.50	15.00	120.00	135.00	1-12

LET A GUIDE SHOW YOU THE WAY

Why not book a Wales Official Tourist Guide for your next visit to Wales. Fees are very reasonable and a driver/guide can take the strain out of navigation and map reading whilst you sit back and enjoy your tour. Members of the Wales Official Tourist Guide Association are the only qualified tourist guides in Wales and the association is registered with the Wales Tourist Board. Any kind of guided tours are undertaken — from hourly tours by car or coach from a designated centre, to extended tours of any duration throughout Wales.

For more information contact Gwennie Johnson, W.O.T.G.A., Cae'r Felin, Chwilog, Criccieth, Gwynedd LL53 6SW.
Tel: (0766) 810889.

HARLECH   Map Ref Ae7

Small, stone-built town dominated by remains of 13-th-century castle — site of Owain Glyndwr's last stand. Dramatically set on a high crag, the castle commands a magnificent panorama of rolling sand dunes, sea and mountains. Home of 18-hole Royal St. David's Golf Club. Shell Island nearby; theatre and swimming pool. Visitors can explore the Chambers of the old Llanfair Slate Caverns just south of Harlech. 🚆

Hotels

Estuary Motel

Talsarnau, Harlech,
Gwynedd LL47 6TA
Tel: (0766) 771155

COMMENDED

Modern purpose built motel set in Snowdonia National Park close by glorious beaches, beautiful mountain scenery and Royal St. David's Golf Course. All rooms en-suite, TV, central heating etc. Licensed bar and restaurant. Disabled persons are welcome and the single level facilities make for easy wheelchair access.

HW T SP	NIGHTLY B&B PER PERSON		WEEKLY D,B&B PER PERSON		🛏 10 🛌 10
	MIN £	MAX £	MIN £	MAX £	OPEN
	16.00	19.00	170.80	189.70	1-12

LLANBEDR   Map Ref Da3

Llanbedr and neighbouring Pensar form a duo of attractive villages on the Ardudwy coast near Harlech. Maes Artro village a popular family tourist attraction. Close to Shell Island at Mochras, and Slate Caverns. The wild Rhinog Mountains in the background are excellent for walking. Explore them from lovely Llyn Cwm Bychan. 🚆

Hotels

Ty Mawr Hotel

Llanbedr, Gwynedd
LL45 2NH
Tel: (034123) 440

COMMENDED

*AA/RAC** Hospitality Award. Fully licensed country house in Snowdonia National Park near the sea and mountains. All ten bedrooms have bathroom en-suite, tea/coffee making facilities, colour TV and family videos. The hotel is tastefully furnished with an excellent menu for residents and non residents in the restaurant and real ale and meals served in the bar lunchtime and evening. Wood burning stoves, open fires and central heating for a warm stay! Honeymoon suites a speciality. Car park.*

HW T SP C	NIGHTLY B&B PER PERSON		WEEKLY D,B&B PER PERSON		🛏 10 🛌 10
	MIN £	MAX £	MIN £	MAX £	OPEN
	25.00	28.00	238.00	252.00	1-12

Victoria Inn

Llanbedr, Gwynedd
LL45 2LD
Tel: (034) 123213

👑👑 COMMENDED

Recently refurnished to the highest standards. This cosy inn now offers five en-suite bedrooms, tastefully furnished for your every comfort. The Victoria stands in the centre of the village on the banks of the River Artro. Delicious bar meals are available. Colour TV in bedrooms. Robinsons Traditional Draught Beers.

HW T SP	NIGHTLY B&B PER PERSON		WEEKLY D,B&B PER PERSON		🛏 5 🛁 5
	MIN £	MAX £	MIN £	MAX £	OPEN 1-12
	20.50	20.50	–	–	

WALES
It's magic

TAL-Y-LLYN
Map Ref Dc5

Lakeside village in magnificent setting below Cader Idris mountain, ideally placed for fishing and walking. Narrow-gauge Tallyllyn Railway, which runs to a nearby halt, connects with Tywyn.

Hotels

Tynycornel Hotel

Tal-y-llyn, Tywyn,
Gwynedd LL36 9AJ
Tel: (0654) 77282 / 223

👑👑 COMMENDED

Uniquely situated in the Snowdonia National Park, Tynycornel Hotel overlooks Talyllyn, its own 220 acre lake, whose waters reflect majestic Cader Idris (2927'). In an internationally acclaimed place of Outstanding Natural Beauty, the hotel has developed a reputation to match its location. Extensively and sensitively refurbished. Tynycornel 15 en-suite bedrooms enjoy spectacular views. An excellent restaurant and fine wine list compliment excellent facilities and high standards maintained in a friendly, relaxed atmosphere.

�” C SP	NIGHTLY B&B PER PERSON		WEEKLY D,B&B PER PERSON		🛏 15 🛁 15
	MIN £	MAX £	MIN £	MAX £	OPEN 1-12
	34.50	44.50	301.00	371.00	

TYWYN
Map Ref Da5

Seaside resort on Cardigan Bay, with beach activities, sea and river fishing and golf among its leading attractions. Good leisure centre. Narrow-gauge Tallyllyn Railway runs inland from here and St. Cadfan's Stone and Llanegryn Church are important Christian sites. In the hills stand Castell-y-Bere, a native Welsh castle, and Bird Rock a haven for birdlife. ⇌

Hotels

Greenfield Hotel & Restaurant

High Street, Tywyn,
Gwynedd LL36 9AD
Tel: (0654) 710354

👑👑 COMMENDED

AA*RAC*. Comfortable family run hotel situated opposite heated swimming pool, sports hall and car park. Close to cinema, shops, beach, bus, British Rail and Talyllyn rail stations. Residents lounge, licensed bar. Full central heating, choice of menu. Reductions for children. Ideal area for golf, fishing, walking and touring Snowdonia National Park. Brochure on request.

T SP	NIGHTLY B&B PER PERSON		WEEKLY D,B&B PER PERSON		🛏 13 🛁 2
	MIN £	MAX £	MIN £	MAX £	OPEN 1-12
	13.50	16.00	125.00	140.00	

TAL-Y-LLYN

Reminders of Wales's traditions and heritage are commonplace in Ceredigion. Aberystwyth preserves its Victorian character – it's even got a camera obscura (a popular amusement in bygone times) and a marvellous 'museum in a music hall'). Aberaeron's handsome Georgian harbour can be viewed from a unique aerial ferry, based on a 19th-century original. At Devil's Bridge (go there by steam train from Aberystwyth), you can see why the dramatic gorge was described in the 19th century as a 'dread chasm'. And New Quay's picturesque stone quayside, now busy with colourful holiday craft, still displays its old table of harbour tolls.

Drovers used to gather in Tregaron's square before setting off with their livestock to markets along the English Border. You can trace their footsteps by motoring over Wales's most spectacular drovers' route, the Abergwesyn Pass, a narrow road which winds its way eastwards across the empty 'Roof of Wales'

ABERAERON Map Ref Fc4

Most attractive little town on Cardigan Bay, with distinctive Georgian-style architecture. Pleasant harbour, marine aquarium, coastal centre, honey-bee exhibition, a recreation Aeron of Express, an extraordinary aerial ferry across harbour first built in 1885. Sailing popular; good touring centre for coast and inland. Aberarth Leisure Park nearby.

Guest Houses

Moldavia

7 & 8 Belle Vue Terrace, Aberaeron, Dyfed SA46 0BB Tel: (0545) 570107

AWARD COMMENDED

Spacious bedrooms offer panoramic views of picturesque Aberaeron Harbour and mountains beyond. All rooms have H&C, central heating, shaver point. Ground floor facilities for disabled guests. Special rates for family room. Children always welcome. Large safe garden and flower filled conservatory to relax in. Beverages always available. Ideally situated for touring, walking, fishing, riding, bird watching. Beach, shops, restaurants close by. Easy parking. We enjoy having visitors and provide a personal service.

HW	T	NIGHTLY B&B PER PERSON		WEEKLY D,B&B PER PERSON		🛏	3
						🛏	0
		MIN £	MAX £	MIN £	MAX £	OPEN	
		13.50	13.50			1-12	

ABERPORTH Map Ref Fa5

Popular seaside village. Safe swimming on two beaches and good sea fishing. Scenic cliff walks. Convenient for visiting other coastal villages along Cardigan Bay.

Hotels

Morlan Motel

Aberporth, Cardigan, Dyfed SA43 2EN Tel: (0239) 810611

Situated in the centre of the village 300 yards from two sandy beaches. All rooms are en-suite and centrally heated with tea and coffee making facilities. Fully licensed bar and pool table. The restaurant offers a good choice of menus and bar meals are available day and evening. Cheap spring and autumn breaks available. It is an ideal base for touring the delights of the West Wales coast and the Teifi Valley.

HW	T	NIGHTLY B&B PER PERSON		WEEKLY D,B&B PER PERSON		🛏	15
🐾	SP					🛏	15
		MIN £	MAX £	MIN £	MAX £	OPEN	
		15.00	16.00	147.00	154.00	1-12	

ABERYSTWYTH
Map Ref Fe2

Premier resort of the Cardigan Bay coastline. Fine promenade, cliff railway, camera obscura, pier and many other seaside attractions. Excellent museum in restored Edwardian theatre. University town, lively Arts Centre with theatre and concert hall. National Library of Wales stands commandingly on hillside. Good shopping. Vale of Rheidol narrow-gauge steam line runs to Devil's Bridge Falls. ⇥

Hotels

Bay Hotel

35-37 Marine Terrace, Aberystwyth, Dyfed SY23 2BX Tel: (0970) 617356 Fax: (0970) 612198

Family owned hotel for 17 years catering for holidays, group holidays, meetings and conferences. On sea front, central for shops, own car park. 32 bedrooms, 22 en-suite. Restaurant, bar, function rooms for 130 guests. Laundry available. School parties, educational groups catered for. Brochure/tariff Bay Hotel, Aberystwyth, Free Post.

HW	T	NIGHTLY B&B PER PERSON		WEEKLY D,B&B PER PERSON		🛏	32
	C					🛏	22
		MIN £	MAX £	MIN £	MAX £	OPEN	
		24.00	27.00	210.00	220.00	1-12	

WALES It's magic

Belle Vue Royal Hotel

Marine Terrace, Aberystwyth,
Dyfed SY23 2BA
Tel: (0970) 617558/
625380 Fax: (0970) 612190

COMMENDED

Situated on the seafront overlooking Cardigan Bay. An ideal centre for fishing, golf, (free to residents Monday to Friday) and touring Mid Wales. All bedrooms have colour television, telephone, tea/coffee, radio and baby listening service. Both 'a la carte and table d'hôte menus are available. Royal's grill room has recently opened. A wide range of bar snacks available in either of our two bars. AA**RAC**, Ashley Courtenay, Les Routiers.

C SP	NIGHTLY B&B PER PERSON		WEEKLY D,B&B PER PERSON		🛏 42
					🍴 25
	MIN £	MAX £	MIN £	MAX £	OPEN
	25.00	28.00	230.00	250.00	1-12

Conrah Country House Hotel

Chancery, Aberystwyth,
Dyfed SY23 4DF
Tel: (0970) 617941
Telex: 35892 Fax: (0970) 624546

COMMENDED

Discreet Welsh country house hotel in 22 acres of quiet grounds, 3 miles from Aberystwyth. A warm welcome, delicious local food, good wines, high standards of service. Elegant withdrawing and writing rooms. Flowers, log fires and luxury en-suite bedrooms. Heated indoor swimming pool. Special short breaks throughout the year.

HW T SP TW	NIGHTLY B&B PER PERSON		WEEKLY D,B&B PER PERSON		🛏 22
					🍴 20
	MIN £	MAX £	MIN £	MAX £	OPEN
	30.00	42.50	249.00	324.00	1-12

Llety Gwyn Hotel

Llanbadarn Fawr,
Aberystwyth,
Dyfed SY23 3SR
Tel: (0970) 623965

Eight rooms en-suite, TV, radio, tea/coffee all rooms. Sun bed, gym, games room, satellite TV, sauna, TV lounge. Parking. Large dining room, licensed. Suitable disabled ramps all entrances. Pleasant garden. Swings for children. 1 1/2 miles sea front. Ideal touring and walking. Good home cooking. Known locally for good food. Warm Welsh welcome Jones family.

T SP TW	NIGHTLY B&B PER PERSON		WEEKLY D,B&B PER PERSON		🛏 14
					🍴 8
	MIN £	MAX £	MIN £	MAX £	OPEN
	16.50	24.00			1-12

Windsor Private Hotel

41 Queens Road, Aberystwyth,
Dyfed SY23 2HN
Tel: (0970) 612134

Situated close to seafront and shops. All rooms have hot/cold, shaving point, tea/coffee facilities, TV. Some rooms have private shower. TV lounge. Ideal for tennis, golf, bowls. Residential licence and fire certificate in force. Discount for children sharing. Windsor Hotel is privately run by proprietors.

HW T	NIGHTLY B&B PER PERSON		WEEKLY D,B&B PER PERSON		🛏 10
					🍴 4
	MIN £	MAX £	MIN £	MAX £	OPEN
	11.00	14.00	122.50	143.50	1-12

Guest Houses

Glynwern Guest House

Llanilar, Aberystwyth,
Dyfed SY23 4NY
Tel: (09747) 203

L

Glynwern is an attractive house set in its own extensive grounds, with own gardens fronting the River Ystwyth. The river affords free private fishing for Glynwern guests. Two double bedrooms with wash-basins, one twin and two single rooms. Comfortable lounge and pleasant dining room. Central heating. Open all year. You can spend a peaceful, restful or exploring holiday, either way Glynwern will offer a most friendly welcome amidst rural surroundings. No dogs allowed. SAE for reply.

T	NIGHTLY B&B PER PERSON		WEEKLY D,B&B PER PERSON		🛏 4
	MIN £	MAX £	MIN £	MAX £	OPEN
	16.00	18.00	–	–	1-12

WALES
It's magic

NIGHTFALL AT ABERYSTWYTH

Hemstal Guest House

69 North Parade, Aberystwyth,
Dyfed SY23 2JN
Tel: (0970) 624398

Family run guest house. Approx 250 yards from sea front, located in town centre. Hot and cold in all rooms, central heating, fire certificate, TV lounge. Bed and breakfast, optional evening meals. Very reasonable terms. Homely. Write or telephone for details. Guests personally cared for by proprietors Jean and Elwyn Thomas.

HW SP T	NIGHTLY B&B PER PERSON		WEEKLY D,B&B PER PERSON		🛏 6 —	
	MIN £	MAX £	MIN £	MAX £	OPEN 1-12
	22.00	00.00	000.00	000.00	

Farmhouse

Tycam Farm

Capel Bangor, Aberystwyth,
Dyfed SY23 3NA
Tel: (097084) 662

Peaceful dairy/sheep farm in glorious Rheidol Valley, 7 1/2 miles Aberystwyth, only 2 1/2 miles off A44. Real home comfort and farmhouse cooking. Lounge/ dining room (separate tables), colour TV. Perfect centre for walking, bird watching, sightseeing, 1/2 mile superb salmon, sewin, trout fishing on farm, plus nearby lakes. Pony trekking, golf and beaches within easy reach. 2 fine double rooms, all with central heating, bathroom, toilet etc. Ample car parking.

HW SP T	NIGHTLY B&B PER PERSON		WEEKLY D,B&B PER PERSON		🛏 2 —	
	MIN £	MAX £	MIN £	MAX £	OPEN 1-12
	13.00	15.00	130.00	150.00	

BORTH   Map Ref Db7

Popular holiday village with marvellous expanse of firm sands, ideal for beach games. Fine views from Ynyslas dunes to north across Dovey Estuary. Golf links, promenade 2 miles long. "Animalarium" farm attraction.

Hotels

Cliff Haven Hotel

Cliff Road, Borth,
Dyfed SY24 5NG
Tel: (0970) 871659
Fax: (0970) 871175   COMMENDED

Enjoy spectacular views of our safe clean sandy beach. Eat delicious food. Relax in our health club and swimming pool. Play golf, go pony trekking. Rooms with en-suite facilities, colour television. Delight in the welcome we give every one. Families, oldies and singles alike.

HW SP	NIGHTLY B&B PER PERSON		WEEKLY D,B&B PER PERSON		🛏 8 🛏 8	
	MIN £	MAX £	MIN £	MAX £	OPEN 1-12
	25.00	28.00	165.00	180.00	

Golf Hotel

Borth, Dyfed SY24 5HY
Tel: (0970) 871362   MERIT

Small family run hotel overlooking safe sandy beach near railway station. Single, double and family rooms with H&C, shaver point, colour TV, tea making facilities. Special rates children sharing. Lounge bar, licensed restaurant offering wide range of menu. Ideal for golfing, riding, bird watching, guided hill walking holidays available or just relax in a pleasant atmosphere. Fire certificate granted. Parties welcome. Terms on request.

HW T	NIGHTLY B&B PER PERSON		WEEKLY D,B&B PER PERSON		🛏 10 —	
	MIN £	MAX £	MIN £	MAX £	OPEN 3-12
	15.00	16.00	135.00	150.00	

CARDIGAN   Map Ref Fa5

Market town on mouth of River, close to beaches and resorts. Good shopping facilities, accommodation, inns. Golf and fishing. Base for exploring inland along wooded Teifi Valley and south to the Pembrokeshire Coast National Park. Y Felin Corn Mill and ruined abbey at neighbouring St. Dogmael's. Wildlife park nearby.

Hotels

Allt-y-Rheini Hotel

Cilgerran, Cardigan,
Dyfed SA43 2TJ
Tel: (0239) 612286

Informal family run hotel set in 4 1/2 acres of grounds overlooking beautiful countryside and only 5 minutes from local beaches. Rooms with en-suite, colour television, and tea/coffee making facilities. Relax in the lounge or take a drink in our conservatory bar. Restaurant offers traditional Welsh fayre and traditional home cooking. Putting green, croquet lawn, solarium and hairdressing salon. Children welcome. Plenty of car parking.

HW T	NIGHTLY B&B PER PERSON		WEEKLY D,B&B PER PERSON		🛏 5 🛏 3	
	MIN £	MAX £	MIN £	MAX £	OPEN 1-12
	22.00	25.00	195.00	215.00	

WINDSURFING OFF BORTH

Penbontbren Farm Hotel

Glynarthen, Cardigan,
Dyfed SA44 6PE
Tel: (0239) 810248

COMMENDED

Tastefully converted pine furnished stone buildings, two miles Cardigan Bay. Excellent cuisine including special diets. Family rooms offer telephone, colour TV, bathroom en-suite, heating, hot drinks tray. Small bar, residents lounges, occasional harp music. Attractions include farm museum/crafts, nature trail in 90 acres. Bargain breaks. Ground floor rooms adapted for disabled. AA**RAC**.

	NIGHTLY B&B PER PERSON		WEEKLY D,B&B PER PERSON		🛏 10
HW T 🐕 C SP ✂ TW	MIN £ 23.00	MAX £ 26.00	MIN £ 196.00	MAX £ 217.00	🛏 10 OPEN 1-12

LET A GUIDE SHOW YOU THE WAY

Why not book a Wales Official Tourist Guide for your next visit to Wales. Fees are very reasonable and a driver/guide can take the strain out of navigation and map reading whilst you sit back and enjoy your tour. Members of the Wales Official Tourist Guide Association are the only qualified tourist guides in Wales and the association is registered with the Wales Tourist Board. Any kind of guided tours are undertaken — from hourly tours by car or coach from a designated centre, to extended tours of any duration throughout Wales.
For more information contact Gwennie Johnson, W.O.T.G.A., Cae'r Felin, Chwilog, Criccieth, Gwynedd LL53 6SW. Tel: (0766) 810889.

Guest Houses

Berwyn

St. Dogmaels, Cardigan,
Dyfed SA43 3HS
Tel: (0239) 613555

Privately situated with magnificent views overlooking River Teifi. Central for beautiful beaches, golf, fishing, boat trips, Welsh crafts. Enjoy breakfast with gorgeous views. Relax on 2 acres delightful grounds. En-suite with TV. Bedrooms with vanity suites, tea/coffee making facilities. Central heating. TV lounge. Pay phone. Ample parking. (Croeso) Welsh welcome.

	NIGHTLY B&B PER PERSON		WEEKLY D,B&B PER PERSON		🛏 3
T	MIN £ 12.50	MAX £ 15.50	MIN £ 000.00	MAX £ 000.00	🛏 1 OPEN 2-10

Brynhyfryd Guest House

Gwbert Road, Cardigan,
Dyfed SA43 1AE
Tel: (0239) 612861

COMMENDED

One of Cardigan's longest established guest houses where a high standard of comfort, cleanliness and good food is always assured. Situated in a pleasant area of the town within two miles of the beautiful coast of Cardigan Bay. All bedrooms have colour television and tea/coffee facilities, en-suites available. Guests lounge, evening meals, easy parking. AA/RAC Listed. Brochure.

	NIGHTLY B&B PER PERSON		WEEKLY D,B&B PER PERSON		🛏 7
T	MIN £ 13.00	MAX £ 14.00	MIN £ 125.00	MAX £ 130.00	🛏 2 OPEN 1-12

LAMPETER   Map Ref Fe5

Farmers and students mingle in this distinctive small central Dyfed town, in the picturesque Teifi Valley. Concerts are often held in St. David's University College and visitors are welcome. Golf and angling, range of small shops and old inns. Visit the landscaped Gerddi Cae Hir Gardens, Cribyn.

Hotels

Falcondale Country House Hotel

Lampeter, Dyfed
SA48 7RX
Tel: (0570) 422910

COMMENDED

A 3 star Victorian mansion situated within 14 acres of parkland, overlooking the university market town of Lampeter. All bedrooms en-suite with telephone, hairdryer, tea/coffee makers, TV, radio, baby listening. 2 bars, conservatory, lift and elegantly appointed restaurant offering table d'hôte plus a very extensive 'a la carte menu. A tennis court plus 18 hole putting green are provided, with golf, pony and horse riding, bowls, swimming pool, sea, salmon and lake fishing, with the safe beaches of Cardigan Bay 20 minutes drive.

	NIGHTLY B&B PER PERSON		WEEKLY D,B&B PER PERSON		🛏 20
HW T SP	MIN £ 27.50	MAX £ 33.00	MIN £ 225.00	MAX £ 295.00	🛏 20 OPEN 1-12

LLANDYSUL

Map Ref Fc6

Pleasant Teifi-side village in a historic textile-producing area where woollen mills still work – and welcome visitors. Salmon fishing very popular; canoeing at certain times of year.

Guest House

Plas Cerdin

Ffostrasol,
Llandysul,
Dyfed SA44 4TA
Tel: (023975) 329

HIGHLY COMMENDED

Relax and enjoy the peaceful, friendly atmosphere of our modern split level house. Situated 350 yards from A486 Llandysul-New Quay road. Large TV lounge with panoramic views. Three double bedrooms (two with en-suite shower/toilet), two single rooms, all with washbasins, shaver points. Good fresh food. Tea/coffee facilities available. Ample parking.

NIGHTLY B&B PER PERSON		WEEKLY D,B&B PER PERSON		
MIN £	MAX £	MIN £	MAX £	5 / 2
12.00	14.00	125.00	140.00	OPEN 1-12

LLANON

Map Ref Fd3

Village near Aberaeron on Cardigan Bay coast. Mainly shingle beach nearby. Good centre from which to explore Mid Wales coast and country.

Hotel

Plas Morfa

Llanon, Nr. Aberaeron,
Dyfed SY23 5HT
Tel: (09748) 415

MERIT

Situated 40 yards from the beach, midway between Aberystwyth and Aberaeron. Sea views from all en-suite bedrooms and the high standard 'a la carte restaurant. Choice of cocktail bar or character cellar bar which converts from disco to function room or air gun shooting range. Bar meals, large screen video. Safe car parking. Recommended bird-watching area, close to wildlife centre, butterfly farm, sea aquarium. Beautiful walks.

HW T C SP

NIGHTLY B&B PER PERSON		WEEKLY D,B&B PER PERSON		
MIN £	MAX £	MIN £	MAX £	8 / 8
18.00	22.00	168.00	190.00	OPEN 1-12

NEW QUAY

Map Ref Fc4

Picturesque little resort with old harbour on Cardigan Bay. Lovely beaches and coves around and about. Good for sailing and fishing. Resort sheltered by protective headland.

Hotel

Black Lion Hotel

New Quay, Dyfed
SA45 9PT
Tel: (0545) 560209

New Quay, famous for its boating, fishing and resident dolphin population is ideal for the family holiday. Overlooking Cardigan Bay the hotel is 3 minutes from the beach and harbour. Comfortable rooms, mostly en-suite, all with colour TV and tea/coffee facilities. Olde worlde bar where Dylan Thomas was a regular. Good food and well stocked cellars. Private car park. Beer garden overlooking the bay.

T C SP

NIGHTLY B&B PER PERSON		WEEKLY D,B&B PER PERSON		
MIN £	MAX £	MIN £	MAX £	8 / 7
17.00	25.00	140.00	160.00	OPEN 2-11

Tŷ Hen Farm Hotel

Llwyndafydd,
Nr. New Quay,
Dyfed SA44 6BZ
Tel: (0545) 560346

MERIT

The farm hotel offers en-suite rooms C.TVs, drink making facilities in a peaceful relaxed setting. No smoking. The Leisure centre offers a large indoor heated pool (lessons available), sauna, solarium, fitness centre, bowls/skittles. Luxury restaurant and bar. Please send for brochure.

HW T SP

NIGHTLY B&B PER PERSON		WEEKLY D,B&B PER PERSON		
MIN £	MAX £	MIN £	MAX £	7 / 7
21.00	28.00	194.00	240.00	OPEN 1-12

NEW QUAY HARBOUR

WALES *It's magic*

TRE-SAITH — Map Ref Fb5

Small village above sands on a popular stretch of Cardigan Bay coast near Aberporth with tiny coves and quiet beaches: many pleasant coastal walks; waterfall plunges down steep cliffs.

Hotel

Glandwr Manor Hotel

Tre-saith, Aberporth, Dyfed
SA43 2JH
Tel: (0239) 810197

COMMENDED

Situated in 5 acres of the beautiful Tre-saith Valley, 6 minutes walk to superbsandy beach, with safe bathing. Comfortable bar with beamed ceiling, log fire. Restaurant offers good selection of food and wine with fresh cream desserts always on the menu. Most bedrooms ensuite. Family suites with double bedroom, adjoining rooms with bunks and bathroom. Tea & coffee making facilities. AA*.

T	NIGHTLY B&B PER PERSON		WEEKLY D,B&B PER PERSON		7
	MIN £	MAX £	MIN £	MAX £	5
	16.50	19.00	145.00	175.00	OPEN 3-10

Guest Houses

Bryn Berwyn Guest House

Tre-saith,
Cardigan,
Dyfed, SA43 2JG
Tel: (0239) 811126

COMMENDED

Bryn Berwyn guest house benefits from spectacular views of the sea and surrounding countryside. We offer all home comforts, home cooking and table licence. All bedrooms have en-suite, colour television. AA Listed. Large garden with play area, five hole pitch and putt for children and parents. Also large car park.

HW T SP	NIGHTLY B&B PER PERSON		WEEKLY D,B&B PER PERSON		7
	MIN £	MAX £	MIN £	MAX £	7
	14.50	23.00	130.00	210.00	OPEN 1-12

Iscoed

Tre-saith,
Cardigan,
Dyfed SA43 2JG
Tel: (0239) 810030

HIGHLY COMMENDED

Quietly situated, less than ten minutes walk to the beach and waterfall at Tre-saith. Emphasis is placed on good home-made food, which includes wholemeal bread and fresh vegetables from our own garden. Guests are welcome to bring their own wine for dinner. A large menu choice is offered at breakfast time.

T	NIGHTLY B&B PER PERSON		WEEKLY D,B&B PER PERSON		3
	MIN £	MAX £	MIN £	MAX £	1
	14.00	16.00	120.00	130.00	OPEN 3-10

TRE-SAITH BEACH

SLIDE PACKS

The following slide packs are available for purchase from the Wales Tourist Board:

North Wales Scenery	£2.00	(4 slides)
Mid Wales Scenery	£2.00	(4 slides)
South Wales Scenery	£2.00	(4 slides)
Historic Sites	£3.00	(6 slides)

Contact: Photo Librarian, WTB, Brunel House, 2 Fitzalan Road, Cardiff CF2 1UY

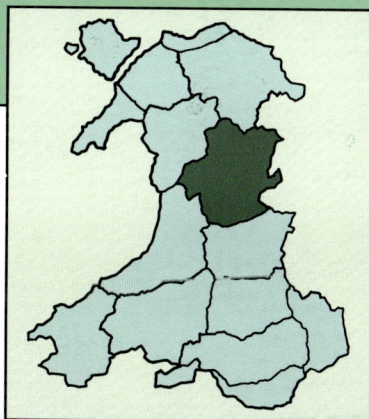

This area takes in everything from wild, high mountains dotted with isolated stone farmsteads to gentle, fertile border country where you'll see old black-and-white buildings which are typical of the Marches borderlands. Montgomeryshire is farming country through-and-through. Visitors can mingle with farming folk during market days, livestock sales and sheepdog trials.

It's the perfect place for those who like to get a map out and explore tall-hedged country lanes that lead to timeless, tranquil villages. And they might even find remote Pistyll Rhaeadr, Wales's highest waterfall, on their travels. Let a narrow-gauge steam train take you on a trip through the hills around Welshpool. And don't miss two castles that couldn't be more different – the National Trust's sumptuous, stately Powis Castle, and Montgomery Castle, a spectacularly located medieval ruin on its rocky perch above a pretty little town.

69

CARNO
Map Ref De6

Village bounded by wild moorland on main north-south (A470) road not far from Llanidloes and Newtown. Talerddig railway cutting 4 miles west was deepest cutting in the world when build in 1861.

LAKE VYRNWY
Map Ref Ea3

Man-made lake of dramatic beauty, hidden away amongst remote mountains and forests. Visitor Centre near dam. Shores are a haven for birds and wild life. Village of Llanwddyn below dam. Spectacular roads climb into the hills from the lakeside.

LLANBRYNMAIR
Map Ref De5

Scattered mountain-ringed village on Afon (River) Twymwyn, a tributary of the Dyfi. Travel south from here on the B4518 to the huge man-made lake of Llyn Clywedog — an inspiring mountain route.

Guest Houses

Dolafon Guest House

Carno, Powys
SY17 5LG
Tel: (0686) 420648

At the heart of lovely Mid Wales. Situated in a acre of grounds on the Newtown to Machynlleth road about 26 miles from the coast. Walking, fishing, shooting and a variety of other activities available locally. Licensed. Colour television and tea making facilities in all rooms, two with bathroom en-suite. Hot and cold water, central heating, guest lounge, dining room. Ample parking, evening meal by arrangement. Packed lunches on request.

HW		NIGHTLY B&B PER PERSON		WEEKLY D,B&B PER PERSON			3
							2
		MIN £	MAX £	MIN £	MAX £	OPEN	
		12.00	16.00	147.00	–	1-12	

Hotels

Lake Vyrnwy Hotel

Lake Vyrnwy,
Llanwddyn, Powys SY10 0LY
Tel: (069173) 692
Fax: (069173) 259

The hotel nestled on a wooded hillside surrounded by mountains and moorland commands breathtaking lake views. Rooms are individually decorated and furnished and the whole atmosphere is quietly elegant, cosy warm and abounding in tranquility and charm. Renowned also for its sporting facilities including excellent fishing. Cuisine is grand "country style". A perfect retreat.

HW	T	NIGHTLY B&B PER PERSON		WEEKLY D,B&B PER PERSON			30
	SP						30
TW		MIN £	MAX £	MIN £	MAX £	OPEN	
		22.75	47.75	253.75	416.50	1-12	

Guest Houses

Cyfeiliog Guest House

Bont Dolgadfan,
Llanbrynmair, Powys SY19 7BB
Tel: (06503) 231

L
MERIT

Licensed guest house in pretty hamlet beside the River Twymyn. Centrally heated throughout. Open fire in beamed lounge. Relaxed friendly atmosphere. TV, books, information, maps. Wonderful holiday centre. Walking, bird watching, touring, golf etc. Sea 25 miles. 2 twin, 1 family bedrooms. Evening meals, packed lunches, vegetarians welcome, other special diets by arrangement.

HW	T	NIGHTLY B&B PER PERSON		WEEKLY D,B&B PER PERSON			3
							–
		MIN £	MAX £	MIN £	MAX £	OPEN	
		11.50	11.50	130.00	130.00	1-12	

LLYN CLYWEDOG

LLANFAIR CAEREINION
Map Ref Fb5

Pleasant town set amid rolling hills and forest in lovely Vale of Banwy; best known as terminus for narrow-gauge Welshpool and Llanfair Light Railway.

Hotels

Goat Hotel

Llanfair Caereinion,
Powys SY21 0QS
Tel: (0938) 810428

The Goat is an 18th century inn, full of character and charm. Our six lovely bedrooms have every modern comfort, central heating, welcome tray, telephone and radio. Our Queen Anne suite is ideal for special occasions. In our lounge you can enjoy real ale and hearty meals or why not relax over a candlelit dinner in our cosy restaurant. Garden and car park.

HW T 🐾 SP	NIGHTLY B&B PER PERSON		WEEKLY D,B&B PER PERSON		🛏 6 🛁 4
	MIN £	MAX £	MIN £	MAX £	OPEN 1-12
	14.00	18.00	000.00	000.00	

WALES *It's magic*

LLANFYLLIN Map Ref Eb3

Historic small country town, in rolling peaceful Powys farmlands. Lake Vyrnwy and 240ft Pistyll Rhaeadr waterfall are popular beauty spots nearby. Visit the Bird and Butterfly World, an attraction with birds from all over the world and Tropical House.

Hotels

Cain Valley Hotel

High Street, Llanfyllin,
Powys SY22 5AQ
Tel: (069184) 366

16th Century inn, of immense character, situated amidst beautiful countryside. A superb base for walking, fishing, riding, golfing. Convenient for Snowdonia and coastal resorts. All en-suite, colour TV, tea/coffee making facilities. The hotel is renowned for its wealth of beams and Jacobean staircase. Family run, friendly staff offering wide range of wines, two bars, recommended in good beer guide. Interesting food, bar meals or 'a la carte. Log fires in winter. Child reductions.

HW T 🐾 SP ✈	NIGHTLY B&B PER PERSON		WEEKLY D,B&B PER PERSON		🛏 14 🛁 14
	MIN £	MAX £	MIN £	MAX £	OPEN 1-12
	17.00	20.00	147.00	179.00	

Farmhouses

Cwm Alan Farm

Llanfyllin,
Powys SY22 5HX
Tel: (069184) 301   L

Situated overlooking the River Alan in peaceful valley with beautiful unspoilt views. Spacious rooms with tea/coffee making facilities. Close to Lake Vyrnwy and Bala with breathtaking mountain passes. Ideal base for touring Wales. Walking, fishing, shooting, pony trekking available locally. Evening meal by arrangement. For further details contact J. Emberton.

T 🐾 SP	NIGHTLY B&B PER PERSON		WEEKLY D,B&B PER PERSON		🛏 3 🛁 1
	MIN £	MAX £	MIN £	MAX £	OPEN 1-12
	11.00	15.00	110.00	140.00	

PISTYLL RHAEADR

MONTGOMERY CANAL

71

LLANGURIG Map Ref Gc1

First village on fledgling River Wye, nearly 1,000ft up in the mountains. A craft centre and a monastic 14th-century church. Good touring centre for lakes and mountains of central Wales. Ideal walking countryside.

Guest Houses

The Old Vicarage

Llangurig,
Nr. Llanidloes,
Powys SY18 6RN
Tel: (05515) 280

AWARD

HIGHLY
COMMENDED

Charming Victorian guest house in superb country close to Elan Valley and Plynlimon Hills. Ideal base for walking and touring the lakes and mountains of central Wales. Peaceful location H&C all rooms (some en-suite). TV lounges. Choice evening meals. Vegetarians and special diets. Pets welcome. Tourist Board Award for comfort and service. AA listed.

	NIGHTLY B&B PER PERSON		WEEKLY D,B&B PER PERSON		🛏 4
TW	MIN £	MAX £	MIN £	MAX £	🚿 2
	13.50	17.50	145.00	165.00	OPEN 3-10

MACHYNLLETH
Map Ref Dc5

Historic market town near beautiful Dovey Estuary. Owain Glyndwr's Parliament House in the wide, handsome main street is now a museum and brass rubbing centre; superbly equipped Plas Leisure Centre offers wide range of activities. Ancient and modern meet here; the inventive National Centre for Alternative Technology is 3 miles away, just off the A487 to Dolgellau. Felin Crewi Water Mill off A489 2 miles to the east. ⇌

Hotels

The White Lion Coaching Inn

Heol Pentrerhedyn,
Machynlleth, Powys
SY20 8ND
Tel: (0654) 703455
Fax: (0654) 703746

Established coaching inn in historical Machynlleth. Ideally situated for golf, fishing, walking, water sports, Snowdonia, beautiful scenery and new leisure centre. Comfortable and friendly atmosphere, superb cuisine with personal hospitality providing a range of en-suite and standard rooms all with H&C, CH, colour TV, tea/coffee facilities. All rooms tastefully co-ordinated. Large car park and gardens. RAC Inn Two Tankard Award, Les Routiers, BHRCA, AA. Weekend, midweek breaks speciality. Access, Visa, Amex, Diners accepted.

	NIGHTLY B&B PER PERSON		WEEKLY D,B&B PER PERSON		🛏 9
TW	MIN £	MAX £	MIN £	MAX £	🚿 6
	37.00	52.00	000.00	000.00	OPEN 1-12

Ynyshir Hall Country House Hotel

Eglwysfach, Machynlleth,
Powys SY20 8TA
Tel: (0654) 781209   COMMENDED

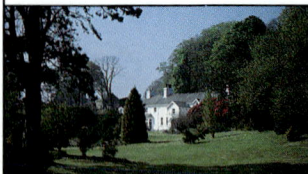

This captivating manor house once owned by Queen Victoria perfectly blends modern comfort and old world elegance. Its 12 acres of picturesque landscaped gardens nestling amidst mountain scenery and the Dyfi Estuary offer peace and tranquility. Taste and design echo throughout the house with 10 individually furnished en-suite bedrooms and public rooms, graced with antiques, oriental rugs and works of art. The much acclaimed restaurant offers English, French and Welsh cuisine.

		NIGHTLY B&B PER PERSON		WEEKLY D,B&B PER PERSON		🛏 9
SP	TW	MIN £	MAX £	MIN £	MAX £	🚿 9
		35.00	60.00	225.00	375.00	OPEN 1-12

Farmhouses

Bacheiddon Farm

Aberhosan, Machynlleth,
Powys SY20 8SG
Tel: (0654) 702229

850 acre beef and sheep Hill Land Award Farm 1985. Six miles from the market town of Machynlleth and within easy reach of the sea and Snowdonia National Park. Three double en-suite bedrooms with tea/coffee facilities, home cooking, own spring water. Lounge with TV and reading material. Brochure from Mrs A. Lewis.

NIGHTLY B&B PER PERSON		WEEKLY D,B&B PER PERSON		🛏 3
MIN £	MAX £	MIN £	MAX £	🚿 3
16.00	00.00	154.00	000.00	OPEN 5-10

NATIONAL CENTRE FOR ALTERNATIVE TECHNOLOGY

NEWTOWN Map Ref Eb6

Busy Severn Valley market town and one-time home of Welsh flannel industry. Textile history recalled in small museum; another collection centres around Robert Owen, pioneer socialist, who lived here; town also has interesting W. H. Smith Museum; Solid old buildings, river promenade, street market and the lively Theatr Hafren. ≈

Farmhouses

Lower-Gwestydd Farm

Newtown,
Powys SY16 3AY
Tel: (0686) 626718

AWARD   COMMENDED

Beautiful half timbered 17th century listed farmhouse full of character. Just off B4568 road, north of Newtown. 2 rooms en-suite, all centrally heated, tea, coffee facilities, radio alarms, separate dining room, lounge with colour TV. Large garden providing fresh produce for table, own beef, lamb and chicken offering "Taste of Wales". Easy day trips to lakes, mountains, seaside, little trains with fishing, pony trekking and golf nearby. Lovely views from this 200 acre mixed farm with country walks. A warm welcome to all. Farmhouse Award. Health and hygiene certificate.

HW T TW	NIGHTLY B&B PER PERSON		WEEKLY D,B&B PER PERSON		🛏 3 🛏 2
	MIN £	MAX £	MIN £	MAX £	OPEN 1-12
	13.50	14.000	136.00	136.00	

PENYBONTFAWR Map Ref Eb3

Secluded village amid forests and lakes, near the spectacular 240ft Pistyll Rhaeadr waterfalls. Pony trekking and walking country, with hills and woods all around. Lake Vyrnwy Visitor Centre nearby.

Farmhouses

Penyceunant

Penybontfawr, Oswestry,
Shropshire SY10 0PF
Tel: (069174) 459

L   COMMENDED

Penyceunant is a 200 year old farmhouse in an elevated position (800ft) above the Tanat Valley. Substantial rooms with spectacular views include washbasin, colour TV, easy chair and tea/coffee making facilities. Ideal as a secluded retreat yet well placed for touring West Wales coast. Snowdonia, Shrewsbury and Chester within an hour's drive. Lake Vyrnwy, Pistyll Rhaeadr and Berwyns within walking distance. 'Evening meals available. Weekends and school holidays. Enquiries :chga Francis.

HW T SP	NIGHTLY B&B PER PERSON		WEEKLY D,B&B PER PERSON		🛏 2
	MIN £	MAX £	MIN £	MAX £	OPEN 3-10
	12.50	14.00	123.00	132.00	

WELSHPOOL Map Ref Ec5

Old market town of the borderlands, full of character, with half-timbered buildings and welcoming inns. Attractive canalside museum. Good shopping centre; golf and angling. Powis Castle is an impressive stately home with a Clive of India museum. Ride the narrow-gauge Welshpool and Llanfair Light Railway, visit the Moors Wildlife Collection. ≈

Hotels

The Royal Oak Hotel

The Cross, Welshpool,
Powys SY21 7DG
Tel: (0938) 552217   MERIT

A privately owned hotel dating back to the 17th century to the time of the Jacobites. The Royal Oak has long been the ideal place to stay for visiting historic places surrounding Welshpool, Powis Castle, Llanfair Light Railway, Clywedog and Claerwen Dams. The hotel has 25 bedrooms with all modern facilities. A 60 seater restaurant with a reputation for good food, wine and warm atmosphere. Weekend breaks available.

T SP	NIGHTLY B&B PER PERSON		WEEKLY D,B&B PER PERSON		🛏 24 🛏 24
	MIN £	MAX £	MIN £	MAX £	OPEN 1-12
	27.00	30.00	217.00	245.00	

WALES
It's magic

73

Wynnstay Hotel

Church Street, Oswestry,
Salop SY11 2SZ
Tel: (0691) 655261
Fax: (0691) 670606

Typical of the Georgian period, the hotel over the years has gone through many changes and in 1988/1989 was extensively renovated in the style of a Georgian country house hotel. The Wynnstay is unique in that it has its own 200 year old walled Crown Bowling Green, set in beautiful surroundings, it is used most days in the season by the Wynnstay Bowling Club and hotel guests. Welshpool 12 miles, Llangollen 18 miles, half and hour's drive to Chester and Shrewsbury.

	NIGHTLY B&B PER PERSON		WEEKLY D,B&B PER PERSON		🍴 26
	MIN £	MAX £	MIN £	MAX £	🛏 26
	32.50	57.50	247.00	402.50	OPEN 1-12

WELSHPOOL AND LLANFAIR LIGHT RAILWAY

POWIS CASTLE

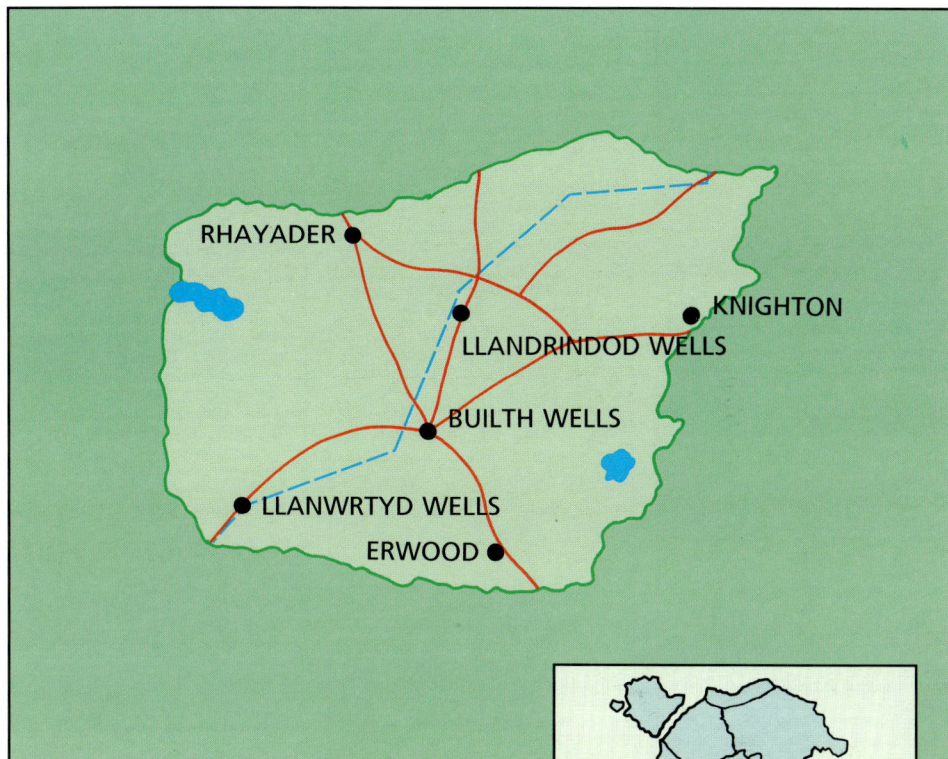

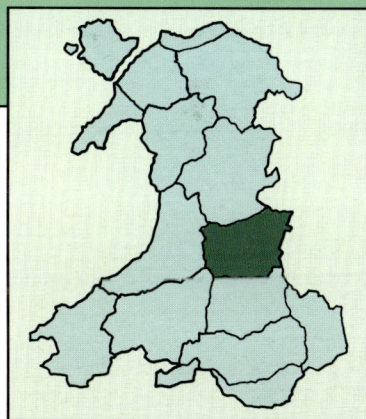

The name accurately reflects the character of this region. The images most closely associated with rural Wales – green, undulating countryside, characterful farming towns, rushing mountain streams, trout and salmon rich rivers – all come to life in the Heart of Wales. Pony trekking is popular around Rhayader and Llanwrtyd Wells. Builth Wells hosts the largest agricultural gathering in Wales when the Royal Welsh Show comes to town annually in late July. And at nearby Llandrindod Wells, with its Victorian Festival in August, you can – if you are curious enough – still take the spa waters that, according to the locals, cure almost everything.

Genteel Llandrindod is a popular inland resort with an excellent selection of places to stay. It's surrounded by superb scenery – close by, for example, are the Elan Valley lakelands, a spectacular string of man-made lakes within the folds of the untravelled Cambrian Mountains.

BUILTH WELLS
Map Ref Ge4

Solidly built old country town which plays host every July to Royal Welsh Agricultural Show, Wales's largest farming gathering. Lovely setting on River Wye amid beautiful hills. Lively sheep and cattle markets. Good shopping for local products, touring centre for Mid Wales and border Country. River walk, Wyeside Arts Centre.

Hotels

The Lion Hotel

Broad Street, Builth Wells,
Powys LD2 3DT
Tel: (0982) 553670
Fax: (0982) 553999

A former coaching inn now a 2 star hotel commanding a prominent position beside the beautiful River Wye. Most rooms en-suite and all have colour TV, tea/coffee facilities, telephone, baby listening and central heating. Extensive restaurant menu and wine list. Choice of 2 bars serving home-made bar snacks and real ale. Car parking. Pets welcome. Excellent base for touring or walking scenic Mid Wales. Ideally situated for golf and salmon fishing. Mini breaks available throughout year.

HW T C SP	NIGHTLY B&B PER PERSON		WEEKLY D,B&B PER PERSON		20 16
	MIN £	MAX £	MIN £	MAX £	OPEN 1-12
	21.00	26.50	134.00	198.00	

Guest Houses

Caepandy Farm

Garth Road, Builth Wells,
Powys LD2 3NS
Tel: (0982) 553793

L

Caepandy farm just off A483 one mile from Builth. Modernised 17th century farmhouse with beautiful views of the Irfon Valley and surrounding countryside within easy reach of Elan Valley, Black Mountains, Brecon Beacons. Lots of walks beside River Wye. Golf, fishing, leisure centre nearby. Tea/coffee making all rooms. H&C all rooms.

HW T	NIGHTLY B&B PER PERSON		WEEKLY D,B&B PER PERSON		2 –
	MIN £	MAX £	MIN £	MAX £	OPEN 1-12
	10.50	12.00	70.00	77.00	

Farmhouses

Disserth Mill

Disserth, Builth Wells,
Powys LD2 3TN
Tel: (0982) 553217

L

Disserth Mill is on a by road 250 meters off A483, 3 miles north of Builth, 4 miles Llandrindod for golf, swimming. Brook running through garden where guests can sit and relax after home cooked meal. Beach 50 miles, hills for the walker and good area for fossil hunters. Hot and cold water, shaver points in bedrooms. Lounge with TV. Separate tables for dining. Full central heating.

HW T C	NIGHTLY B&B PER PERSON		WEEKLY D,B&B PER PERSON		2 –
	MIN £	MAX £	MIN £	MAX £	OPEN 4-10
	11.00	12.00	119.00	126.00	

New Hall Farm Guest House

Llandewircwm,
Builth Wells, Powys
LD2 3RX
Tel: (0982) 552483

Situated 1½ miles from Builth Wells market town and Royal Welsh showground. Magnificent unspoiled scenery overlooking the Wye Valley and Aberedw Hills. Picturesque walking area, centrally situated for all places and activities in central Wales. Easy access to parking. Comfortable accommodation in 17th century farmhouse renovated to a high standard. Good home cooked meals. Personal welcome and services from proprietor who has the WTB Farmhouse Award. Brochure available.

HW T SP	NIGHTLY B&B PER PERSON		WEEKLY D,B&B PER PERSON		6 2
	MIN £	MAX £	MIN £	MAX £	OPEN 1-12
	14.00	18.00	147.00	175.00	

WALES
It's magic

ELAN VALLEY

ERWOOD   Map Ref Ha5

Pretty Wye-side village in narrow wooded valley. the good ale in the "local" inspired the idea of Punch magazine. Superb fishing and walking country.

Guest Houses

Old Vicarage

Erwood, Builth Wells,
Powys LD2 3EX   L
Tel: (0982) 560680

Situated just off A470 near Erwood. Attractive guest house set in own grounds overlooking Wye Valley. Three bedrooms all with H&C, shavolites, tea/coffee facilities one room Colour TV. Guests own TV lounge. Black Mountains, Brecon Beacons, Elan Valley, walks, bird-watching, trekking, golf, swimming nearby. Erwood 5 minutes walk with two homely inns. Children welcome. Guests own bathroom. Separate toilet. CH. Homegrown produce for meals. Also bara-brith with afternoon tea.

HW T 🐕 SP	NIGHTLY B&B PER PERSON		WEEKLY B,B&B PER PERSON		🛏 3 🛁 –	
	MIN £	MAX £	MIN £	MAX £	OPEN 1-12	
	9.50	10.50	94.50	101.00		

KNIGHTON   Map Ref Hb2

"Tref y Clawdd", the town on the dyke, stands in a deep wooded valley where the 8th-century Offa's Dyke defines the ancient border between Wales and England. Some of the best-preserved stretches of the ancient dyke can be found in the undisturbed hills near the town. Superb hill walking country — call at the town's Offa's Dyke Centre. ⇌

CALL
Holidays WALES
(0792) 645555

Hotels

Milebrook House Hotel

Milebrook, Knighton, Powys
LD7 1LT   👑👑👑
Tel: (0547) 528632   COMMENDED

Situated in the beautiful Teme Valley amidst three acres of gardens, riverside and wildflower meadow. Trout fly fishing, the best food and wine. All rooms en-suite with colour TV. Restaurant open to non residents. Roaring log fires in winter. Resident owners, Rodney and Beryl Marsden. Telephone for reservations or brochure.

T SP	NIGHTLY B&B PER PERSON		WEEKLY D,B&B PER PERSON		🛏 6 🛁 6	
	MIN £	MAX £	MIN £	MAX £	OPEN 1-12	
	26.50	26.50	225.00	225.00		

Guest Houses

The Fleece House

Market Street, Knighton,   👑
Powys LD7 1BB
Tel: (0547) 520168

Set in the old town a short distance from Offa's Dyke Association Office. Originally a coaching inn reputed to have been built on the remains of the castle. Oak beams, olde worlde atmosphere. Extensively modernised, centrally heated, hot and cold, shaver points all bedrooms. Lounge with colour television. Licensed bar, separate dining tables. Fire certificate. Weekly guided walking tours in own mini coach available.

HW T SP ⼎✕	NIGHTLY B&B PER PERSON		WEEKLY D,B&B PER PERSON		🛏 6 🛁 2	
	MIN £	MAX £	MIN £	MAX £	OPEN 1-12	
	12.50	17.50	112.00	145.00		

LLANDRINDOD WELLS   Map Ref Ge3

Victorian spa town with spacious streets and impressive architecture. You can still take the waters at Rock Park Gardens. Victorian-style visitor centre and excellent museum tracing history of spa. A popular inland resort with golf, fishing, bowling, boating and tennis available. Good selection of hotels. Excellent touring centre for Mid Wales hills and lakes. Annual Victorian Festival in August. ⇌

Hotels

The Bell Country Inn

Llanyre, Llandrindod Wells,
Powys LD1 6DY
Tel: (0597) 823959
Fax: (0597) 825899

This comfortable country hotel has ten en-suite bedrooms, TV, hairdryer, telephone, trouser press, tea maker. Lavish award winning restaurant with local produce a speciality. Ideal for golfing, fishing, walking, bird-watching etc. Centrally located in the heart of Wales. 1 1/2 hours from Bristol or Birmingham, 3 1/2 hours London. If you want to tour Wales this comfortable retreat in the heart of the rolling hills of Mid Wales is the ideal location.

HW T 🐕 C SP ⼎✕ TW	NIGHTLY B&B PER PERSON		WEEKLY D,B&B PER PERSON		🛏 10 🛁 10	
	MIN £	MAX £	MIN £	MAX £	OPEN 1-12	
	25.00	30.00	275.00			

Griffin Lodge Hotel

Temple Street,
Llandrindod Wells
Powys LD1 5HF
Tel: (0597) 822432

MERIT

Charming licensed Victorian hotel centrally situated within walking distance of station. Set back from the road, our hotel has adequate car parking, friendly atmosphere, comfortable lounge and good reputation for food with wide choice of menu. Most bedrooms en-suite with tea/coffee making facilities, radio and colour television. A warm welcome awaits you.

		NIGHTLY B&B PER PERSON		WEEKLY D,B&B PER PERSON		🛏 8
🐕	SP					🛁 5
		MIN £ 14.75	MAX £ 19.00	MIN £ 144.50	MAX £ 170.00	OPEN 2-12

The Llanerch 16th Century Inn

Waterloo Road,
Llandrindod Wells, Powys
LD1 5BG
Tel: (0597) 822086

Set in own grounds by town centre offering traditional food, ales and hospitality in a relaxed atmosphere. All rooms have tea/coffee making facilities. Rooms with private facilities have colour TV. Resident lounges. Children's play area, patio, terrace, garden. Car parking. Golf, fishing, rambling all close by. Children welcome.

HW	T	NIGHTLY B&B PER PERSON		WEEKLY D,B&B PER PERSON		🛏 11
🐕	C					🛁 6
	SP	MIN £ 16.00	MAX £ 20.00	MIN £ 150.00	MAX £ 175.00	OPEN 1-12

Guest Houses

Corven Hall

Howey,
Llandrindod Wells
Powys LD1 5RE
Tel: (0597) 823368

AWARD   MERIT

Victorian house of character with large grounds in peaceful setting, surrounded by beautiful unspoilt countryside. 1 1/2 miles Llandrindod Wells. South of Howey off A483. The house is licensed, centrally heated, comfortable and spacious. Traditional cooking, home-made and freshly prepared. Large dining room, TV lounge, bar. Most bedrooms en-suite, tea/coffee facilities. Ground floor accommodation. Walking, touring, bird-watching country, fishing, golf, pony trekking in area. WTB Guest House Award. Brochure on request.

HW	T	NIGHTLY B&B PER PERSON		WEEKLY D,B&B PER PERSON		🛏 10
🐕	SP					🛁 8
✕	TW	MIN £ 12.00	MAX £ 14.50	MIN £ 119.00	MAX £ 129.00	OPEN 1-11

LET A GUIDE SHOW YOU THE WAY

Why not book a Wales Official Tourist Guide for your next visit to Wales. Fees are very reasonable and a driver/guide can take the strain out of navigation and map reading whilst you sit back and enjoy your tour. Members of the Wales Official Tourist Guide Association are the only qualified tourist guides in Wales and the association is registered with the Wales Tourist Board. Any kind of guided tours are undertaken — from hourly tours by car or coach from a designated centre, to extended tours of any duration throughout Wales.

For more information contact Gwennie Johnson, W.O.T.G.A., Cae'r Felin, Chwilog, Criccieth, Gwynedd LL53 6SW. Tel: (0766) 810889.

ANGLING AT LLANDRINDOD WELLS

78

SOUTH WALES

This region is full of contrasts. Visitors to South Wales can head for the hills or make for the beach, stay at an historic market town or in the heart of the city.

The differences between the National Parks in South Wales – the grassy Brecon Beacons and the salty Pembrokeshire Coast – sum up the variety to be found here. The Pembrokeshire Coast National Park in the far south-west is one of Europe's finest stretches of untouched coastline. Contrasts abound even here. In the north, there's a rugged, rocky shoreline dotted with small resorts and places to stay such as the tiny cathedral city of St. David's. In the more popular south, there's an excellent concentration of hotels and guest houses around sandy Tenby (its clifftop hotels command magnificent views) and the watersports centre of Saundersfoot.

The Gower Peninsula was the first part of Britain to be declared an 'Area of Outstanding Natural Beauty'. The peninsula's small, south-facing sandy beaches shelter in crescent-shaped bays along a coastline of towering cliffs.

Nearby Swansea is right on Gower's doorstep. This attractive city by the sea has more of those South Wales contrasts – compare, for example, Swansea's dazzling new marina and Maritime Quarter with its traditional fresh foods market which sells everything from Welsh lamb to that unique local delicacy, laverbread.

Cardiff, Wales's capital, is an architecturally magnificent city with a modern shopping complex, Victorian arcades, superb Civic Centre and city-centre castle. More and more visitors are now discovering Cardiff's cosmopolitan charms (it's so easy to get to by road and rail). And more and more visitors are discovering the nearby South Wales 'Valleys', an area of unexpected beauty and varied attractions.

The Brecon Beacons National Park, an exhilarating swathe of moor and grassy upland rises almost to 3,000 ft. Stay at places like Llandovery, Brecon and Abergavenny, three attractive towns on the edge of the park, and explore the mountains, lakelands and limestone caverns of this magnificent national park. And there are yet more seductive landscapes on the border of Wales along the leafy Wye Valley, another 'Area of Outstanding Natural Beauty'.

BRECON BEACONS FROM CRADOC GOLF COURSE

The incomparable coastline around Wales's south-western tip is all within the Pembrokeshire Coast National Park. The park's 225 square miles encompasses secluded coves, towering headlands, huge beaches and tranquil backwaters. Tenby, with its pastel-painted harbourside houses and and narrow medieval streets, is a gem of a resort which, together with the neighbouring sailing centre of Saundersfoot, serves as a popular, picturesque base.

Further west, around Dale, Broad Haven and Newgale, there are more magnificent sands, surfing beaches and walks along a seashore rich in wildlife. The tiny cathedral city of St. David's heralds the start of North Pembrokeshire's rocky bays and undiscovered beaches, a savagely beautiful coastline stretching all the way to Poppit Sands.

There are plenty of attractions for the whole family including historic Pembroke Castle, an action-packed day out at Oakwood Park and the opportunity to meet the animals at Folly Farm. The Tall Ships will gather on the Milford Haven Waterway during the week prior to the Cutty Sark 'Tall Ships' race which begins on July 15.

BROAD HAVEN
Map Ref Jb5

Sand and green hills cradle this holiday village in the midst of the Pembrokeshire Coast National Park. Good beach, accommodation, shops. Good National Park Information Centre.

Hotels

Broad Haven Hotel

Broad Haven,
Haverfordwest,
Pembrokeshire, Dyfed SA62 3JN
Tel: (0437) 781366

Relaxing family run hotel facing safe sandy beach in Pembrokeshire Coast National Park. Superb scenery and coastal walks. Children's games room, pool, table tennis, sound proofed dance hall. Popular locals bar. Excellent cuisine with fresh fish daily. Enchanting islands of Skomer, Ramsey and Skokholm nearby with their bird and seal colonies. AA/RAC Listed.

T SP	NIGHTLY B&B PER PERSON		WEEKLY D,B&B PER PERSON		🛏 39
	MIN £	MAX £	MIN £	MAX £	🛏 34
	17.00	22.00	155.00	185.00	OPEN 1-12

SKOMER ISLAND

CROES-GOCH
Map Ref Jb3

Small village, useful spot for touring Pembrokeshire Coast National Park — especially its peaceful, rugged northern shores — and nearby holiday centes of St. David's and Fishguard.

Farmhouses

Trearched Farm Guest House

Croes-Goch,
Haverfordwest,
Dyfed SA62 5JP
Tel: (0348) 831310

AWARD   MERIT

18th century farmhouse set in spacious grounds with small lake. Arable farm of 68 acres. Footpath link to Coast Path 2§1/4§ miles. Ideally situated for touring North and South Pembrokeshire. Variety of beaches within seven miles, St. David's five miles, Fishguard 8 miles. Tea, coffee making facilities in all bedrooms. Iron and hairdryers available for guest's use. AA/ RAC Listed.

HW T	NIGHTLY B&B PER PERSON		WEEKLY D,B&B PER PERSON		🛏 ??
	MIN £	MAX £	MIN £	MAX £	
	14.00	16.00	–	–	OPEN 1-11

DALE
Map Ref Jb6

Sheltered yachting village at mouth of Milford Haven waterway. Henry VII landed near here and marched on to take the crown at the Battle of Bosworth in 1485. Many good beaches nearby. Skokholm and Skomer islands off-shore — both marvellous for sea birds.

Hotels

Post House Hotel

Dale, Haverfordwest,
Pembrokeshire, Dyfed
SA62 3RE
Tel: (0646) 636201

COMMENDED

Seven bedroomed family run licensed hotel. Double and twin bedded rooms, (one downstairs). Five have en-suite facilities, showers in most others. Good food in comfortable surroundings. Restaurant serving local seafood etc. Residents lounge, colour television, large double glazed conservatory overlooking garden. 100 yards from bay in picturesque National Park coastal village of Dale. Area renowned for natural beauty. Walking, water sports or visiting famous bird islands of Skokholm and Skoner and Grassholm. Closed February.

T	NIGHTLY B&B PER PERSON		WEEKLY D,B&B PER PERSON		🛏 7
	MIN £	MAX £	MIN £	MAX £	🛏 5
	13.50	17.00	135.00	150.00	OPEN 1-12

WALES
It's magic

FISHGUARD Map Ref Jc2

Lower Fishguard is a cluster of old wharfs and cottages around a beautiful harbour. "Under Milk Wood" with Richard Burton was filmed here in 1971. Shopping in Fishguard town. Good walks along Pembrokeshire Coastal Path and in the country. Nearby Goodwick is the Irish ferry terminal, with a direct rail link from London. Excellent range of craft workshops in area, including Tregwynt Woollen Mill. Music Festival in July. ⇌

Hotels

Fishguard Bay Hotel

Quay Road, Goodwick,
Fishguard, Dyfed, SA64 OBT
Tel: (0348) 873571 Telex: 48602
Fax: (0348) 873030

The largest hotel in North Pembrokeshire having a unique setting in ten acres of woodland with terraced paths leading to the magnificent cliff scenery around Strumble Head. Ideal touring base for South West Wales and Pembrokeshire Coast National Park. Perfect for overnight stops en route or returning from Ireland. Within yards of the ferry terminal. Centrally heated. Lift, colour TV lounge residents lounge. A la carte restaurant. Open to non residents. Mid week breaks available from October to March. Colour brochure available.

HW	T	NIGHTLY B&B PER PERSON		WEEKLY D,B&B PER PERSON		🛏 62
🐾	SP					🛁 38
		MIN £	MAX £	MIN £	MAX £	OPEN
		24.00	38.00	200.00	325.00	1-12

Manor House Hotel

Main Street, Fishguard,
Pembrokeshire, Dyfed,
SA65 9HG   MERIT
Tel: (0348) 873260

Georgian town house overlooking picturesque lower Fishguard Harbour. Charming garden has impressive sea views with easy access for Pembrokeshire Coastal Footpath. Spacious bedrooms are individually furnished to high standard. Comfortable residents lounge, delightful licensed restaurant offering wide choice of home cooked meals using local produce wherever possible. Special terms for weekend short break holidays, autumn, winter, spring. German and French spoken by Viennese born resident proprietor.

🐾	SP	NIGHTLY B&B PER PERSON		WEEKLY D,B&B PER PERSON		🛏 6
						🛁 2
		MIN £	MAX £	MIN £	MAX £	OPEN
		15.00	19.00	147.00	175.00	1-12

Stone Hall

Welsh Hook, Wolfscastle,
Haverfordwest, Dyfed
SA62 5NS   COMMENDED
Tel: (0348) 840212
Fax: (0348) 840815

Country house hotel converted from the original 14th century manor house set in a secluded location in 10 acres of gardens and woodland. Situated 6 miles from the beautiful unspoilt Pembrokeshire coastline. In the cosy oak beamed restaurant we serve genuine French cuisine which is recommended by Egon Ronay.

HW	T	NIGHTLY B&B PER PERSON		WEEKLY D,B&B PER PERSON		🛏 5
						🛁 5
		MIN £	MAX £	MIN £	MAX £	OPEN
		22.50	24.00	–	–	1-12

Guest Houses

Ivy Bridge

Drim Mill Dyffryn, Goodwick,
Fishguard, Dyfed SA64 0FT
Tel: (0348) 872623   MERIT

A warm welcome awaits you at Ivy Bridge. All rooms are en-suite, with colour TV and hot drinks facilities. Try our indoor heated swimming pool, whirlpool, games room and solarium, or relax by the open fire in the lounge. Good home cooking, vegetarian guests welcomed. Ample car parking. Family suite available. Full central heating. Licensed bar.

HW	T	NIGHTLY B&B PER PERSON		WEEKLY D,B&B PER PERSON		🛏 6
🐾	SP					🛁 6
		MIN £	MAX £	MIN £	MAX £	OPEN
		16.00	18.00	149.00	159.00	1-12

Rhos Felen

Scleddau, Fishguard,
Pembrokeshire, Dyfed   COMMENDED
SA65 9RD
Tel: (0348) 873711

Family run country house in 3 acres. Putting green. 2 miles Fishguard and harbour. Ideal touring base for coastal path, beaches, Preseli Hills and St. David's. CH, guest lounge, colour TV, H&C, shaver points. Single, double, family rooms, (cots). Reduced rates under twelves. Tea and coffee facilities. Adjoining restaurant open Easter to October for coffees, light lunches, snacks, teas. Home cooking. Special diets catered for. Large car park. Weekend and mid-week breaks all year.

HW	T	NIGHTLY B&B PER PERSON		WEEKLY D,B&B PER PERSON		🛏 4
🐾	SP					🛁 –
		MIN £	MAX £	MIN £	MAX £	OPEN
		10.00	14.00	105.00	135.00	1-12

HAVERFORDWEST
Map Ref Jc5

Ancient town — now a good base for exploring the Pembrokeshire Coast National Park — and the administrative and shopping centre for the area. Medieval churches and narrow streets; museum in the castle grounds, which occupy an outcrop overlooking the town. Most attractive redeveloped riverside and old wharf buildings. Sutherland art collection in Picton Castle, a few miles east. Many other attractions nearby, including Scolton Manor Country Park, "Motormania" exhibition, Selvedge Farm Museum and Nant-y-Coy Mill.

Hotels

The Denant Mill Inn

Dreenhill, Dale Road,
Haverfordwest, Pembrokeshire,
Dyfed SA62 3TS
Tel: (0437) 766569

Converted 16th century mill in a "lost world" valley. Seven acres unspoiled woodland, 700 yard trout brook. Close to beaches, coastal walks, Skomer Island, surfing, sailing. Weekly clay pigeon shooting. Lunch time bar snacks, 'a la carte restaurant. All rooms centrally heated, H&C, washbasin. Comfortable television lounge. Large gardens. Recommended by CAMRA Beer and food guides. Ideal geology, field studies, cycling groups. Real ale, real food, real hospitality, uniquely different.

HW T	NIGHTLY B&B PER PERSON		WEEKLY D,B&B PER PERSON		🛏 8
🐕 C 🚲✕	MIN £	MAX £	MIN £	MAX £	🛁 2
	15.00	17.00	153.00	186.00	OPEN 1-12

Hotel Mariners

Mariners Square,
Haverfordwest, Pembrokeshire,
Dyfed SA61 2DU
Tel: (0437) 763353 Fax: (0437) 764258

Ideal centre for touring Pembrokeshire coastline and countryside, 20 minutes to Fishguard and Irish Ferry. 17th century hotel all rooms have colour TV, radio, telephone, tea/coffee facilities and en-suite bathroom. Ample car parking. Popular bars, bar snacks and restaurant. Open to non residents. Special weekend breaks all year.

HW T 🐕 SP	NIGHTLY B&B PER PERSON		WEEKLY D,B&B PER PERSON		🛏 32
	MIN £	MAX £	MIN £	MAX £	🛁 31
	30.00	37.00	282.00	317.00	OPEN 1-12

HERITAGE OF A NATION (VHS/BETA)

Narrated by Richard Burton, this 25-minute video presents the heritage of Wales from prehistoric to modern times. Wale's natural beauty is also depicted within some memorable sequences.

LOWER FISHGUARD HARBOUR

Pembroke House Hotel

Spring Gardens,
Haverfordwest, Pembrokeshire,
Dyfed SA61 2EJ
Tel: (0437) 763652

A charming Georgian terraced house of architectural interest in town centre providing an excellent base for touring Pembrokeshire. The restaurant has maintained a high standard of cuisine for many years. En-suite rooms with colour television, central heating, direct dial telephones, tea/coffee facilities. Ample parking at rear of hotel.

T 🐕 C SP	NIGHTLY B&B PER PERSON		WEEKLY D,B&B PER PERSON		🛏 21
	MIN £	MAX £	MIN £	MAX £	🛁 19
	25.00	27.5	210.00	227.50	OPEN 1-12

Guest Houses

Greenacre

Spittal, Haverfordwest,
Pembrokeshire, Dyfed
SA62 5RE
Tel: (0437) 731201

MERIT

Quiet guest house in centre of Pembrokeshire, convenient for coastline and Preseli Hills. Fishing at Llysyfran Reservoir. Riding nearby. Full central heating, all rooms H&C, shaver points, ground floor bedrooms. Access to rooms and TV lounge at all times. Ample parking. Warm welcome.

HW T 🐕 SP	NIGHTLY B&B PER PERSON		WEEKLY D,B&B PER PERSON		🛏 3
	MIN £	MAX £	MIN £	MAX £	🛁 –
	12.00	16.00	90.00	120.00	OPEN 1-10

Farmhouses

Crossways

Spittal, Cross Farm,
Spittal, Haverfordwest,
Pembrokeshire Dyfed SA62 5DB
Tel: (043787) 253

A new farmhouse offering bed and breakfast in one double room with en-suite facilities. One twin room with exclusive use of main bathroom, coffee/tea in bedrooms. Comfortable lounge, access any time. Situated amidst beautiful countryside. Locally there are good restaurants and many places of interest to visit. Farmhouse Award Two Crowns. Here you'll find the warmest welcome. Luxurious comfort, relaxing peace and quiet.

T SP		NIGHTLY B&B PER PERSON		WEEKLY D,B&B PER PERSON		🛏 2
		MIN £	MAX £	MIN £	MAX £	🐾 1
		13.00	15.00	–	–	OPEN 1-12

Cuckoo Mill Farm

Pelcomb Bridge, Haverfordwest,
Dyfed SA62 6EA
Tel: (0437) 762139

L

Situated peacefully in central Pembrokeshire. Two miles out of Haverfordwest. Six miles coastline walks, beaches. Mixed livestock working farm. Two comfortable bedrooms with night storage heaters, bathroom with toilet, shower, lounge with and open fire. Personal attention. Good home cooking, using home produce. Evening meal at short notice. Children and pets welcome.

HW T C SP	NIGHTLY B&B PER PERSON		WEEKLY D,B&B PER PERSON		🛏 2
	MIN £	MAX £	MIN £	MAX £	🐾 –
	10.00	13.00	1000.00	119.00	OPEN 1-11

Knock Farm

Camrose, Haverfordwest,
Dyfed SA62 6HW
Tel: (0437) 762208

L

Knock Farm is a 275 acre working dairy farm situated in a scenic valley 10 minutes drive from Pembrokeshire's sandy beaches and 2 miles from the county town of Haverfordwest. Children welcome. Lots of farm animals for them to see. Good home cooking prepared from home produce. TV lounge, central heating throughout and log fire.

HW T C SP	NIGHTLY B&B PER PERSON		WEEKLY D,B&B PER PERSON		🛏 2
	MIN £	MAX £	MIN £	MAX £	🐾 –
	10.00	13.00	100.00	119.00	OPEN 1-11

LAMPHEY   Map Ref Jd6

Pretty village near Pembroke, only a short distance from one of the most spectacular stretches of cliff scenery in entire Pembrokeshire Coast National Park. Lamphey Bishop's Palace one time home of bishops of St. David's. Host of attractions nearby. ⬆

Hotels

Bethwaite's Lamphey Hall Hotel

Lamphey, Pembroke,
Dyfed SA71 5NR
Tel: (0646) 672394
Fax: (0646) 672369

COMMENDED

Enjoy the varied charm of unspoiled Pembrokeshire. Just 1 1/2 miles from national parks. Lampey Hall stands in its own grounds offering every comfort. All bedrooms en-suite. Fully licensed. Table d'hôte, 'a la carte menus, bistro bar. Within easy reach beaches. Warm welcome. Good food, choice of wines. Packed lunches. Telephone for brochure.

HW T C SP	NIGHTLY B&B PER PERSON		WEEKLY D,B&B PER PERSON		🛏 10
	MIN £	MAX £	MIN £	MAX £	🐾 10
	30.00	35.00	234.00	245.00	OPEN 1-12

MARLOES BEACH

MARLOES   Map Ref Jb5

Marloes Sands nearby, a remote stretch of the Pembrokeshire Coast National Park — one of its finest beaches — overlooking Skomer Island, a haven for puffins and other seabirds. Safe for surfing and swimming; boat trips to the island from nearby Martin's Haven.

Guest Houses

The Foxes

Marloes, Haverfordwest,
Dyfed SA62 3AY
Tel: (0646) 636527

Single, double, family, twin bedrooms, H:CHG, wash-basins, central heating. Situated centre village. Sandy beaches. Boat trips Skomer/Grassholm bird islands-see puffins nesting. Miles coastal path walks, lovely wild flowers. Children welcome, reduced rates. Licensed restaurant meals from £1.50. Ample parking. Access rooms all times. Pets welcome. Fire certificate. Opposite Marloes village clock.

HW T	NIGHTLY B&B PER PERSON		WEEKLY D,B&B PER PERSON		🛏 5
	MIN £	MAX £	MIN £	MAX £	🐾 –
	24.00	32.00	000.00	000.00	OPEN 1-12

MILFORD HAVEN
Map Ref Jc6

Important port on edge of Pembrokeshire Coast National Park; Nelson called it one of the best natural harbours he had seen. Fine walks and gardens. Torch Theatre, Maritime Museum and Leisure Centre. Excellent touring base. Home of the 1991 Cutty Sark Tall Ships Race. ⇌

MOYLGROVE
Map Ref Je2

Small coastal village on North Pembrokeshire coast. Ceibwr beach is a secluded cove and the Coast Path is close at hand for spectacular clifftop walks. Just under 5 miles away is Nevern with its ancient church and Celtic Cross; Pentre Ifan Cromlech, one of Wales's finest prehistoric monuments, also close by.

NARBERTH
Map Ref Je5

Small market town, ancient castle remains (private). Charming local museum. Convenient for beaches of Carmarthen Bay and resorts of Tenby and Saundersfoot. Nearby are a host of attractions, including activity-packed Oakwood Adventure and Leisure Park, Heron's Brook Country Park, Folly Farm and Blackpool Mill. ⇌

Hotels

Ferry Inn

Hazelbeach, Llanstadwell, Neyland, Milford Haven, Pembrokeshire Dyfed SA73 1EG
Tel: (0646) 600270

👑

We welcome you to our family run inn, situated on the water's edge, enjoying fine views of the Cleddau Estuary, en route of the Pembrokeshire Coastal Path. An ideal base for your holiday, whether touring, fishing, sailing, walking or enjoying the magnificent Tall Ships Race in 1991. Our seven bedrooms all have tea/coffee facilities, dining room, licensed bars, games room. Children most welcome. River front/patio garden. Close to Neyland Marina.

HW	T	NIGHTLY B&B PER PERSON		WEEKLY D,B&B PER PERSON		🛏 7	
		MIN £	MAX £	MIN £	MAX £	🛏 1	
		14.00	20.00	147.00	189.00	OPEN 1-12	

Guest Houses

The Old Vicarage Country Guest House

Moylgrove, Nr. Cardigan, Dyfed SA43 3BN
Tel: (0239) 86 231   COMMENDED

👑 👑

Spacious Edwardian Vicarage in an acre of paddock and gardens with views overlooking Cardigan Bay. Bedrooms with vanity units, wash basins, some with en-suite bathrooms. Tea and coffee making facilities in all bedrooms. Elegant dining room with individual tables, comfortable lounge with colour TV. Centrally heated and double glazed throughout. In the Pembrokeshire National Park, one mile from the Coastal Path at Ceibwr. Dinner available on request. Full facilities for disabled guests.

🐕 ✖	NIGHTLY B&B PER PERSON		WEEKLY D,B&B PER PERSON		🛏 6	
	MIN £	MAX £	MIN £	MAX £	🛏 3	
	15.00	22.50	165.00	205.00	OPEN 1-12	

Guest Houses

Highland Grange Farm Guest House

Roberston Wathen, Narberth, Pembrokeshire, Dyfed SA67 8EP
Tel: (0834) 860952

👑 👑

220 acre farm central for touring Pembrokeshire. Set back off A40 road. Lovely modern farmhouse. Organic vegetable garden. Delicious home cooking. 3 course dinner. Ideal for families, (babysitting). Ground floor accommodation suitable for elderly. Inn 200 yards. Beach 8 miles. Family, double, twin, single rooms. Golf and adventure complex nearby. Naomi Jones welcomes enquiries. Stamp for brochure please.

HW	T	NIGHTLY B&B PER PERSON		WEEKLY D,B&B PER PERSON		🛏 6	
SP	✖	MIN £	MAX £	MIN £	MAX £	🛏 1	
		12.00	14.00	120.00	128.00	OPEN 1-12	

RIVER CLEDDAU,
MILFORD HAVEN WATERWAY

NEWPORT　Map Ref Jd2

Ancient castled village on Pembrokeshire coast. Fine beaches – bass and sea trout fishing. Pentre Ifan burial chamber is close by. Backed by heather-clad Preseli Hills and overlooked by Carn Ingli Iron Age Fort.

Hotels

The Salutation Inn

Felindre Farchog,
Crymych, Dyfed SA41 3UY
Tel: (0239) 820564　　COMMENDED

Beautifully situated in the Pembrokeshire Coast National Park, 5 minutes from Newport beach and the Preseli Hills. Facilities nearby include riding, golf, fishing, sailing, birdwatching, walking, canoeing and lazing quietly. Modern and traditional rooms. Pleasant restaurant, good food. A really relaxing place to stay.

	NIGHTLY B&B PER PERSON		WEEKLY D,B&B PER PERSON		🛏 9	
					🍴 9	
	MIN £	MAX £	MIN £	MAX £	OPEN	
	19.00	26.00	186.00	246.00	1-12	

PEMBROKE　Map Ref Jd6

Ancient borough built around Pembroke Castle, birthplace of Henry VII. Fascinating Museum of the Home and next-door Sea Historical Gallery. In addition to impressive castle, well-preserved sections of old town walls. Sandy bays within easy reach, yachting, fishing – all the coastal activities associated with estuaries. Plenty of things to see and do in the area, including visit to beautiful Upton Castle Grounds.

Bangeston Farm

Stackpole, Pembroke,
Dyfed SA71 5BX
Tel: (0646) 683986

Homely farmhouse in peaceful countryside with coastal outlook three miles from Pembroke close to Bosherston Lily Ponds, clean beaches, coastal walks and bird life. Good home cooking, hearty breakfasts, separate dining tables, lounge with colour TV. Tea making facilities and H&C in all bedrooms. A warm welcome awaits. Leaflet available, enquiries to Selina Mathias.

	NIGHTLY B&B PER PERSON		WEEKLY D,B&B PER PERSON		🛏 3	
					🍴 0	
	MIN £	MAX £	MIN £	MAX £	OPEN	
	12.00	12.00	115.00	115.00	4-09	

SAUNDERSFOOT　Map Ref Je6

Popular resort on South Pembrokeshire coast within the National Park. Picturesque harbour and sandy beach. Very attractive sailing centre. Good sea fishing. In the wooded hills to the north is the fascinating Stepaside Industrial Heritage Centre.

Hotels

Bay View Hotel

Pleasant Valley, Stepaside,
Saundersfoot,　　MERIT
South Pembrokeshire
Dyfed SA67 8LR
Tel: (0834) 813417

Small family hotel with friendly atmosphere. Children really welcome. Situated in its own private peaceful surroundings away from crowded places, within easy reach of numerous beaches and delightful walks. Nearest beach ½ miles, Saundersfoot 1½ miles, Tenby 5 miles. Some rooms en-suite, cots, high chairs, babysitting, washing facilities, crazy golf, mini golf, swings, outdoor heated swimming pool. Entertainment weekly in season. TV lounge, residential licence, lunchtime snacks available. Ample Parking. Brochure from Jean and Mike Artingstall.

	NIGHTLY B&B PER PERSON		WEEKLY D,B&B PER PERSON		🛏 12	
T					🍴 7	
	MIN £	MAX £	MIN £	MAX £	OPEN	
	12.00	15.95	110.00	140.00	4-09	

Coppett Hall Beach Hotel

Saundersfoot,
Dyfed SA69 9AJ
Tel: (0834) 813380

This family run hotel is perfectly situated adjoining Coppett Hall Beach where you can walk straight onto the sandy beach from the hotel grounds. It is also a very short flat walk to the shops and harbour of Saundersfoot.

	NIGHTLY B&B PER PERSON		WEEKLY D,B&B PER PERSON		🛏 16	
SP					🍴 12	
	MIN £	MAX £	MIN £	MAX £	OPEN	
	16.00	22.00	150.00	165.00	1-12	

SAUNDERSFOOT BEACH

Manian Lodge Hotel

Begelly, Kilgetty,
Dyfed SA68 0XE
Tel: (0834) 813273

Privately owned family hotel near Saundersfoot. All rooms have en-suite, tea making facilities, licensed bar, TV room, full central heating, home cooked meals, children catered for, pets welcome, laundry room. Ideally situated for touring the beautiful Pembroke countryside. Local horse riding, boating, fishing, golf. 10% reduction for OAPs up to 29th June and from 2nd September.

	SP	NIGHTLY B&B PER PERSON		WEEKLY D,B&B PER PERSON		🛏 6
		MIN £	MAX £	MIN £	MAX £	🛏 6
		14.50	14.50	100.00	140.00	OPEN 3-10

Merlewood Hotel

St. Brides Hill, Saundersfoot,
Dyfed SA69 9NP
Tel: (0834) 812421

COMMENDED

Set in peaceful surroundings with own garden and superb views of Saundersfoot beach and village. Food cooked by resident proprietors, table d'hôte menu. Heated swimming pool, play area, mini golf, launderette. Entertainment main season. Rooms en suite with TV, tea maker, radio, baby listening. Family suites available. 5 minutes from village/beach. Ample car parking. Colour brochure available.

HW	SP	NIGHTLY B&B PER PERSON		WEEKLY D,B&B PER PERSON		🛏 34
		MIN £	MAX £	MIN £	MAX £	🛏 28
		25.00	27.50	175.00	195.00	OPEN 3-10

Pleasant Valley House

Pleasant Valley, Stepaside,
Nr Saundersfoot, South
Pembrokeshire
Dyfed SA67 8NY
Tel: (0834) 813607

COMMENDED

Situated in a peaceful wooded valley, aptly named Pleasant Valley. 500 yds from Wisemans Bridge Beach, thirty minutes leisurely coastal stroll into Saundersfoot. Picturesque surroundings and within easy reach of beautiful sandy beaches. We have ample parking, licensed bar and a 32' x 16' swimming pool. Large residential lounge, varied menu. Friendly relaxed atmosphere. Colour brochure available.

SP	NIGHTLY B&B PER PERSON		WEEKLY D,B&B PER PERSON		🛏 9
	MIN £	MAX £	MIN £	MAX £	🛏 1
	10.50	12.50	101.50	115.50	OPEN 3-10

Guest Houses

Cliff House

Wogan Terrace, Saundersfoot,
Pembrokeshire
Dyfed SA69 9HA
Tel: (0834) 813931

COMMENDED

Friendly, comfortable and ideally situated in heart of the village, 100 yards from beach. Superb sea views, elegant spacious dining room and relaxing TV lounge. Double, twin or family rooms all with H&C, shaver point, tea and coffee facilities and central heating. Luxury en-suite facilities in several rooms. Excellent cuisine using fresh local produce.

	NIGHTLY B&B PER PERSON		WEEKLY D,B&B PER PERSON		🛏 6
	MIN £	MAX £	MIN £	MAX £	🛏 3
	12.00	15.00	117.00	138.00	OPEN 1 12

SOLVA
Map Ref Jb4

Picturesque Pembrokeshire coast village with small perfectly sheltered harbour and excellent craft shops. Pembrokeshire Coast Path offers good walking. Exotic butterflies at Nectarium. Famous cathedral at nearby St. David's.

Farmhouses

Llanddinog Old Farmhouse

Solva, Haverfordwest,
Dyfed SA62 6NA
Tel: (0348) 831224

Peacefully situated in spacious grounds. This 16th century farmstead is ideally situated for sandy beaches, surfing, boat trips, fishing, riding, walking, birdwatching. Close St. David's, Solva Harbour, coastal path, Preseli Mountains. Homely atmosphere, home produced foodstuffs, local fish. One large family bedroom and one double, washbasins, cots, Bathroom with shower. Heating, colour TV, dining room, highchair. Bathroom with shower. Heating, colour TV, dining room, picnics and flasks prepared. Ample parking. Laundry facilities. Dogs accepted. Chidren's play garden, rope swings, pond, small animals and birds. SAE Mrs Griffiths.

HW	T	NIGHTLY B&B PER PERSON		WEEKLY D,B&B PER PERSON		🛏 2
	SP	MIN £	MAX £	MIN £	MAX £	🛏 0
		12.00	13.00	126.00	133.00	OPEN 1-12

SOLVA HARBOUR

Lochmeyler Farm

Pen-y-Cwm, Nr. Solva,
Pembrokeshire, Dyfed
SA62 6LL
Tel: (0348) 837724/837705

COMMENDED

A 220 acre dairy farm, Lochmeyler is situated 4 miles from Solva harbour, 3 miles from the Coastal Footpath. Saunter around our farm trails and ponds, unwind on mature lawns. All rooms en-suite (some with 4 poster beds), with TV, video, tea making facilities, hairdryer and telephone. Traditional and vegetarian menus. Children over 10 years old welcome. RAC Highly Acclaiamed. AA Farmhouse Award. Taste of Wales member.

HW T ♘ SP ⚫ TW	NIGHTLY B&B PER PERSON		WEEKLY D,B&B PER PERSON		🛏 6 🐾 6
	MIN £	MAX £	MIN £	MAX £	OPEN 1-12
	00.00	15.00	000.00	150.00	

ST. DAVID'S

Map Ref Ja4

Smallest cathedral city in Britain, shrine of Wales's patron saint. Magnificent ruins of Bishop's Palace beside ancient cathedral nestling in hollow. Set in Pembrokeshire National Park, with fine beaches nearby; superb scenery on nearby headland. Craft shops, sea life centres, painting courses, boat trips to Ramsey Island, farm parks and museums; ideal for walking and birdwatching.

Hotels

Ocean Haze Hotel & Restaurant

Haverfordwest Road,
St. David's, Pembrokeshire,
Dyfed SA62 6QN
Tel: (0437) 720826

Friendly family run hotel situated on outskirts of St. David's within walking distance of Cathedral. Fully licensed bar, residents' lounge, games room and children's play area. Most rooms en-suite, sea views, colour TV, tea/coffee, rooms en-suite. A la carte, table d'hôte, bar snacks available. We also cater for disabled guests.

HW T ♘ SP	NIGHTLY B&B PER PERSON		WEEKLY D,B&B PER PERSON		🛏 9 🐾 6
	MIN £	MAX £	MIN £	MAX £	OPEN 1-12
	18.50	22.50	199.50	227.50	

Warpool Court Hotel

St. David's,
Pembrokeshire,
Dyfed SA62 6BN
Tel: (0437) 720300
Fax: (0437) 720676

Delightful country house hotel housing famous antique tile collection. Beautiful sea views, easy walking distance to St. David's and coast. All rooms en-suite with radio, colour TV, feature film system, telephone. Covered heated pool (April/Oct), tennis, sauna, games room. Delightful, private grounds. Well known for exceptional hospitality and good food. Please request our brochure.

HW T ♘ SP	NIGHTLY B&B PER PERSON		WEEKLY D,B&B PER PERSON		🛏 25 🐾 25
	MIN £	MAX £	MIN £	MAX £	OPEN 1-12
	33.00	60.00	308.00	539.00	

Whitesands Bay Hotel

St. David's, Haverfordwest,
Dyfed SA62 6PT
Tel: (0432) 720297

Friendly family hotel commanding panoramic views of Ramsey Island and Whitesands Bay, adjacent to the Pembrokeshire Coastal Path, famous Whitesands beach, golf links (fees gratis to residents) and easy walking distance from St. David's magnificent Cathedral and Bishop's Palace. En-suite bedrooms with modern facilities. Good freshly prepared food available in our restaurant overlooking the Atlantic Ocean. Various leisure activities and cultural interests locally or just relax and enjoy the peaceful and beautiful surroundings.

HW T ♘ SP ⚫	NIGHTLY B&B PER PERSON		WEEKLY D,B&B PER PERSON		🛏 15 🐾 12
	MIN £	MAX £	MIN £	MAX £	OPEN 1-12
	24.00	32.50	247.50	305.50	

Guest Houses

Glan-y-Môr Guest House

Caerfai Road,
St. David's, Dyfed SA62 6QT
Tel: (0437) 721788

With magnificent views over St. Brides Bay and situated in the Pembrokeshire Coast National Park just a short walk from St. David's. All rooms have wash basins, shaver points and central heating, (3 rooms with en-suite facilities). TV lounge, restaurant and residentially licensed bar. Parking. Large gardens. We are open all year.

SP ⚫	NIGHTLY B&B PER PERSON		WEEKLY D,B&B PER PERSON		🛏 9 🐾 3
	MIN £	MAX £	MIN £	MAX £	OPEN 1-12
	16.00	–	–	–	

CALL
Holidays WALES
☎ (0792) 645555

Farmhouses

Torbant Farm Guest House

Croes-Goch,
Haverfordwest, Pembrokeshire,   MERIT
Dyfed SA62 5JN
Tel: (0348) 831276

Torbant is a large 300 year old farmhouse, comfortably brought up to date with heating, H & C, tea/coffee in all bedrooms (some en-suite), on a working dairy farm. Single, double, family rooms. Fully licensed with good varied meals. Children especially catered for with reduced rates and early suppers. Large garden and safe play area. The sea and many beautiful beaches, spectacular coastal walks and abundant wildlife just 1½ miles away. Brochure available. AA/ RAC. Relais Routier.

T SP	NIGHTLY B&B PER PERSON		WEEKLY D,B&B PER PERSON		6 3
	MIN £	MAX £	MIN £	MAX £	OPEN 4-10
	12.00	16.00	115.00	140.00	

Trevaccoon Farm

St. David's, Haverfordwest
Pembrokeshire,
Dyfed SA62 6DP   MERIT
Tel: (0348) 831438

Relax and enjoy the peace and beauty of Trevaccoon, a 17th century farmhouse in peaceful country/coastal setting with panoramic sea views over the picturesque Pembrokeshire National Park. Some large family rooms, en-suite bathrooms, TV lounge, visitors' kitchen, central heating. Pets, children, walkers, vegetarians welcome. 50% discount children. Free golf to guests at St. David's City Golf Club. Licensed for that glass of wine to compliment Vikki's farmhouse cooking. Ideal year round.

HW T SP	NIGHTLY B&B PER PERSON		WEEKLY D,B&B PER PERSON		7 5
	MIN £	MAX £	MIN £	MAX £	OPEN 1-12
	14.50	18.00	146.00	171.00	

TENBY   Map Ref Je6

Popular South Pembrokeshire resort with two wide beaches. Fishing trips from the attractive Georgian harbour, and boat trips to nearby Caldy Island. The medieval walled town has a maze of charming narrow streets and fine old buildings, including Tudor Merchant's House (National Trust). Galleries and craft shops, excellent museum on headland, good range of amenities. Attractions include Manor House Leisure Park and "Silent World" Aquarium. ⇌

Hotels

Atlantic Hotel

The Esplanade, Tenby,
Dyfed SA70 7DU
Tel: (0834) 2881 / 4176   COMMENDED
Fax: (0834) 2881

First class cuisine and service compliment the high standard of the beautifully appointed restaurant and rooms at the Atlantic. Jacuzzi, solarium, indoor heated pool add to its popularity. All en-suite rooms have radio, colour TV, tea making facilities, baby listening. Children welcome. Car park. Private cliff garden direct to beach. AA**RAC** award winning hotel.

T SP	NIGHTLY B&B PER PERSON		WEEKLY D,B&B PER PERSON		35 35
	MIN £	MAX £	MIN £	MAX £	OPEN 1-12
	21.00	33.00	242.00	328.00	

WALES
It's magic

Buckingham Hotel

Esplanade, Tenby,
Dyfed SA70 7DU
Tel: (0834) 2622   MERIT

Overlooking the South Beach with glorious views of Caldy Island. Friendly, family run hotel offering quiet relaxing atmosphere. Excellent breakfast and dinner from our table d'hôte menu. All rooms en-suite, colour TV and tea/coffee facilities. Special occasion ask for elegant room with 4 poster bed etc.

HW T SP	NIGHTLY B&B PER PERSON		WEEKLY D,B&B PER PERSON		8 7
	MIN £	MAX £	MIN £	MAX £	OPEN 4-11
	15.00	20.00	145.00	180.00	

Castle View Private Hotel

The Norton, Tenby,
Pembrokeshire, Dyfed
SA70 8AA
Tel: (0834) 2666

Delightfully situated on seafront overlooking North Bay and Castle Hill. Spacious lounge overlooking the sea. All bedrooms with colour TV and en-suite facilities. Table licence. Central for coach and train. Limited parking on premises. Under supervision of resident proprietors. AA and RAC Listed.

SP	NIGHTLY B&B PER PERSON		WEEKLY D,B&B PER PERSON		10 10
	MIN £	MAX £	MIN £	MAX £	OPEN 4-11
	18.00	21.00	168.00	189.00	

TENBY HARBOUR

The Court Hotel

Lamphey, Pembroke,
Dyfed SA71 5NT
Tel: (0646) 672273
Telex: 48587
Fax: (0646) 672480

A super leisure centre awaits you at this AA***RAC country hotel near coast and golden beaches. Spacious grounds, indoor swimming pool, sauna, gym, solarium. Renowned for comfort, bedrooms en-suite. Purpose designed family studios. Satellite TV, telephone, tea makers, hairdryer, radio, trouser press. Honeymoon breaks. Yacht charter. Children free. Egon Ronay Recommended. A Best Western hotel.

HW T ♨ C SP	NIGHTLY B&B PER PERSON		WEEKLY D,B&B PER PERSON		🛏 30 🛏 30
	MIN £	MAX £	MIN £	MAX £	OPEN 1-12
	39.00	50.00	259.00	371.00	

SUNSET OVER TENBY HARBOUR

Fourcroft Hotel

The Croft, Tenby,
Dyfed SA70 8AP
Tel: (0834) 2886
Fax: (0834) 2888

COMMENDED

Sea front hotel with private garden to beach. AA**RAC**. Comfortable, spacious lounges, restaurant and conservatory. Bedrooms with every amenity. Lift, swimming and spa pools. Sauna, multi-gym, snooker, pool, table tennis, bowls. Delicious interesting food and wine. Caring staff and cheerful service. Brochure from Osborne family, proprietors since 1964.

T ♨ SP ✗ TW	NIGHTLY B&B PER PERSON		WEEKLY D,B&B PER PERSON		🛏 38 🛏 38
	MIN £	MAX £	MIN £	MAX £	OPEN 3-11
	31.00	36.00	235.00	255.00	

Hildebrand Hotel

Victoria Street, Tenby,
South Pembrokeshire,
Dyfed SA70 7DY
Tel: (0834) 2403

MERIT

The Hildebrand, conveniently situated near the beautiful South Beach with Caldy Island as a backdrop, offers a high standard of decor in your room, with colour TV, radio, intercom, heating, tea/coffee facilities, most have private bathroom. Cellar bar, spacious lounge complimented by excellent food, served by experienced friendly hosts Veronica and Jim Martin.

♨ SP	NIGHTLY B&B PER PERSON		WEEKLY D,B&B PER PERSON		🛏 11 🛏 8
	MIN £	MAX £	MIN £	MAX £	OPEN 1-12
	12.00	20.00	160.00	182.00	

Ripley St. Mary's Hotel

St. Mary's Street, Tenby,
Pembrokeshire,
Dyfed SA70 7HN
Tel: (0834) 2837

Situated in quiet "floral" street, within walled town, 75 yards sea front and Paragon Gardens. Car parks within short distance. All bedrooms have colour TV, heating and tea makers. Personally managed by Alan and Kath Mace who enjoy a high reputation for their friendly welcome and good home cooking. AA Listed, RAC Acclaimed.

T ♨ SP	NIGHTLY B&B PER PERSON		WEEKLY D,B&B PER PERSON		🛏 14 🛏 8
	MIN £	MAX £	MIN £	MAX £	OPEN 4-10
	16.00	20.00	150.00	190.00	

Sea Breezes Hotel

The Norton, Tenby,
Dyfed SA70 8AA
Tel: (0834) 2753

Cosy and comfortable, friendly and informal, just yards from seafront, shops and amenities. All rooms have TV, tea maker and heating, also separate bar and TV lounge. Some rooms en-suite. Vegetarian and special diets catered for. AA and RAC Listed.

HW T C	NIGHTLY B&B PER PERSON		WEEKLY D,B&B PER PERSON		🛏 8 🛏 6
	MIN £	MAX £	MIN £	MAX £	OPEN 3-11
	16.00	20.00	140.00	180.00	

Tall Ships Hotel

34 Victoria Street,
Tenby, Dyfed SA70 7DY
Tel: (0834) 2055   COMMENDED

A small family hotel run by resident proprietors Marianne and Dilwyn Richards. Close to the South Beach, public car park and all amenities. All rooms have heating, colour TV, clock radio, tea and coffee tray. Attractive dining room, excellent home cooking with choice of menu. Well stocked cellar bar. Credit cards accepted.

SP	NIGHTLY B&B PER PERSON		WEEKLY D,B&B PER PERSON		🛏 9
	MIN £	MAX £	MIN £	MAX £	🛏 5
	124.00	17.50	115.00	155.00	OPEN 3-10

Guest Houses

Fairway

The Golf Links, South Beach,
Tenby, Dyfed SA70 7EL
Tel: (0834) 2141   COMMENDED

Delightful house in peaceful location overlooking sand dunes and golf links, offering comfort, four course candlelit dinners and parking, yet only 200 yards from golf club and beach. Sorry no children or pets. Non smokers preferred. Please write or phone for brochure.

🕭✳	NIGHTLY B&B PER PERSON		WEEKLY D,B&B PER PERSON		🛏 4
	MIN £	MAX £	MIN £	MAX £	🛏 4
	13.00	15.00	120.00	135.00	OPEN 4-09

TENBY HARBOUR

Flemish Court

St. Florence, Tenby,
Dyfed SA70
Tel: (0834) 871413

Flemish Court is the home of June and Eric who have successfully turned it into a lovely, small select guest house where you will be assured of a real welcome. All rooms have colour TV, tea making and many other facilities mainly found in larger hotels. Food will be excellent, varied and plentiful. Lovely lounge and pleasant gardens. Dining room has lovely views over gardens and countryside. Most rooms have shower/toilet. All have hot and cold. We are sure you would enjoy your holiday with us and you will realise the value you have found real value for money. Please send for brochure by writing or phoning.

🐕 SP	NIGHTLY B&B PER PERSON		WEEKLY D,B&B PER PERSON		🛏 6
✳	MIN £	MAX £	MIN £	MAX £	🛏 4
	12.95	13.95	90.00	112.00	OPEN 1-12

Oxford Lodge Guest House

Lower Frog Street, Tenby,
Dyfed SA70 7HT
Tel: (0834) 2934   MERIT

Small family run guest house situated within Tenby's historic town walls, close to South Beach and all amenities. Comfortable rooms with tea making facilities, hairdryer, heating. We offer excellent and varied food. Extensive wine list. Access at all times. Friendly, personal service.

🐕 SP	NIGHTLY B&B PER PERSON		WEEKLY D,B&B PER PERSON		🛏 16
🕭✳	MIN £	MAX £	MIN £	MAX £	🛏 3
	13.00	16.50	130.00	150.00	OPEN 3-11

Sutherlands

3 Picton Road, Tenby,
Dyfed SA70 7DP
Tel: (0834) 2522   L

Well established small family run guest house close to beach and town centre. Friendly informal atmosphere. Excellent home cooking and a varied daily menu. Tea and coffee facilities in all rooms at no extra charge.

HW T	NIGHTLY B&B PER PERSON		WEEKLY D,B&B PER PERSON		🛏 5
✳	MIN £	MAX £	MIN £	MAX £	🛏 0
	10.00	12.00	90.00	105.00	OPEN 1-12

TRE-FIN   Map Ref Jb3

Quiet tiny village on North Pembrokeshire coast. Near cathedral city of St. David's.

Guest Houses

Bryngarw Guest House

Abercastle Road, Tre-fin,
Haverfordwest,   COMMENDED
Pembrokeshire, Dyfed
SA62 5AR
Tel: (0348) 831211

Modern 5 bedroomed en-suite, licensed guest house in 2½ acres, sea views. Solarium. Large parking area. Tea/coffee making facilities. Downstairs bedrooms available. Varied menu. Taste of Wales. No hidden extras. Peaceful surroundings. Tre-Fin coastal village between St. David's/Fishguard. Every effort is made to make your stay enjoyable. Brochure Ray and Jane Gratton.

HW T	NIGHTLY B&B PER PERSON		WEEKLY D,B&B PER PERSON		🛏 5
TW ✳	MIN £	MAX £	MIN £	MAX £	🛏 5
	15.00	18.00	130.00	150.00	OPEN 5-10

At Llandovery, you can stand in the cobbled old market square and still see why the 19-th-century traveller and writer George Borrow described it as 'the pleasantest little town' in Wales. Llandovery's timeless charm epitomises the traditional town-and country-character of the Vales of Dyfed.

The landscape is dominated by the two great valleys carved by the Towy and Teifi rivers. Rich farmlands in the Vale of Towy are flanked by the brooding Black Mountain and the Brechfa Forest. Along the rushing Teifi, thick woods crowd down to the riverbanks where coracles are still used to fish for salmon and trout. This is an area of cattle and sheep markets – don't miss bustling Carmarthen on market day – and a magical coastline so vividly captured in the writings of Dylan Thomas (the boathouse where he lived in sleepy Laugharne is open to the public).

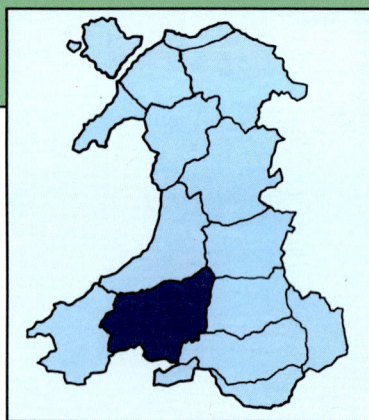

CARMARTHEN
Map Ref Kc2

County town of Dyfed in pastoral Vale of Towy. Lively market and shops, Livestock market. Carmarthen Castle was an important residence of the native Welsh princes but only the gateway and towers remain. Golf, fishing, tennis and well-equipped lesiure centre. Remains of Roman amphitheatre. Immaculate museum in beautiful historic house on outskirts of town. Gwili Railway and ornamental Middleton Hall Amenity Area. ⇌

Guest House

Glasfryn Guest House

Brechfa, Carmarthen,
Dyfed SA32 7QY
Tel: (0267) 202306

COMMENDED

Situated in the heart of Brechfa Forest surrounded by moss covered hills. A small family owned country guest house ideally located for salmon and sewin fishing, pony trekking, walking, shooting, birdwatching. Hot and cold in all rooms, 2 double rooms, 1 twin. Excellent home cooking, large dining room. ½ from nearest town, 45 minutes from beach.

HW	T	NIGHTLY B&B PER PERSON		WEEKLY D,B&B PER PERSON		🛏 3
🐾	C	MIN £	MAX £	MIN £	MAX £	🛏 -
⦸		12.50	12.50			OPEN 1-12

CARMARTHEN

LLANDEILO
Map Ref Ga7

Farming centre at an important crossing on River Towy and handy as touring base for Carreg Cennen Castle, impressively set on high crag, and remains of Dryslwyn Castle. Limited access to Dinefwr Castle in parklands on edge of town. Gelli Aur Country Park nearby has 90 acres, including a nature trail, arboretum and deer herd. Call also at the Trapp Arts and Crafts Centre near Carreg Cennen. ⇌

Hotels

The Plough Inn at Rhosmaen

Rhosmaen, Llandeilo,
Dyfed SA19 6NP
Tel: (0558) 823431
Fax: (0558) 823969

HIGHLY COMMENDED

Giulio and Diane Rocca, hosts for over twenty years at this friendly inn on the A-40, extend a warm welcome to all those who seek relaxation in the beautiful Towy Valley. The very best of local produce, salmon and sewin, venison, Welsh lamb and beef, cooked simply or in delicious continental recipes. Beautifully appointed en-suite bedrooms with panoramic views. Conference facilities, gym and sauna. Please phone or write for colour brochure.

C	NIGHTLY B&B PER PERSON		WEEKLY D,B&B PER PERSON		🛏 12
	MIN £	MAX £	MIN £	MAX £	🛏 12
	20.00	22.50			OPEN 1-12

Guest Houses

Brynawel Restaurant & Guest House

19 New Road, Llandeilo,
Dyfed SA19 6DD
Tel: (0558) 822925

MERIT

Under new ownership, tastefully refurbished throughout. Centrally heated. Fire certificate. Television, washing, shaving, tea making facilities in all rooms. Quiet comfortable lounge. Centrally located for shops and buses. Easy access from M4. Golf, riding, fishing, historic buildings and delightful country walks nearby. Leisurely drive to Gower and Pembrokeshire coast and Brecon Beacons National Park. En-suite family room, cot, ample parking. Evening meal by prior arrangement. Licensed.

HW	T	NIGHTLY B&B PER PERSON		WEEKLY D,B&B PER PERSON		🛏 5
		MIN £	MAX £	MIN £	MAX £	🛏 3
		14.00	16.00			OPEN 1-12

CARREG CENNEN CASTLE

CALL
Holidays WALES
📞 (0792) 645555

93

LLANDOVERY
Map Ref Gb6

An important market town on the A40 with a ruined castle; its Welsh name Llanymddyfri means "The church among the Waters". Nearby is the cave of Twm Sion Catti — the Welsh Robin Hood. Good touring centre for Brecon Beacons and remote Llyn Brianne area. ≈

Guest Houses

Myrtle Hill Licensed Guest House

Llansadwrn, Llanwrda,
Dyfed SA19 8HL

Tel: (0550) 777530

MERIT

Old farmhouse with magnificent views in beautiful unspoilt country. All bedrooms with en-suite bathrooms, tea/coffee facilities and hairdryers. Two comfortable sitting rooms, one 'no smoking'. Access at all times. Excellent food, freshly prepared, using own garden produce. Ideally situated for exploring South, West and Mid Wales. Lovely walking country, abundant wildlife. Fishing, pony trekking available locally. Autumn and Winter breaks. Send for brochure.

	NIGHTLY B&B PER PERSON		WEEKLY D,B&B PER PERSON			3
						3
	MIN £	MAX £	MIN £	MAX £	OPEN 2-12	
	15.50	16.00	153.00	157.00		

Y Neuadd Guest House & Photo Holidays

Pentre Ty Gwyn, Llandovery,
Dyfed SA20 0RN

Tel: (0550) 20603

COMMENDED

Small, comfortable guest house and photography centre. All rooms own shower, toilet, tea/coffee. Attractive lounge with log fire. Secluded but easily accessible in hidden valley on edge of Brecon Beacons National Park. Ideal for touring Mid/South Wales, walking, birdwatching, photography. Evening meals by arrangement. Professional photographer plus darkroom available. Llandovery 3 miles.

	NIGHTLY B&B PER PERSON		WEEKLY D,B&B PER PERSON			3
						3
	MIN £	MAX £	MIN £	MAX £	OPEN 2-11	
	14.00	14.00	140.00	140.00		

Farmhouses

Cwmgwyn Farm

Llangadog Road, Llandovery,
Dyfed SA20 0EQ

Tel: (0550) 20410

L

Welcome to our 17th century modernised farmhouse overlooking the River Towy which provides a picturesque view of the Towy Valley. Peaceful, ideal for walking. A working livestock farm, two miles from Llandovery market town on A4069 road. Ideal centre for touring. One family room and one double room, TV lounge and dining room.

T	NIGHTLY B&B PER PERSON		WEEKLY D,B&B PER PERSON			2
						–
	MIN £	MAX £	MIN £	MAX £	OPEN 3-9	
	11.00	12.50				

THE VALLEYS REVISITED

Our full colour brochure on the South Wales Valleys features tours of industrial heritage sites, leisure activities, an events list, a comprehensive guide to the Valleys rail network and a detailed map of the area. An accommodation supplement featuring a range of both serviced and self catering accommodation can be included on request.

CEFN SIDAN SANDS,
PEMBREY COUNTRY PARK

LLANELLI
Map Ref Kd4

Bustling town with good shopping, covered market and pleasant parklands. Pembrey Country Park, adjoining 7 miles of sandy beach, has a Visitor Centre and offers guided walks, pony trekking, ski slope, adventure playground and much more. The Welsh Motor Sports Centre is nearby and Kidwelly Castle and Industrial Museum must be visited; also the unusual Carmarthen Bay Wind Energy Demonstration Centre. ≈

Guest Houses

Victoria Guest House

88A Queen Victoria Road, Llanelli,
Dyfed SA15 2TH

Tel: (0554) 753050

L

This family run guest house is ideally situated close to town centre, beaches, swimming pool, parks, golf course, Motor Sport Centre and Pembrey Country Park. Recently refurbished. Most bedrooms with private bathroom. All bedrooms have colour television, tea making facilities. Good home cooking. Spacious television lounge. Separate dining room. Car park. Full central heating and a warm and friendly welcome to everyone.

	NIGHTLY B&B PER PERSON		WEEKLY D,B&B PER PERSON			9
						6
	MIN £	MAX £	MIN £	MAX £	OPEN 1-12	
	12.00	15.00	84.00	112.00		

LLANGADOG
Map Ref Ga7

Small market town set on two tributaries of the nearby Towy. Convenient for walking and touring the Black Mountain. The road over Black Mountain to Brynaman is one of the most scenic in South Wales. Bethlehem, 2 miles south, has a famous Christmas postmark! ⇌

Guest Houses

Pen-y-Bont

Llangadog, Dyfed SA19 9EN
Tel: (0550) 777126

Charming old guest house on fringe of Brecon Beacons National Park in tranquil surroundings. Ideal for peaceful holidays and short/long breaks. Newly refurbished accommodation includes bath or shower for each room, restful lounge with colour TV, charming dining room, and pretty bedrooms. The cottage garden with babbling stream is frequented by wildlife. Excellent cuisine, fresh produce daily. Car park. Our aim is your happiness and comfort and to spoil you.

	NIGHTLY B&B PER PERSON		WEEKLY D,B&B PER PERSON			3
	MIN £	MAX £	MIN £	MAX £	OPEN	3
	14.00	14.00	157.50	157.50	1-12	

COUNTRYSIDE NORTH OF LLANDOVERY

SLIDE PACKS

The following slide packs are available for purchase from the Wales Tourist Board:

North Wales Scenery	£2.00	(4 slides)
Mid Wales Scenery	£2.00	(4 slides)
South Wales Scenery	£2.00	(4 slides)
Historic Sites	£3.00	(6 slides)

Contact: Photo Librarian, WTB, Brunel House, 2 Fitzalan Road, Cardiff CF2 1UY

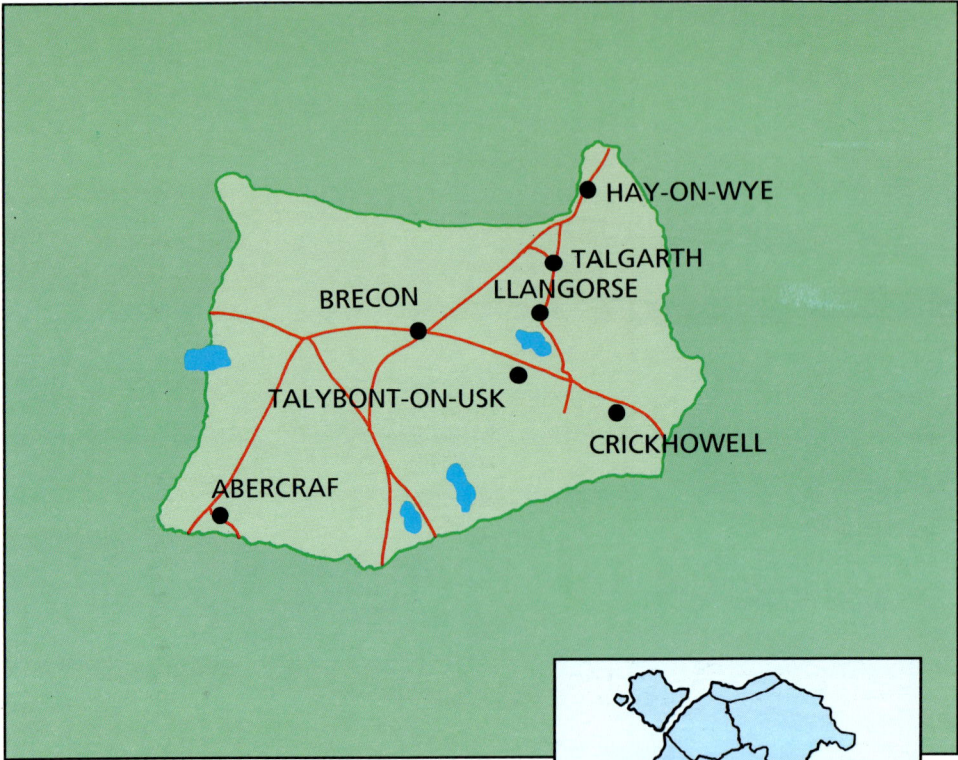

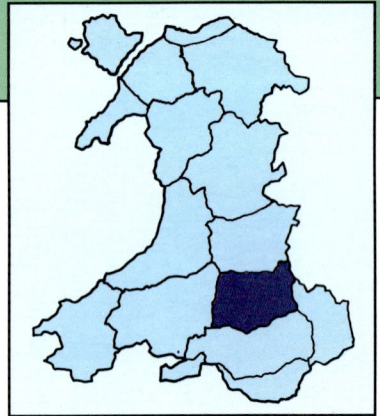

Handsome Brecon is ideally located for exploring the 519-square-mile Brecon Beacons National Park. The grassy slopes of the Beacons themselves, rising above the town, are only one of four mountain ranges within this huge park. To the east, there are the borderland Black Mountains, to the west the lonely wilderness of Fforest Fawr and the challenging Black Mountain. This high, fresh country, rising to almost 3,000 ft, is watered by innumerable lakes and rivers – such as the remote Llyn y Fan Fawr or reedy Llangorse Lake near Brecon.

This great outdoors attracts walkers and pony trekkers, hang gliders and canoeists, anglers and golfers – even canal cruises along the peaceful Monmouthsire and Brecon Canal.

The wide, open spaces up in the hills decline into sheltered valleys dotted with pretty places to stay – book-filled Hay-on-Wye, or the old stagecoach town of Crickhowell.

Plenty of events such as the Brecon Jazz Festival and Hay Literary Festival help to enliven the summer scene.

BRECON
Map Ref Ge6

Main touring centre for the 519 square miles of the Brecon Beacons National Park. Handsome old town with thriving market, castle, cathedral, priory and interesting Brecknock and South Wales Borderers museums. Wide range of inns, guest houses and hotels, and good shopping. Centre for riding and pony trekking. Golf, fishing and canal cruising available. Very popular summer jazz festival.

Hotels

Old Castle Farm Hotel

Llanfaes, Brecon, Powys
LD3 8DL
Tel: (0874) 2120

A 17th century farmhouse with all modern facilities west of the market town of Brecon, half mile from town centre, and in easy reach of mountain centre, golf, pony trekking, swimming. The hotel caters for 26 persons. All rooms have en-suite, TV, radio and tea/coffee making facilities. Licensed bar/lounge. Private car park. Access to hotel at all times. Washing facilities available.

HW		NIGHTLY B&B PER PERSON		WEEKLY D,B&B PER PERSON		🛏 11
						🛏 11
		MIN £	MAX £	MIN £	MAX £	OPEN 2-11
		15.00	18.00	133.00	147.00	

SOUTH WALES VALLEYS (VHS/BETA)

A 15-minute look at a distinctive part of Wales where a rich industrial heritage co-exists with a surprising natural beauty and range of attractions.

The Olde Masons Arms Hotel

Hay Road, Talgarth, Brecon, Powys LD3 0BB
Tel: (0874) 711688
MERIT

16th century hotel with country cottage ambience, amidst the Black Mountains and Brecon Beacons. Enjoy weekend and midweek breaks. All rooms en-suite, colour TV, radio, hot beverage tray. Freshly cooked cuisine to delight every palate. Fully licensed lounge bar and restaurant. Ideal for walking, pony trekking and fishing.

🐕	SP	NIGHTLY B&B PER PERSON		WEEKLY D,B&B PER PERSON		🛏 7
						🛏 7
		MIN £	MAX £	MIN £	MAX £	OPEN 1-12
		21.50	25.00	190.00	225.00	

Old Gwernyfed Country Manor

Felindre, Three Cocks, Brecon, Powys LD3 0SU
Tel: (04974) 376
COMMENDED

Built 1600. Our beautiful Elizabethan home offers peace and tranquility in 12 acres isolation in Black Mountains. Hay-on-Wye 5 miles. Charles 1 stayed in 1645. Interesting features remain-minstrells gallery, carved code, Armada mast, trap doors etc. Service is personal and friendly, food interesting and fresh. Vistas are magnificent. Local amenities include gliding, hill walking, trekking, clay shooting, canoeing, sailing etc.

HW	T	NIGHTLY B&B PER PERSON		WEEKLY D,B&B PER PERSON		🛏 11
🐕	SP					🛏 9
		MIN £	MAX £	MIN £	MAX £	OPEN 3-11
		21.00	35.00	231.00	315.00	

Guest Houses

Beacons Guest House

16 Bridge Street, Brecon, Powys LD3 8AH
Tel: (0874) 3339
MERIT

Friendly Georgian guest house close to town centre, River Usk and Brecon Beacons. En-suite bedrooms with beverage tray and colour TV. Cosy bar, residents' lounge and private parking. Ideal location for attractions, outdoor activities. Groups, pets and children welcome. Excellent home cooking, Taste of Wales recommended. AA Listed. Please telephone or write for brochure. Credit cards accepted.

HW	T	NIGHTLY B&B PER PERSON		WEEKLY D,B&B PER PERSON		🛏 10
🐕	SP					🛏 7
🍴	TW	MIN £	MAX £	MIN £	MAX £	OPEN 1-12
		13.00	15.00	123.50	135.50	

The Old Rectory

Llanddew, Brecon, Powys
LD3 9SS
Tel: (0874) 2058
MERIT

Situated 1½ miles from Brecon in own grounds with magnificent views of Brecon Beacons. Family run guest house, offering every comfort with personal hospitality and excellent home produced meals. H&C, colour TV, tea, coffee facilities all rooms. Private lounge, central heating, ample parking, croquet on lawns, golf course, pony trekking, country walks nearby.

HW	T	NIGHTLY B&B PER PERSON		WEEKLY D,B&B PER PERSON		🛏 3
	SP					🛏 0
		MIN £	MAX £	MIN £	MAX £	OPEN 1-12
		12.00	14.00	130.00	144.00	

WALES
It's magic

Trewalter House

Llangorse, Brecon,
Powys LD3 0PS
Tel: (087484) 442

Jean and Peter Abbott welcome you to their charming former farmhouse in Brecon Beacons National Park. Peaceful setting with magnificent panoramic views. All rooms tastefully decorated, en-suite bathrooms, colour TV, tea/coffee making. Ideal centre for touring, walking Brecon Beacons and Black Mountains. One mile Llangorse Lake. Ample parking. Short breaks minimum two nights DBB.

HW T SP	NIGHTLY B&B PER PERSON		WEEKLY D,B&B PER PERSON		🛏 3 🛏 3
	MIN £	MAX £	MIN £	MAX £	OPEN
	20.00	20.00	182.00	182.00	1-11

BRECON BEACONS

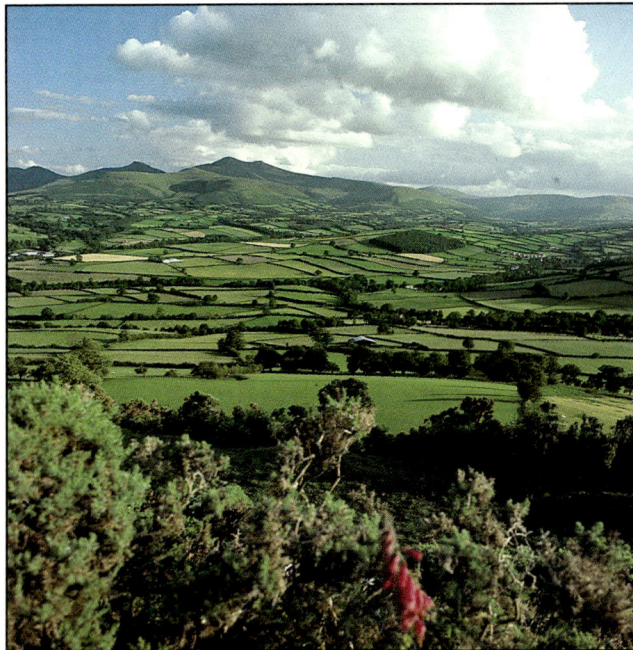

Farmhouses

Brynfedwen Farm

Trallong Common, Sennybridge,
Brecon, Powys
LD3 8HW
Tel: (0874) 82505   AWARD   👑👑 COMMENDED

Brynfedwen "hill of the birch trees", is a family farm set high above the Usk Valley commanding splendid views of the Brecon Beacons. Well situated for all country pursuits or just relaxing. Period, centrally heated farmhouse. All three rooms are en-suite, including self contained flat designed for disabled visitors. Good home fare. Children welcome. Telephone number from May 1991 (0874) 636505.

HW T SP	NIGHTLY B&B PER PERSON		WEEKLY D,B&B PER PERSON		🛏 3 🛏 3
	MIN £	MAX £	MIN £	MAX £	OPEN
	14.00	—	140.00	—	1-12

CRICKHOWELL
Map Ref Hb7

Small, pleasant country town beautifully situated on the River Usk. Walking, fishing, pony trekking and riding facilities. Remains of Norman castle, 14th century Tretower Court and earlier castle worth a visit.

Hotels

Dragon House Hotel

High Street, Crickhowell,   👑
Powys NP8 1BE   👑👑
Tel: (0873) 810362
Fax: (0873) 811868

Charming 18th century hotel in picturesque market town within the Brecon Beacons National Park. Ideal for business or pleasure and year round outdoor pursuits. Individually furnished rooms have telephone and tea/coffee facilities. Colour TV and hairdryer in en-suite rooms. Some non smoking rooms. Our cosy bar and restaurant with real log fire serves freshly prepared meals. Resident's lounge. Car park.

T SP	NIGHTLY B&B PER PERSON		WEEKLY D,B&B PER PERSON		🛏 17 🛏 9
	MIN £	MAX £	MIN £	MAX £	OPEN
	16.00	25.00	140.00	180.00	1-12

HAY-ON-WYE
Map Ref Hb5

Small market town on the Offa's Dyke path, nestling below the Black Mountains on a picturesque stretch of the River Wye. A mecca for book lovers — there are antiquarian and second-hand bookshops, some huge, all over the town. Attractive crafts centre. Literature Festival in early summer attracts big names.

Hotels

Old Black Lion

Lion Street, Hay-on-Wye,
Hereford HR3 5AD
Tel: (0497) 820841
COMMENDED

A 13th century inn nestling quietly in the centre of the town. Single, double and family rooms with TV, phone in all rooms. Resident's lounge. Ideally situated for Hay's books and fishing. Internationally known for its sophisticated country cuisine.

HW T 🐕 SP	NIGHTLY B&B PER PERSON		WEEKLY D,B&B PER PERSON		🛏 10 🛁 9
	MIN £	MAX £	MIN £	MAX £	OPEN 1-12
	16.50	19.75	203.00	203.00	

Guest Houses

York House

Hardwick Road, Cusop,
Hay-on-Wye, Powys HR3 5QX
Tel: (0497) 820705

Peter and Olwen Roberts welcome you to their traditional Victorian guest house, quietly situated in beautiful gardens on the edge of Hay. Sunny mountain views enjoyed by the well equipped rooms (most en-suite). Ideal for a relaxing holiday browsing the book shops, exploring the National Park and Kilvert country or just enjoying our freshly prepared home cooking. Private parking and AA/RAC Listed. Regret no smoking indoors. Credit cards accepted.

🐕 ⊟✕	NIGHTLY B&B PER PERSON		WEEKLY D,B&B PER PERSON		🛏 5 🛁 3
	MIN £	MAX £	MIN £	MAX £	OPEN 1-12
	15.50	20.00	157.50	188.85	

TALGARTH   Map Ref Ha6

Small market town between Brecon and Hay-on-Wye, in foothills of the Black Mountains. Centre for walkers, pony trekkers and anglers. Bronllys Castle nearby.

Guest Houses

Upper Trewalkin Farm

Pengenffordd,
Talgarth, Brecon,
Powys LD3 0HA
Tel: (0874) 711349
AWARD
HIGHLY COMMENDED

Within the Brecon Beacons National Park, Upper Trewalkin, a family run sheep and cattle farm has superb views of the Black Mountains. A short distance from Brecon and Hay-On-Wye and within easy reach of so many attractions of Wales and the Marches. Good food and every comfort assured. Separate brochure available on request.

HW T	NIGHTLY B&B PER PERSON		WEEKLY D,B&E PER PERSON		🛏 3 🛁 1
	MIN £	MAX £	MIN £	MAX £	OPEN 4-10
	13.00	15.00	145.00	159.00	

WALES
It's magic

TRETOWER COURT

TALYBONT ON USK
Map Ref Ge7

Village in picturesque setting on banks of River Usk and Monmouthshire-Brecon Canal. Within the Brecon Beacons National Park. Surrounding hills perfect for walking and pony trekking. Brecon nearby.

Hotels

Aberclydach House

Aber, Talybont on Usk,
Powys LD3 7YS
Tel: (087487) 361
Fax: (087487) 436
COMMENDED

Warm, friendly run hotel set in pleasant gardens and surrounded by hills in the heart of the Brecon Beacons National Park. Ideally situated for lovely walks, pony trekking and all kinds of water sports. Aberclydach House has a well stocked bar with over 40 different malt whiskies.

SP ⊟✕	NIGHTLY B&B PER PERSON		WEEKLY D,B&B PER PERSON		🛏 11 🛁 11
	MIN £	MAX £	MIN £	MAX £	OPEN 1-12
	29.00	—	264.00	—	

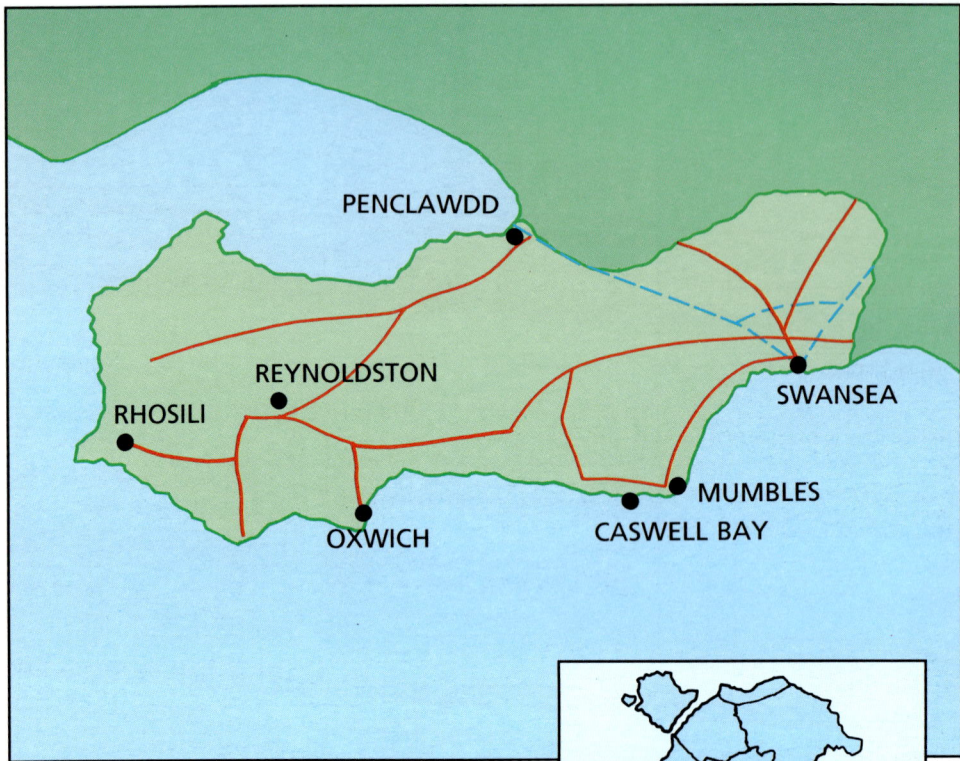

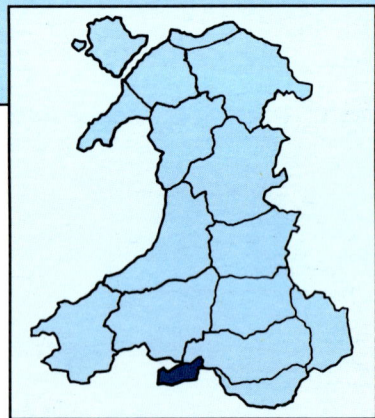

Swansea's stylish marina and Maritime Quarter have won accolades for the way in which they have brought new life to the waterfront of this city-by-the-sea. Swansea also has its traditional side – visit Wales's finest fresh-food market, where you can buy that peculiar Welsh delicacy laverbread and fresh cockles direct from the pickers of Penclawdd.

The Gower Peninsula, only a stone's throw from the city, was the first part of Britain to be declared an 'Area of Outstanding Natural Beauty', is a lovely promontory of sheltered, south-facing bays – at Langland, Caswell, Oxwich and Port-Eynon. The peninsula comes to an end in spectacular fashion along the precipitous Worms Head and the endless beach at Rhosili, where surfers ride the waves. At Gower's approach stands The Mumbles, a strangely named, attractive little sailing and water sports centre guarded by one of this area's many castles at Oystermouth.

MUMBLES — Map Ref La4

Small resort on Swansea Bay with attractive waterfront and headland pier; centre for all watersports and sailing. On fringe of Gower Peninsula, a designated Area of Outstanding Natural Beauty. Oystermouth Castle and Clyne Valley Country Park and Gardens nearby.

Hotels

Beach House Hotel

734 Mumbles Road,
Southend, Mumbles,
Swansea, West Glamorgan SA3 4EL
Tel: (0792) 367650

Situated on the sea front with superb views across Swansea Bay. All bedrooms have colour TV, teasmade, telephone, hairdryer. Choice of rooms with/without en-suite bathroom. Central heating. Lounge bar, licensed restaurant. Suitable for children over five. Full fire certificate. Open all year.

	NIGHTLY B&B PER PERSON		WEEKLY D,B&B PER PERSON		🛏 11
	MIN £	MAX £	MIN £	MAX £	🛏 6
	18.00	25.00	—	—	OPEN 1-12

Osborne Hotel

Rotherslade Road,
Langland Bay, Swansea,
West Glamorgan SA3 4QL
Tel: (0792) 366274
Fax: (0792) 363100

Golf course 18 hole ¼ mile. Overlooking beaches. Sea fishing ¼ mile. Surfing 50 yards, tennis ¼ mile. Swansea 4 miles. Gower peninsula.

T 🍴 C SP	NIGHTLY B&B PER PERSON		WEEKLY D,B&B PER PERSON		🛏 36
	MIN £	MAX £	MIN £	MAX £	🛏 32
	37.50	47.50	238.00	290.00	OPEN 1-12

OXWICH — Map Ref Kd5

Popular Gower Peninsula Beach with 3 miles of glorious sand and extensive dunes: easily accessible. Nature trail visitor centre.

RHOSILI BEACH

Hotels

Oxwich Bay Hotel

Oxwich, Gower, Swansea,
West Glamorgan SA3 1LS
Tel: (0792) 390329/390491
Fax: (0792) 391254

The Oxwich Bay Hotel is superbly located fronting the bay, within seconds of two glorious miles of golden sands. All rooms are en-suite with bath/shower and WC. The bay is safe for swimming and all water sports. Small touring caravan site and one self-catering caravan for hire. Colour brochure sent with pleasure.

C SP	NIGHTLY B&B PER PERSON		WEEKLY D,B&B PER PERSON		🛏 13
	MIN £	MAX £	MIN £	MAX £	🛏 13
	15.00	30.00	160.65	244.65	OPEN 1-12

REYNOLDSTON — Map Ref Kd5

Gower peninsula village near sandy beaches of Oxwich, Port-Eynon and Rhosili. Gower Farm Park Nearby.

Farmhouses

Greenways

Hills Farm, Reynoldston, Gower,
West Glamorgan SA3 1AE
Tel: (0792) 390125

Greenways is situated in beautiful countryside near main road. Central to all Gower Bays adjacent to Cefn Bryn, a walkers paradise. Working farm with own produce. Hot and cold in bedrooms central heating, TV lounge, separate tables. Pets by arrangement. Car park. Send SAE please to D W John.

🐕	NIGHTLY B&B PER PERSON		WEEKLY D,B&B PER PERSON		🛏 3
	MIN £	MAX £	MIN £	MAX £	🛏 0
	12.00	15.00	—	—	OPEN 3-10

WALES It's magic

SWANSEA Map Ref La4

Gateway to the Gower Peninsula, Britain's first designated Area of Outstanding Natural Beauty. Superb new marina complex and Maritime quarter — excellent leisure centre, with Maritime and Industrial Museum nearby. Art gallery, Superbowl, dry ski slope and marvellous 'Plantasia' exotic plants attraction. Good shopping. Covered market with destinctively Welsh atmosphere: try the cockles, laverbread and Gower potatoes. Swansea Festival and 'Fringe' Festival in October. Theatres and cinemas, parks and gardens, restaurants and wine bars.

Hotels

Langland Court Hotel

Langland Court Road,
Langland, Swansea,
West Glamorgan SA3 4TD
Tel: (0792) 361545
Fax: (0792) 362302

Set in a quiet residential area of Langland. All rooms en-suite after complete refurbishment. The public area still retains the character of the past with oak panelled entrance hall, dining room and galleried staircase. From the extensive gardens, fine views of the sea. Lovely cliff walks, beaches and bays, golf, leisure centre, maritime quarter, theatre and cinemas all nearby. The Quadrant Centre has some of the finest shops in the area.

HW T C SP TW	NIGHTLY B&B PER PERSON		WEEKLY D,B&B PER PERSON		🛏 21 🐾 21
	MIN £	MAX £	MIN £	MAX £	OPEN 1-12
	32.00	34.00	270.00	295.00	

Guest Houses

Belmont Guest House

2 Mirador Crescent, Uplands,
Swansea, West Glamorgan
SA2 0QY
Tel: (0792) 466812

Small, friendly, quietly situated with own adjoining private car park. Convenient for city centre or Gower Peninsula. Ideally situated for business or pleasure. All centrally heated, bedrooms equipped with tea/coffee, colour TV, H&C, shaver point, clock radio, full fire certificate. Small groups welcome. Proprietors Mair and Tony Aston.

HW T SP	NIGHTLY B&B PER PERSON		WEEKLY D,B&B PER PERSON		🛏 6 🐾 0
	MIN £	MAX £	MIN £	MAX £	OPEN 1-12
	14.00	15.50	60.00	70.00	

Cwmdulais House

Cwmdulais, Pontarddulais,
Swansea, West Glamorgan
SA4 1NP
Tel: (0792) 885008

Family run licensed country guest house. Newly refurbished to a high standard. Situated on a peaceful bridle path. Only 8 miles from city centre and 3 miles off Junction 47 M4. Well placed for the area's many attractions. Good home cooking, special diets catered for. Dogs and horses welcome. Reductions for children and long stay. Brochure available.

HW T	NIGHTLY B&B PER PERSON		WEEKLY D,B&B PER PERSON		🛏 4 🐾 1
	MIN £	MAX £	MIN £	MAX £	OPEN 1-12
	15.50	17.00	147.00	157.50	

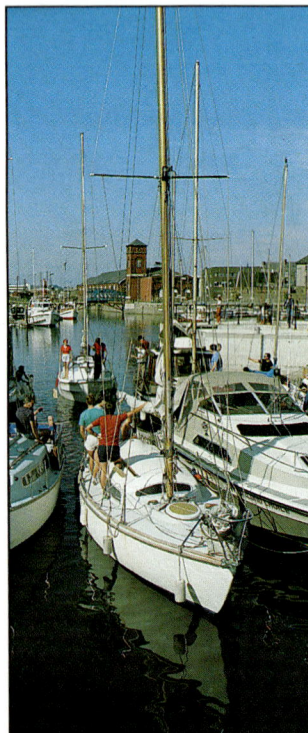

Grosvenor House

Mirador Crescent, Uplands,
Swansea, West Glamorgan COMMENDED
SA2 0QX
Tel: (0792) 461522

"Commended" by Wales Tourist Board. Pat and Brian extend a warm welcome. Quietly situated, private car parking available. Easy walking city centre, near beautiful parks, sports, Gower. Full central heating, comfortable TV lounge, separate dining room, evening meal optional. All bedrooms have colour TV, tea/coffee making facilities, radio clock alarm, H&C. Business or pleasure your comfort is our priority.

T	NIGHTLY B&B PER PERSON		WEEKLY D,B&B PER PERSON		🛏 8 🐾 0
	MIN £	MAX £	MIN £	MAX £	OPEN 1-12
	15.00	20.00	135.00	145.00	

WALES *It's magic*

SWANSEA MARINA

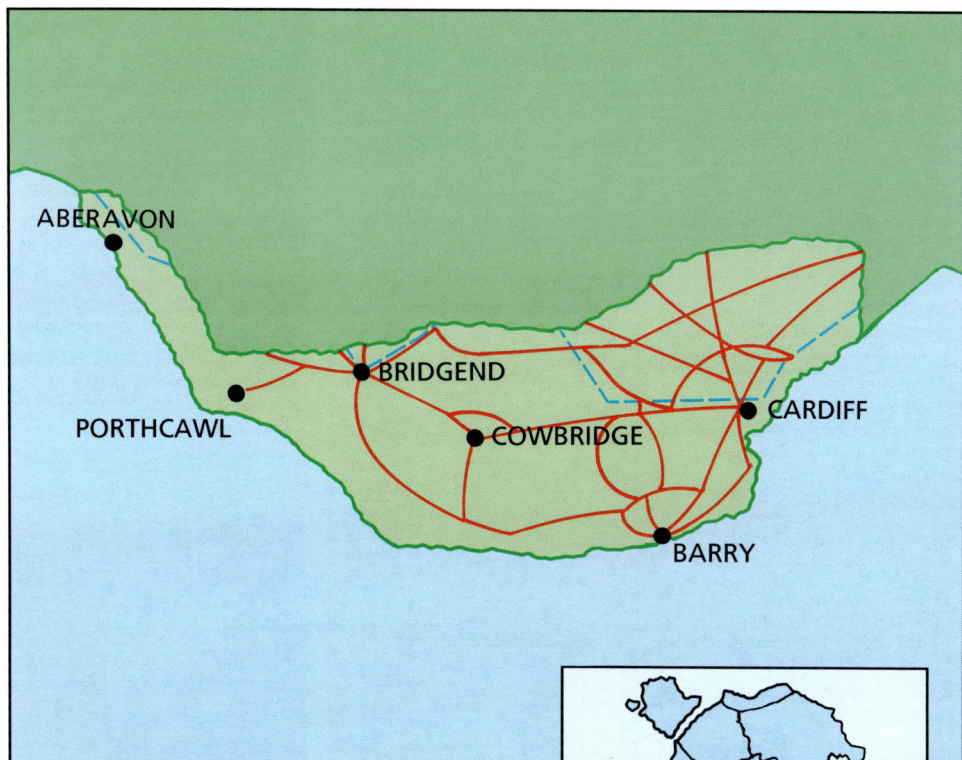

Cardiff has now come into its own – and deservedly so – as a popular visitor centre. There's so much to enjoy and appreciate in this cosmopolitan capital – a much-praised Civic Centre, amazing city-centre castle (a Roman fort, Norman castle and fabulous Victorian mansion all rolled into one!), treasure-packed National Museum, St. David's Concert Hall, superb shopping and entertainment. And if that's not enough, there's the Welsh Folk Museum at St. Fagans on the city's outskirts, where the Wales of bygone times lives on. It's all so easy to get to – less than two hours by train from London, or a short, swift drive along the motorway.

On its doorstep is the Vale of Glamorgan, an area of rich farmlands dotted with charming villages. And fringing this greenery is a coastline of great variety that includes the towering cliffs of the Glamorgan Heritage Coast. Penarth has a delightful Victorian pier and modern marina, while the lively resorts of Barry Island and Porthcawl offer traditional seaside fun.

ABERAVON   Map Ref Lb4

Popular sandy beach near Port Talbot. The Afan Lido is a major sports and entertainment centre. Spacious promenade. Central location on the South Wales coast for visiting Swansea, Cardiff and South Wales Valleys attractions. Margam Country Park and Penscynor Wildlife Park close by.

Hotels

Aberavon Beach Hotel

Aberavon, Port Talbot,
West Glamorgan   MERIT
SA12 6QP
Tel: (0639) 884949

Modern three star hotel opposite sandy beach with views across Swansea Bay. Easy reach M4 and ideal base to explore South Wales. Excellent restaurant with dinner dance Fridays and Saturdays. Bar snacks always available. All bedrooms with bathroom en-suite, colour TV, radio, telephone, tea/coffee facilities. Children stay free, special rates weekends. Facilities for the disabled. Free entrance to Afan Lido Centre adjacent hotel for squash, swimming, solarium, spa, sauna, steam etc.

HW T	NIGHTLY B&B		WEEKLY D,B&B		🛏 65
🐾 C	PER PERSON		PER PERSON		🛏 65
SP	MIN £	MAX £	MIN £	MAX £	OPEN
	20.00	24.50	189.00	198.50	1-12

THE VALLEYS REVISITED

Our full colour brochure of the South Wales Valleys features tours of industrial heritage sites, leisure activities, an events list, a comprehensive guide to the Valleys rail network and a detailed map of the area. An accommodation supplement featuring a range of both serviced and self catering accommodation can be included on request.

BARRY   Map Ref Ma6

Town on a narrow peninsula near Cardiff. Nearby is Barry Island, a great favourite with fun seekers, with its sandy beaches, pleasure park and range of amusements. The Knap, in contrast, has a quiet pebble beach, swimming pool and boating lake. Sports centre, sailing, bowls and fishing. Visit the Welsh Hawking Centre and two nearby beauty spots — Portkerry Country Park and Dyffryn Gardens. ≋

Hotels

Mount Sorrel Hotel

Porthkerry Road, Barry,
South Glamorgan CF6 8AY
Tel: (0446) 740069
Telex: 497819 G
Fax: (0446) 746600

Ideal touring centre for the Vale, close to beaches and Cardiff. Indoor pool and leisure facilities. Egon Ronay recommended. 50 bedrooms all en-suite, colour TV, teasmade, telephone, excellent restaurant and licensed bars. All newly refurbished to a high standard. Children welcome. Special mini weekend rates available all year. Ample car parking.

HW T	NIGHTLY B&B		WEEKLY D,B&B		🛏 50
🐾 C	PER PERSON		PER PERSON		🛏 50
SP	MIN £	MAX £	MIN £	MAX £	OPEN
	30.00	40.00	240.00	360.00	1-12

BRIDGEND   Map Ref Ld5

Bustling industrial and market town in the rural Vale of Glamorgan. Lively resort of Porthcawl and unspoilt Heritage Coast with cliffs and dunes nearby. Beautiful Bryngarw Country Park and ancient Ewenny Priory on doorstep. Three ruined Norman castles in the area — Coity, Newcastle and Ogmore. ≋

Hotels

Court Colman Hotel

Pen-y-Fai, Bridgend,
Mid Glamorgan CF31 4NG
Tel: (0656) 720212
Fax: (0656) 724544

A beautiful manor house with 16th century origins, set in 6 acres, nr. Bridgend. En-suite bedrooms with colour TV, tea/coffee facilities. Delightful panelling and woodwork. Conference facilities from 10 to 250, weddings and functions a speciality. Extensive à la carte menu and wine list. Cocktail bar. Large public bar attached to the main bulding offering a choice of atmosphere and snacks.

HW T	NIGHTLY B&B		WEEKLY D,B&B		🛏 40
🐾 C	PER PERSON		PER PERSON		🛏 40
SP ✕	MIN £	MAX £	MIN £	MAX £	OPEN
	55.00	65.00	–	–	1-12

Capital of Wales, business, trade and entertainment centre. Splendid civic centre, lovely parkland, modern pedestrianised shopping centre, good restaurants, theatres, cinemas, clubs and sports facilities, including ice rink and Superbowl. Visit St David's Hall for top-class entertainment. Splendid city centre castle. National Museum of Wales has a fine collection of Impressionist and Post-Impressionist paintings. Industrial and Maritime Museum and Techniquest Science centre in docklands. national Stadium is home of Welsh rugby. Wide range of accommodation at all prices. Llandaff Cathedral close by and fascinating collection of old farmhouses and other buildings in Welsh Folk Museum at St. Fagans.

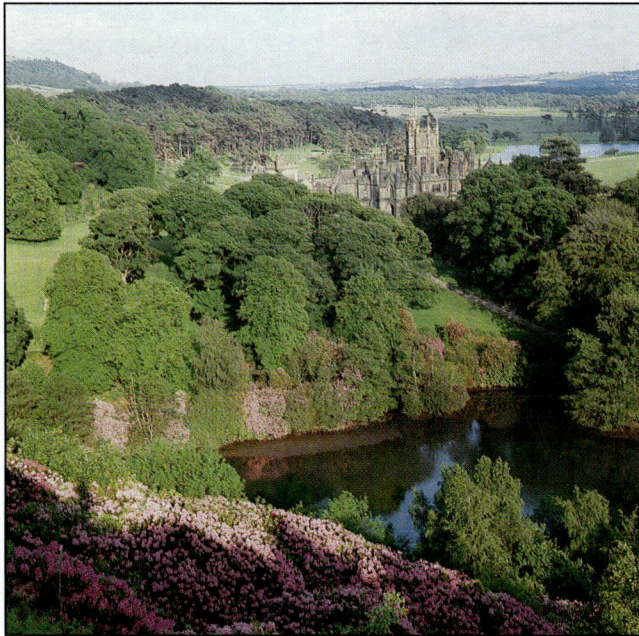

MARGAM COUNTRY PARK

Hotels

Angel Hotel

Castle Street, Cardiff,
South Glamorgan CF1 2QZ
Tel: (0222) 232633
Telex: 498132   COMMENDED
Fax: (0222) 396212

Recently restored, the Angel Hotel is once again in its rightful place as the premier hotel of Cardiff. Skilfully blending elegance and service with quiet efficiency. Situated between Cardiff Arms Park and Cardiff Castle, in the heart of the city, minutes from shopping and business areas. The hotel now offers 91 bedrooms, including 10 suites. All rooms are equipped with telephone, colour television, hairdryer and tea/coffee making facilities. Special packages available.

	NIGHTLY B&B PER PERSON		WEEKLY D,B&B PER PERSON		🛏 91
					🛏 91
	MIN £	MAX £	MIN £	MAX £	OPEN 1-12
	36.50	45.00	260.00	320.00	

Austins

11 Coldstream Terrace,
Cardiff, South Glamorgan
CF1 8LJ
Tel: (0222) 377148

Situated in the centre of Cardiff 300 yards from the castle. 7 single and 5 twin rooms, 5 rooms with private shower. All with hot and cold, shaver points, fixed heating, tea and coffee, colour TV. Full English breakfast. Evening meal by arrangement. 10 minutes walk from bus and train station. Fire certificate held. Warm welcome to all nationalities.

	NIGHTLY B&B PER PERSON		WEEKLY D,B&B PER PERSON		🛏 12
					🛏 5
	MIN £	MAX £	MIN £	MAX £	OPEN 1-12
	12.00	13.00	–	–	

Cardiff International Hotel

Mary Ann Street, Cardiff,
South Glamorgan
CF1 2EQ
Tel: (0222) 341441
Fax: (0222) 223742
Central Reservations: (0800) 282315

Cardiffs' newest hotel, the Cardiff International blends gently into this city of contrasts, where the old and the new meet in perfect harmony. Offering high 4 star standards at 3 star prices and situated in Cardiffs' city centre with its superb recreation, leisure and shopping facilities, within easy reach of the coast and the countryside. The Cardiff International hotel provides the perfect luxurious base for your stay.

	NIGHTLY B&B PER PERSON		WEEKLY D,B&B PER PERSON		🛏 143
					🛏 143
	MIN £	MAX £	MIN £	MAX £	OPEN 1-12
	48.50	–	–	–	

Cathedral Hotel

47-49 Cathedral Road, Cardiff,
South Glamorgan CF1 9HD
Tel: (0222) 236511
Fax: (0222) 236511

We are a friendly family run hotel offering guests the chance of a drink in our cosy residents bar or a meal in our restaurant. All rooms have TV, coffee and tea making facilities and telephones. We are only a few minutes walk from the city centre and castle. We are also opposite the National Sports Centre for Wales for which we have a membership card for guests.

	NIGHTLY B&B PER PERSON		WEEKLY D,B&B PER PERSON		🛏 23
					🛏 18
	MIN £	MAX £	MIN £	MAX £	OPEN 1-12
	15.00	21.00	–	–	

Clare Court Hotel

46/48 Clare Road, Cardiff,
South Glamorgan CF1 7QP
Tel: (0222) 344839

Family run hotel, walking distance to bus and railway station, Cardiff Castle, shopping centre etc. All rooms with en-suite bathrooms, remote control colour TV, radio, telephone, Tea & coffee machine, central heating, satellite TV in lounge. Licensed bar. Evening meals provided.

	NIGHTLY B&B PER PERSON		WEEKLY D,B&B PER PERSON			9
	MIN £	MAX £	MIN £	MAX £		9
	16.00	20.00	140.00	170.00	OPEN 1-12	

Courtfield Hotel

101 Cathedral Road, Cardiff,
South Glamorgan CF1 9PH
Tel: (0222) 227701

This popular and comfortable licensed hotel is located close to Cardiff Castle and city amenities. All centrally heated bedrooms are furnished with hot and cold washing facilities, together with razor point, private direct dial telephone, colour television and complimentary tea and coffee tray. Single, double or family rooms with en-suite bathrooms are available. The licensed restaurant is open to non-residents. All major credit cards are accepted.

T		NIGHTLY B&B PER PERSON		WEEKLY D,B&B PER PERSON			16
C	SP	MIN £	MAX £	MIN £	MAX £		4
		20.00	25.00	–	–	OPEN 1-12	

DYFFRYN GARDENS

Courtlands Hotel

110 Newport Road, Cardiff,
South Glamorgan CF2 1DG
Tel: (0222) 497583

Situated ½ mile from city centre. Licensed bar and dining room. Comfortable residents lounge. Evening meals available on request. Hot and cold snacks available. All bedrooms with tea and coffee facilities, colour television, wash hand-basins, electric shaver points, radio and full central heating. Majority of bedrooms en-suite. Full fire certificate. Free car park.

HW	T	NIGHTLY B&B PER PERSON		WEEKLY D,B&B PER PERSON			7
	C	MIN £	MAX £	MIN £	MAX £		4
		15.00	18.00	168.00	189.00	OPEN 1-12	

Glenmor Hotel

150-152 Newport Road,
Cardiff, South Glamorgan
CF2 1DJ
Tel: (0222) 489545
Fax: (0222) 490230

Located only ten minutes from the city centre and all its major attractions. All rooms are well appointed with full en-suite facilities, colour TV, radio, clock alarm and hot drinks facility, video and satelite transmissions are also available in all rooms. Private secure car park available for those travelling by car.

HW	T	NIGHTLY B&B PER PERSON		WEEKLY D,B&B PER PERSON			18
	SP	MIN £	MAX £	MIN £	MAX £		18
		17.50	20.00	160.00	185.00	OPEN 1-12	

Miskin Manor

Miskin, Pontyclun,
Nr Cardiff, Mid Glamorgan
CF7 8ND
Tel: (0443) 224204   HIGHLY
Fax: (0443) 237606   COMMENDED

An elegant mellow stone Victorian mansion. The building nestles in 20 acres of garden and woodland overlooking River Ely. The well proportioned rooms are all individually decorated offering comfort and luxury. Superb cuisine and fine wines make any stay at Miskin Manor memorable. Extensive leisure facilities and swimming pool on site.

SP		NIGHTLY B&B PER PERSON		WEEKLY D,B&B PER PERSON			35
		MIN £	MAX £	MIN £	MAX £		35
		62.00	84.00	–	–	OPEN 1-12	

The Sandringham Hotel

21 St Mary Street, Cardiff,
South Glamorgan CF1 2PL
Tel: (0222) 232161
Fax: (0222) 383998

Situated in the heart of the city shopping centre, the hotel has recently undergone extensive modernisation. The Grosvenor Room on the first floor accommodates weddings, conferences, private parties for up to 80 persons. Ground floor bar and restaurant open from eleven until eleven, seven days a week and offers a variety of fayre from light snacks to main meals. Renowned for the warmth of its hospitality.

HW	T	NIGHTLY B&B PER PERSON		WEEKLY D,B&B PER PERSON			28
C	SP	MIN £	MAX £	MIN £	MAX £		28
TW		27.50	30.00	212.00	222.00	OPEN 1-12	

Wynford Hotel

Clare Street, Cardiff, South
Glamorgan, CF1 8SD
Tel: (0222) 371983
Fax: (0222) 340477

Very close to the city centre, train and bus stations, the Wynford is a privately owned hotel, personally supervised by the proprietor and priding itself on a warm welcome, attentive service and excellent facilities. Comfortable lounge, two cosy bars, music and dancing, bistro and restaurant. All rooms have colour TV and telephone, and many are with bathroom. French, Spanish and German spoken. Video-linked security car park.

HW T SP	NIGHTLY B&B PER PERSON		WEEKLY D,B&B PER PERSON		🛏 28 🛏 18
	MIN £	MAX £	MIN £	MAX £	OPEN
	16.00	24.00	—	—	1-12

Guest Houses

Acorn Lodge

182 Cathedral Road, Cardiff,
South Glamorgan CF1 9JE L
Tel: (0222) 221373

A fine large Victorian house of character situated in a conservation area. Ideally located central to all attractions and within a few minutes walk of city centre. All rooms to high standard and have tea and coffee, colour television and thermostat variable control central heating. Full choice of breakfast. Car park. On main bus route. Diners, restaurants nearby. Warm welcome, friendly personal service.

🍴	NIGHTLY B&B PER PERSON		WEEKLY D,B&B PER PERSON		🛏 9 🛏 0
	MIN £	MAX £	MIN £	MAX £	OPEN
	13.00	15.00	—	—	1-12

Chapel Guest House

Church Road,
St. Brides, Wentloog, Newport, L
Gwent NP1 9SN
Tel: (0633) 681018

Comfortable accommodation in a converted chapel near the centre of a charming country village between Newport and Cardiff. Pleasant walks and sea fishing, country pub and restaurant adjacent. Family, double and twin rooms, most en-suite, guest lounge. Children welcome. Special rates. Leave M4 junction 28 follow B4239 (3 miles) coastal road towards Cardiff. Ample parking. 20 minutes drive to Wye Valley. 10 minutes to Cardiff, 5 minutes from Tredegar House and Park.

HW T 🐕 SP 🍴	NIGHTLY B&B PER PERSON		WEEKLY D,B&B PER PERSON		🛏 5 🛏 1
	MIN £	MAX £	MIN £	MAX £	OPEN
	13.00	15.00	120.00	134.00	1-12

Lower House Farm

Rhoose Road, Rhoose,
South Glamorgan CF6 9ER L
Tel: ((0446) 710010

This Georgian farmhouse with thatched cottage attached offers tastefully furnished single, double, family rooms. Special rates for children. Lounge with colour television, full central heating. Ideally situated for the Vale of Glamorgan and its Heritage Coast, the South Wales Valleys, the Welsh Folk Museum and Cardiff Wales Airport. A non smoking establishment.

HW T SP 🍴	NIGHTLY B&B PER PERSON		WEEKLY D,B&B PER PERSON		🛏 3 🛏 0
	MIN £	MAX £	MIN £	MAX £	OPEN
	14.00	18.00	—	—	1-12

Sant-y-Nyll

St. Brides-Super-Ely, Cardiff,
South Glamorgan CF5 6EZ
Tel: (0446) 760209

Beautiful Georgian country house in glorious situation overlooking Vale of Glamorgan. Close to Cardiff and M4 but still in quiet countryside. Welsh Folk Museum and many historical places of interest close by. For sportsmen there is tennis, golf and riding available in the area. The Heritage Coast is within 15 minutes drive.

T 🐕	NIGHTLY B&B PER PERSON		WEEKLY D,B&B PER PERSON		🛏 6 🛏 1
	MIN £	MAX £	MIN £	MAX £	OPEN
	15.00	20.00	157.50	175.00	1-12

Farmhouses

Cliff House Farm

Llancarfen, Cardiff, South
Glamorgan CF6 9AD
Tel: (0446) 710223

A 16th century farmhouse set in peaceful countryside, offering magnificent views. If it's quiet, tranquil, quality accommodation you prefer then Cliff House will not disappoint you. Complete with priest hole, converted old bake-house now a lounge, this Victorian/Georgian farmhouse with beautifully appointed bedrooms is ideal for people attending to business in Cardiff or surrounding area. Close to airport. Safe parking. Pleasant walks.

T SP 🍴	NIGHTLY B&B PER PERSON		WEEKLY D,B&B PER PERSON		🛏 3 🛏 2
	MIN £	MAX £	MIN £	MAX £	OPEN
	16.00	22.00	—	—	1-12

WALES *It's magic*

COWBRIDGE
Map Ref Le6

Picturesque town with wide main road and pretty houses — the centre of the Vale of Glamorgan farming community. Fine old inns, shops selling high-class clothes and country wares. 14th century town walls. Good touring centre for South Wales. Visit nearby Beaupre Castle.

CITY HALL, CARDIFF

Farmhouses

Treguff Farm

Llantrithyd, Nr Cowbridge,
South Glamorgan CF7 7LT
Tel: (0446) 750210

L COMMENDED

Relax in the homely atmosphere of this Elizabethan house steeped with historical interest, tastefully furnished spacious accommodation, warm hospitality, excellent food. Featured in the "Style Magazine". Treguff is well worth a visit in the heart of the Vale rich with castles, beaches, country and coastal walks, picturesque villages, near Welsh Folk Museum, Cardiff, St. Donats Castle.

HW T ⚪✕	NIGHTLY B&B PER PERSON		WEEKLY D,B&B PER PERSON		🛏 4
	MIN £	MAX £	MIN £	MAX £	🛏 0
	14.00	16.00	168.00	182.00	OPEN 1-12

108

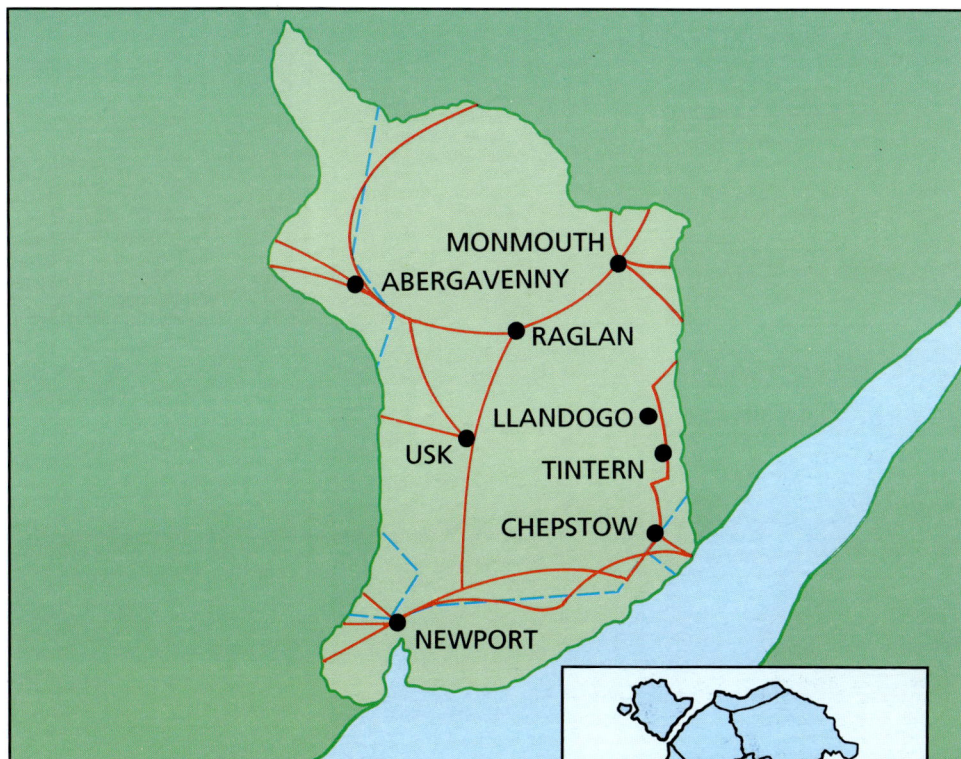

This is a tale of two rivers - the meandering Usk and the languid Wye. The stretch of the Wye between Monmouth and Chepstow – an 'Area of Outstanding Natural Beauty' – provides the leafy setting for the mellow ruins of Tintern Abbey praised by the poet William Wordsworth. Both rivers are famous for their fishing as well as their beauty. The Usk, which follows a pastoral course southwards from Abergavenny to Newport, flows past Caerleon where the Romans established a major base. Their amphitheatre, amazingly well-preserved after all these years, stands close to remains of a barracks and a recently excavated bath-house complex.

This green, history-laden border country has Britain's first stone-built castle at Chepstow. Raglan is the home of one of the later breeds of castle, when fortresses were evolving into more comfortable homes. At Newport, there's home comfort on a grand, gilded scale at opulent Tredegar House, a 17th-century mansion set in a splendid country park.

ABERGAVENNY
Map Ref Mc2

Flourishing market town with backdrop of mountains at south-western gateway to Brecon Beacons National Park. Pony trekking in nearby Black Mountains. Castle with museum. Leisure Centre. Monmouthshire and Brecon Canal runs just to the west of the town. Excellent touring base for lovely Vale of Usk and Brecon Beacons. 🚆

Guest Houses

Belchamps Guest House

1 Holywell Road,
Abergavenny, Gwent NP7 6LP
Tel: (0873) 3204

World wide recommendations for comfort, good food, personal attention. Rooms tastefully furnished, vanity unit, colour TV, tea/coffee making facilities, power points. Bathroom and toilet, separate shower room and toilet. Guests lounge and separate dining room. Access at all times. Full central heating. Guestaccomm Good Room Award. AA Approved. Fire certificate. Adjacent to coach station and town centre. For brochure and tariff ring Ann Rogers.

HW		NIGHTLY B&B PER PERSON		WEEKLY D,B&B PER PERSON		🛏 5
		MIN £	MAX £	MIN £	MAX £	🛏 0
		14.00	16.00	132.00	146.00	OPEN 1-12

Park Guest House

36 Hereford Road,
Abergavenny, Gwent NP7 5RA   MERIT

A warm friendly welcome, personal attention and home cooking of the highest quality are assured in this family run attractive detached Georgian guest house. Close town centre. Tastefully furnished throughout. All bedrooms have tea/coffee making facilities, basins and razor points. Two bathrooms, TV lounge and dining room. Evening meals available. Full licence, fire certificate and ample private parking. Access at all times. Brochure on request.

C	NIGHTLY B&B PER PERSON		WEEKLY D,B&B PER PERSON		🛏 6
	MIN £	MAX £	MIN £	MAX £	🛏 0
	14.00	15.00	150.00	160.00	OPEN 1-12

CHEPSTOW   Map Ref Me4

Attractive hilly town with substantial remains of a great stone castle — reputedly the first to be built in Britain — above the Wye. Fortified gate still stands in main street and medieval walls remain. Good shopping. Museum, Stuart Crystal Engraving Workshop. Sunday market, fine racecourse, excellent walks — beginning of Wye Valley walk and Offa's Dyke Path. Ideal for touring beautiful Wye Valley. 🚆

Guest Houses

Castle View Hotel

16 Bridge Street, Chepstow,
Gwent NP6 5EZ
Tel: (02912) 70349
Fax: (0291) 627397   COMMENDED

Enjoy comfort, good food and personal attention in surroundings retaining 18th century charm. Small luxury hotel with attractive garden. All bedrooms have bathroom, colour TV, movies, telephone, tea tray, hairdryer, mini bar. Award winning restaurant with Ronay/Routiers commended food, making imaginative use of fresh local produce. Full vegetarian menu also available. Real ales. Good large family rooms including Cottage Suite.

HW	T	NIGHTLY B&B PER PERSON		WEEKLY D,B&B PER PERSON		🛏 11
	SP	MIN £	MAX £	MIN £	MAX £	🛏 11
		28.75	30.25	239.00	275.00	OPEN 1-12

WALKING IN THE WYE VALLEY NEAR TINTERN

WALES
It's magic

Guest House

Lower Viney Country Guest House

Viney Hill, Blakeney,
Gloucestershire GL15 4LT
Tel: (0594) 516000

Spacious period house just west of
Gloucester in the Royal Forest of Dean.
All guest rooms have en-suite facilities and
are comfortably furnished. All rooms have
shaver points and tea/coffee making
facilities with full central heating. Evening
meals are available. AA Listed, RAC Highly
Commended and ETB 3 Crowns.

HW T SP 🐕 ✕	NIGHTLY B&B PER PERSON		WEEKLY D,B&B PER PERSON		🛏 6 🛋 6 OPEN 1-12
	MIN £	MAX £	MIN £	MAX £	
	16.00	18.00			

SOUTH WALES VALLEYS (VHS/BETA)

A 15-minute look at a distinctive part
of Wales where a rich industrial
heritage co-exists with a surprising
natural beauty and range of
attractions.

LLANDOGO Map Ref Me2

Ideally located village in the
lovely Wye Valley, halfway
between Monmouth and
Chepstow. Woodland walks,
Offa's Dyke Path, Wye Valley
Walk; ruins of tintern Abbey
nearby.

Hotels

The Sloop Inn

Llandogo, Nr. Monmouth,
Gwent NP5 4TW
Tel: (0594) 530291   MERIT

Half way between Monmouth and
Chepstow, in the heart of the lower Wye
Valley is the village of Llandogo with its
award winning inn. Spotlessly clean, en-
suite character bedrooms, unpretentious
food at realistic prices and a cheerful
atmosphere, make the Sloop Inn a popular
place to stay.

🐕	NIGHTLY B&B PER PERSON		WEEKLY D,B&B PER PERSON		🛏 4 🛋 4 OPEN 1-12
	MIN £	MAX £	MIN £	MAX £	
	19.00	25.00	–	–	

MONMOUTH
Map Ref Me1

Historic market town in
picturesque Wye Valley —
birthplace of Henry V and
Charles Rolls (of Rolls-Royce).
Interesting local history
museum with collection of
Nelson memorabilia. Rare
fortified gateway still spans
the River Monnow. Ruined
castle close to town centre.
Good touring base.

Hotels

The King's Head Hotel

Agincourt, Square Monmouth,
Gwent NP5 3DY
Tel: (0600) 2177
Telex: 497294
Fax: (0600) 3545

The historic King's Head Hotel, in the heart
of an Area of Outstanding Natural Beauty,
preserves its character as a 17th century
coaching inn yet has been elegantly
modernised throughout. All bedrooms en-
suite with colour TV, radio and telephone.

HW T SP 🐕 C ✕	NIGHTLY B&B PER PERSON		WEEKLY D,B&B PER PERSON		🛏 29 🛋 29 OPEN 1-12
	MIN £	MAX £	MIN £	MAX £	
	39.00	41.00	–	–	

MONNOW BRIDGE, MONMOUTH

Riversdale Lodge Hotel

Symonds Yat West,
Ross-on-Wye, Herefordshire
HR9 6BL
Tel: (0600) 890445

Excellent accommodation on the banks of the River Wye. A unique 2 acre setting. Spectacular views of the rapids set in a gorge. Ideal quiet get away place. Beautiful views from most rooms. All rooms en-suite, TV, coffee/tea facilities. Dinner optional. Log burning stoves. Snooker/pool, swimming pool, croquet lawn. Licensed.

HW T	NIGHTLY B&B PER PERSON		WEEKLY D,B&B PER PERSON		🛏 5
	MIN £	MAX £	MIN £	MAX £	🛏 5
	19.00	22.00	206.50	220.50	OPEN 1-12

Talocher Hotel

Wonastow Road, Monmouth,
Gwent NP5 4DN
Tel: (0600) 83482
Fax: (0600) 83450

Talocher has superb views across the Welsh Valleys. The Wye Valley, Tintern and the Forest of Dean are within a few mintues drive. The restaurant and bar serve only fresh food. A gym with sauna and solarium is available for guests. Talocher is the base for Outface Ventures who provide activity holidays and courses, abseiling, canoeing, ATB's, shooting, golf arranged for groups.

HW T	NIGHTLY B&B PER PERSON		WEEKLY D,B&B PER PERSON		🛏 11
C	MIN £	MAX £	MIN £	MAX £	🛏 4
	20.00	25.00	–	–	OPEN 1-12

Guest Houses

Church Farm Guest House

Mitchel Troy, Monmouth,
Gwent NP5 4HZ
Tel: (0600) 2176

A spacious and homely 16th century former farmhouse with oak beams and inglenook fireplaces. Set in large attractive garden with stream. Easy access to A40 and only 2 miles from historic Monmouth. Excellent base for Wye Valley, Forest of Dean and Black Mountains. Own car park. Colour TV, central heating, some en-suite bedrooms, tea/coffee making facilities. Tasty alternatives to English breakfast available.

	NIGHTLY B&B PER PERSON		WEEKLY D,B&B PER PERSON		🛏 6
	MIN £	MAX £	MIN £	MAX £	🛏 2
	13.50	16.00	144.00	168.00	OPEN 1-12

NEWPORT   Map Ref Mc4

Busy industrial, commercial and shopping centre. Interesting murals in main hall of Civic Centre. Newport Museum and Art Gallery in John Frost Square (named after Chartist leader) and Leisure Centre with wave machine. On the outskirts, magnificently restored Tredegar House with extensive country park and 14 Locks Canal Visitor Centre. St. Woolos Cathedral on hill overlooking centre. 🚉

Hotels

Caerleon House Hotel

61 Caerau Road, Newport,
Gwent NP9 4HJ
Tel: (0633) 264869

AA Listed licensed hotel with personal attention provided at all times by the resident owners (22 years). All bedrooms have tea/coffee making facilities, shower and colour TV, residents bar with meals available evenings ½ mile from town centre. Parking. Reductions for children. Close to golf courses and tourist areas and the 1992 Garden Festival.

	NIGHTLY B&B PER PERSON		WEEKLY D,B&B PER PERSON		🛏 8
	MIN £	MAX £	MIN £	MAX £	–
	15.00	16.00	–	–	OPEN 1-12

Country Court Hotel

Chepstow Road, Langstone,
Newport, Gwent NP6 2LX
Tel: (0633) 413737
Telex: 497147
Fax: (0633) 413713
Central Reservations: (0800) 262626

Located 30 minutes from Wye Valley and Forest of Dean. This new hotel is an ideal base for touring the Gower Peninsula, Vale of Glamorgan, not to mention Roman of Bath, Caerleon. Wales capital city, Cardiff is 20 minutes away. Superb indoor pool, steam, sauna, whirlpool, luxurious bedrooms. The perfect base for a family holiday.

HW T	NIGHTLY B&B PER PERSON		WEEKLY D,B&B PER PERSON		🛏 141
SP	MIN £	MAX £	MIN £	MAX £	🛏 141
	48.50	–	262.00	–	OPEN 1-12

The Parkway Hotel

Cwmbran Drive, Cwmbran,
Gwent NP44 3UW
Tel: (0633) 871199
Telex: 497887
Fax: (06333) 69160

A new privately owned luxury hotel set in 7½ acres and designed on a Mediterranean theme. The Parkway is situated between Cwmbran and Newport, located just off the M4 motorway Junction 26. Extensive Health and Leisure Complex including swimming pool, sauna, solarium, spa bath, gymnasium and Promenade Cafe bar. Ideal base for touring Wales.

T	NIGHTLY B&B PER PERSON		WEEKLY D,B&B PER PERSON		🛏 70
SP	MIN £	MAX £	MIN £	MAX £	🛏 70
	31.00	41.25	–	318.30	OPEN 1-12

WALES *It's magic*

The Westgate Hotel

Commercial Street, Newport,
Gwent NP1 1TT
Tel: (0633) 244444
Telex: 498173
Fax: (0633) 246616

Completely refurbished in 1990 this historic hotel offers four star accommodation at reasonable rates. All rooms have private en-suite facilities, colour television, hairdryer, trouser press and a welcoming refreshments tray. Rates include hearty Welsh breakfast and VAT. Excellent food and wine in Chartist's Restaurant, Courts Cafe Bar for all day snacks, Scrum Half pub for great beers and bar food. Situated 1 mile from J26 on M4. Rates from £35 per person.

HW T C SP	NIGHTLY B&B PER PERSON		WEEKLY D,B&B PER PERSON		🛏 69 🛋 69
	MIN £	MAX £	MIN £	MAX £	OPEN
	35.00	40.00	180.00	210.00	1-12

TINTERN ABBEY

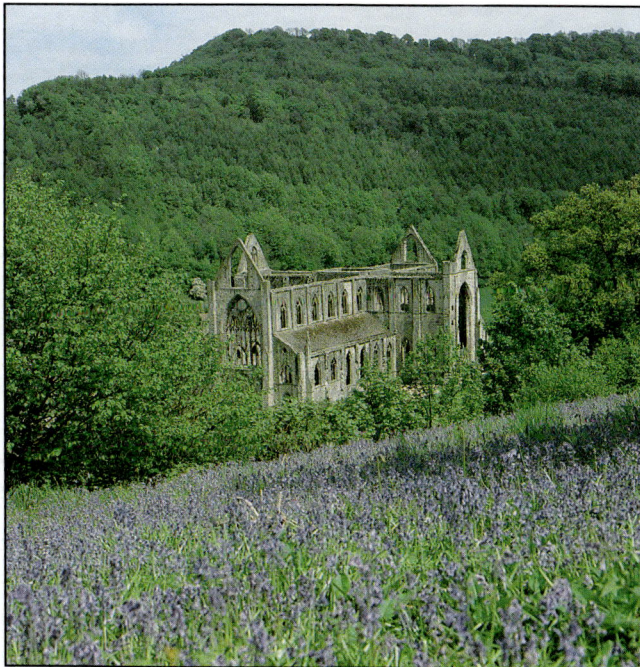

Guest Houses

Brick House Country Guest House

Redwick, Newport,
Gwent NP6 3DX
Tel: (0633) 880230   COMMENDED

Located at the edge of the peaceful village of Redwick yet only three miles from the M4. Furnished in tasteful traditional style. All double rooms have en-suite bathrooms. Local attractions such as Tintern Abbey and the Welsh Folk Museum are within easy reach and our guests can order a fresh home cooked meal.

HW T 🐾	NIGHTLY B&B PER PERSON		WEEKLY D,B&B PER PERSON		🛏 7 🛋 5
	MIN £	MAX £	MIN £	MAX £	OPEN
	19.00	22.00	196.00	206.00	1-12

TINTERN   Map Ref Me2

Riverside village in particularly lovely stretch of Wye Valley. Impressive ruins of Tintern Abbey not to be missed. The former railway station has a visitor's interpretative centre and a picnic site with refreshments. Excellent walks and good fishing.

Hotels

The Royal George Hotel

Tintern, Chepstow,
Gwent NP6 6SF
Tel: (0291) 689205
Fax: (0291) 689448

17 bedrooms all with private facilities, 14 of family size overlooking prize winning gardens and stream. Beautiful, quiet location close to Abbey. Excellent cuisine and service using fresh local produce. Wye salmon a speciality. Dining/function room seating 125 with conference facilities. Two bars. Personal attention of owners. Chef Tony Chippendale.

HW 🐾 C SP TW	NIGHTLY B&B PER PERSON		WEEKLY D,B&B PER PERSON		🛏 18 🛋 15
	MIN £	MAX £	MIN £	MAX £	OPEN
		58.85			1-12

THE VALLEYS REVISITED

Our full colour brochure on the South Wales Valleys features tours of industrial heritage sites, leisure activities, an events list, a comprehensive guide to the Valleys rail network and a detailed map of the area. An accommodation supplement featuring a range of both serviced and self catering accommodation can be included on request.

Guest Houses

The Old Rectory

Tintern, Chepstow,
Gwent NP6 6SG
Tel: (0291) 689519

A warm welcome awaits visitors to this 18th/19th century house exactly on the England/Wales border with beautiful views. Ideal for exploring Forest of Dean, Brecon Beacons Nearby is Chepstow racecourse, golf, riding, fishing. Central heating, log fires. Sample our spring water and enjoy home comforts and cooking in a relaxed and friendly atmosphere.

	NIGHTLY B&B PER PERSON		WEEKLY D,B&B PER PERSON			
	MIN £	MAX £	MIN £	MAX £		5
	11.50	11.50	121.00	121.00	OPEN 1-12	–

SOUTH WALES VALLEYS (VHS/BETA)

A 15-minute look at a distinctive part of Wales where a rich industrial heritage co-exists with a surprising natural beauty and range of attractions.

Valley House

Raglan Road, Tintern,
Nr. Chepstow, Gwent NP6 6TH
Tel: (0291) 689652

A fine Georgian residence situated opposite picturesque woods in the tranquil Angidy Valley, within a mile of Tintern Abbey. Charming, comfortable en-suite rooms all with colour TV and tea/coffee facilities. Hearty breakfasts and home cooked meals are served in our unique dining room with its arched stone ceiling. Relax by log fires in the lounge or in our pleasant gardens. An ideal location for sightseeing, forest walks straight from our doorstep.

HW T	NIGHTLY B&B PER PERSON		WEEKLY D,B&B PER PERSON			4
SP	MIN £	MAX £	MIN £	MAX £		4
	15.00	16.00	168.00	174.00	OPEN 1-12	

LLANDEGFEDD RESERVOIR

USK
Map Ref Md3

Ancient borough on River Usk; excellent salmon fishing and inns. Good walks. Rural Life Museum, grass skiing. Great castle of Raglan 5 miles north: Sailing and other watersports on nearby Llandegfedd reservoir. Good central location for sight-seeing.

Hotels

Glen-yr-Afon Hotel

Pontypool Road, Usk,
Gwent NP5 1SY
Tel: (02913) 2302 & 3202

An elegant country house, providing gracious service and fine home cooked food in a warm friendly atmosphere. Situated in mature, secluded grounds, five minutes walk from the historic village of Usk. It has tastefully decorated bedrooms (all but one with private bathroom), two comfortable lounges (one with colour television, the other containing a fully stocked bar). Under the personal supervision of the proprietor.

SP	NIGHTLY B&B PER PERSON		WEEKLY D,B&B PER PERSON			16
	MIN £	MAX £	MIN £	MAX £		15
	24.15	26.85	154.50	154.50	OPEN 1-12	

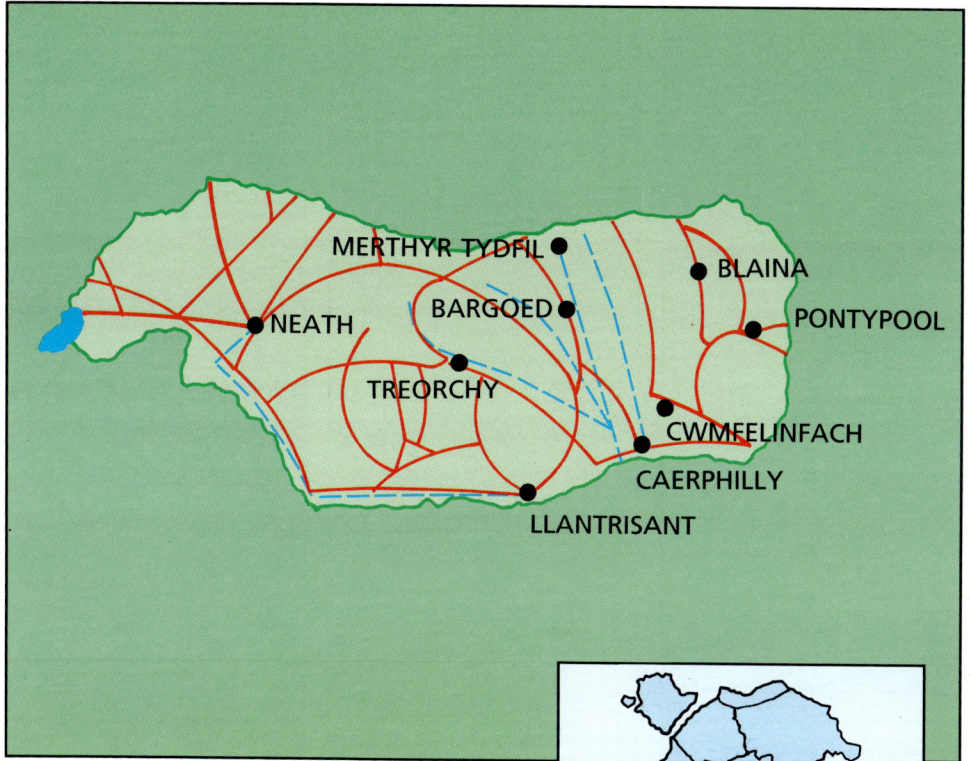

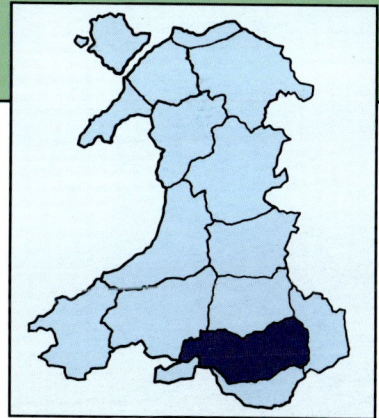

First-time visitors to this part of Wales are invariably surprised – first by the unexpected natural beauty of the Valleys, and also by their wealth of attractions. This is an area of country parks, forest walks and panoramic hilltop views across untouched moorland. Ebbw Vale is already preparing for the 1992 Garden Festival, which will be held on a site embracing valley, mountain and lake.

The Valleys' many and varied attractions include a dry ski slope at Pontypool and narrow-gauge railway at Merthyr Tydfil, a wildlife park near Neath, and – at Caerphilly – one of Europe's greatest castles. The Valleys' fascinating industrial past as a coal and iron producing area is not forgotten. Visitors are taken on conducted underground tours at the Big Pit Mining Museum, Blaenafon. And there are more memories of 'King Coal' at the Welsh Miners' Museum, near Cymmer, and the exciting new Rhondda Heritage Park.

BARGOED — Map Ref Ma3

Town set amidst hillsides in Rhymney Valley between Newport and Merthyr Tydfil with hilltop views over to the Brecon Beacons. Bryn Bach Country Park a few miles to the north. ⇌

Hotels

Parc Hotel

Cardiff Road, Bargoed,
Mid Glamorgan CF8 8SP
Tel: (0443) 837599/839828
Fax: (0443) 834818

Roley and Pauline Butler would like to welcome you to their privately owned and run hotel and restaurant. Comfortable home from home atmosphere, 12 luxury bedrooms with tea/coffee makingfacilities, colour TV and direct dial telephone, 6 en-suite. Extensive 'a la carte lounge bar and lunch time menus offering exquisite first class cusine. Ideal base for exploring the valleys of South Wales and the Beacons and National Park.

HW T 🐕 SP	NIGHTLY B&B PER PERSON		WEEKLY D,B&B PER PERSON		🛏 12 🛁 6	
	MIN £	MAX £	MIN £	MAX £	OPEN 1-12	
	25.00	25.00	225.00	225.00		

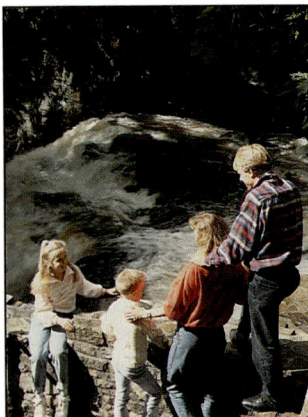

ABERDULAIS FALLS

CALL
Holidays WALES
(0792) 645555

116

BLAINA — Map Ref Mb2

Village in eastern part of the South Wales Valleys. Only a few miles from the southern boundary of Brecon Beacons National Park. Big Pit Mining Museum and historic Clydach Gorge nearby.

Guest Houses

Chapel Farm

Nr Coal Brookevale, Blaina,
Gwent NP3 3DJ
Tel: (0495) 290888

MERIT

15th century renovated farmhouse, farming Welsh mountain sheep. Oak beamed lounge and family bedroom. H&C, showers, evening meal, packed lunches, home cooking. Near miniature railway. Good base for Big Pit Mining Museum, Brecon Beacons, Abergavenny, Bryn Bach Park all in nine miles. Lovely walks and views, riding 4 miles. Children welcome. Drinks licence for table. Reduced rates children sharing. Warm welcome assured to all our guests. Television in lounge.

HW ✂	NIGHTLY B&B PER PERSON		WEEKLY D,B&B PER PERSON		🛏 3 🛁 –	
	MIN £	MAX £	MIN £	MAX £	OPEN 1-12	
	13.00		138.00	145.00		

CAERPHILLY — Map Ref Ma4

A sight not to be missed — 13th century Caerphilly Castle is one of Europe's finest surviving medieval strongholds and has a famous leaning tower. Golf courses, shopping, excellent centre for exploring Valleys and visiting Cardiff. Caerphilly Mountain offers fine views and pleasant walks. Caerphilly cheese made at the Old Courthouse. ⇌

Guest Houses

The Cottage Guest House

Pwllypant, Caerphilly,
Mid Glamorgan CF8 3HW
Tel: (0222) 869160

The owners of this 300 year old cottage offer a warm homely welcome. All bedrooms centrally heated and hot and cold water, tea/coffee making facilities. Television lounge and car park. Owner a registered Wales and England Guide and provides free touring advice. Good convenient restaurants in town. Perfect centre for castles, coast, mountains.

T	NIGHTLY B&B PER PERSON		WEEKLY D,B&B PER PERSON		🛏 3 🛁 –	
	MIN £	MAX £	MIN £	MAX £	OPEN 1-12	
	14.00	15.00				

CWMFELINFACH — Map Ref Mb4

In South Wales Valleys north of Cardiff. Forested slopes around and about — Cwmcarn Forest Drive is nearby; also the Sirhowy Valley Country Park and the Ynys Hywel Visitor Centre.

Hotels

Ynys Hywel Countryside Centre

Cwmfelinfach, Cross Keys,
Gwent NP1 7JX
Tel: (0495) 200113

In the 1000 acre Sirhowy Valley Country Park. Lounge bar and restaurant. All rooms with television and welcome tray. Ideal for country walks. Trim Trail. Programme of special events, themed meals. Landrover rides on request. Also training and conference facilities. Car parking readily available. Member of A Taste Of Wales.

SP ✂ TW	NIGHTLY B&B PER PERSON		WEEKLY D,B&B PER PERSON		🛏 9 🛁 5	
	MIN £	MAX £	MIN £	MAX £	OPEN 1-12	
	26.00		252.00			

WALES
It's magic

MERTHYR TYDFIL
Map Ref Le2

Once the "iron capital of the world"; the museum in Cyfartha Castle, built by the Crawshay family of ironmasters and set in pleasant parkland, tells of those times. Visit the birthplace of hymn-writer Joseph Parry and the Ynysfach Engine House. The narrow-gauge Brecon Mountain Railway makes the most of the town's location on the doorstep of the Brecon Beacons National Park. Garwnant Forest Visitor Centre and scenic lakes in hills to the north. ≈

Hotels

Tregenna Hotel

Park Terrace, Merthyr Tydfil, 👑👑
Mid Glamorgan CF47 8RF 👑👑
Tel: (0685) 723627/82055   COMMENDED
Fax: (0685) 721951

Family run hotel 21 bedrooms all with en-suite facilities, tea, coffee trays, colour TV, telephone. 2 luxurious apartments, suites and 3 detached family houses 5 minutes from hotel. Apartments double bedroom, bathroom, kitchen and TV lounge. Houses 3-4 bedrooms, 2 bathrooms, fitted kitchen, TV lounge, dining room. Special tariff from £16 per person including bed and breakfast at hotel. 5 minutes Brecon Beacons National Park, 2½ hours London Heathrow. All our guests return.

HW · T · B · TW	NIGHTLY B&B PER PERSON		WEEKLY D,B&B PER PERSON		🛏 31 🛏 27
	MIN £	MAX £	MIN £	MAX £	OPEN 1-12
	22.50	-	-	-	

Guest Houses

Llwyn On Guest House

Cwmtâf, Merthyr Tydfil, 👑
Mid Glamorgan CF48 2HS 👑
Tel: (0685) 4384

Situated in the Brecon Beacons National Park 5 miles from Merthyr Tydfil and only 8 miles from the foothills of Pen-y-Fan. Also central for valleys and coastal areas. Overlooking Llwyn On Reservoir, some bedrooms are en-suite. All have colour TV and tea/coffee facilities. Separate guests lounge and dining room. Fire certificate. Walking, fishing, pony trekking, golf nearby. Parking. AA Listed.

C	NIGHTLY B&B PER PERSON		WEEKLY D,B&B PER PERSON		🛏 4 🛏 2
	MIN £	MAX £	MIN £	MAX £	OPEN 1-12
	17.50	20.00	-	-	

NEATH
Map Ref Lb3

Busy town, now emerging from its industrial past. Museum and country park. The Vale of Neath has a wide variety of tourist attractions including and abbey, Penscynor Wildlife Park and Aberdulais Falls and Canal Basin. Superbly located for a choice of activities, surrounded by forests. ≈

CAERPHILLY CASTLE

Hotels

Castle Hotel

The Parade, Neath, 👑👑
West Glamorgan SA11 1RB 👑👑
Tel: (0639) 643581   MERIT
Telex: 48119
Fax: (0639) 641624
Central Reservations: (0582) 400158

Original 17th century coaching inn recently refurbished to four Crown standard. Situated in Neath town centre, the Welsh Rugby Union was formed here. The hotel is ideally situated for Neath Valley, the Gower, Swansea and the Brecon mountains. Excellent restaurant and bars with bar snacks always available. Ideal location for visiting this lovely area.

HW · T · C · SP · B	NIGHTLY B&B PER PERSON		WEEKLY D,B&B PER PERSON		🛏 28 🛏 28
	MIN £	MAX £	MIN £	MAX £	OPEN 1-12
	20.00	32.00	220.00	250.00	

Farmhouses

Gelli Farm

Crynant, Neath, 👑
West Glamorgan SA10 8PP 👑
Tel: (0639) 750209

Gelli Farm, 580 acres of lovely countryside. A la carte restaurant available, home and local produce used. Ideal base for all local attractions.

HW · T	NIGHTLY B&B PER PERSON		WEEKLY D,B&B PER PERSON		🛏 3 🛏 1
	MIN £	MAX £	MIN £	MAX £	OPEN 1-12
	17.00	17.00	-	-	

We're here to help

When you arrive in Wales, call in at a Tourist Information Centre. Staff will be only too pleased to assist with enquiries and offer advice on where to go and what to see both locally and further afield, suggest scenic routes and so on. "What's On" events information will also be available, together with a wide range of tourist literature including all Wales Tourist Board publications.

A network of centres covers all major resorts, towns and key points in Wales.

i TOURIST INFORMATION CENTRES

NORTH WALES
Open All Year

Beddgelert, Gwynedd LL55 4YA
The National Trust Information Point,
Llewellyn Cottage
Tel: (076686) 293

Caernarfon, Gwynedd LL55 2PB
Tourist Information Centre, Oriel Pendeitsh
Tel: (0286) 672232 BB BABA

Colwyn Bay, Clwyd LL29 8BU
Tourist Information Centre/Colwyn Borough Council, Station Road
Tel: (0492) 530478 BB BABA

Holyhead, Gwynedd LL65 1DR
Tourist Information Centre,
Marine Square, Salt Island Approach
Tel: (0407) 762622 BB BABA

Llandudno, Gwynedd LL30 2YU
Tourist Information Centre, Chapel Street
Tel: (0492) 76413 BB BABA

Llanfair P.G., Gwynedd LL61 5UJ
Tourist Information Centre, Station Site
Tel: (0248) 713177 BB BABA

Llangollen, Clwyd LL20 5PD
Tourist Information Centre, Town Hall
Tel: (0978) 860828 BB BABA

Porthmadog, Gwynedd LL49 9LP
Tourist Information Centre, High Street
Tel: (0766) 512981 BB BABA

Rhyl, Clwyd LL18 5NL
Tourist Information Centre, Central Promenade
Tel: (0745) 355068 BB BABA

Ruthin, Clwyd LL15 1BB
Tourist Information Centre, Craft Centre
Tel: (08242) 3992 BB BABA

Open Summer Only

Abersoch, Gwynedd
Village Hall
Tel: (075881) 2929

Bangor, Gwynedd LL57 2TL
Tourist Information Centre,
Theatr Gwynedd, Deiniol Road
Tel: (0248) 352786 BB BABA

Betws-y-Coed, Gwynedd LL24 0AH
Tourist Information Centre/Snowdonia National Park, Royal Oak Stables
Tel: (06902) 426/665 BB BABA

Colwyn Bay, Clwyd
Tourist Information Centre/Colwyn Borough Council, The Promenade, Rhos on Sea
Tel: (0492) 48778 BB

Conwy, Gwynedd
Tourist Information Centre,
Conwy Castle Visitor Centre
Tel: (0492) 592248 BB BABA

Criccieth, Gwynedd LL52 0EY
Criccieth Trade & Tourism Association,
The Sweet Shop, 47 High Street
Tel: (0766) 523303

Halkyn, Clwyd CH8 8DF
Tourist Information Centre,
Little Chef Services A55
Tel: (0352) 780144 BB BABA

Llanberis, Gwynedd LL55 4UB
Tourist Information Centre,
Amgheddfa'r Gogledd/Museum of the North
Tel: (0286) 870765 BB BABA

Mold, Clwyd CH7 1AB
Tourist Information Centre,
Mold Town Council, Town Hall
Tel: (0352) 59331 BB BABA

Prestatyn, Clwyd LL19 9LH
Tourist Information Centre,
Scala Cinema
Tel: (07456) 85 4365 BB BABA

Pwllheli, Gwynedd LL53 6HE
Tourist Information Centre, Y Maes
Tel: (075861) 3000 BB BABA

Wrexham, Clwyd LL12 7AG
Tourist Information Centre,
Memorial Hall
Tel: (0978) 357845

Tourist Information on North Wales also available at

Chester, Cheshire
Chester Visitor Centre, Vicars Lane
Tel: (0244) 318916 BB BABA

Oswestry, Salop
Mile End Services
Tel: (0691) 662488 BB BABA

Sandbach, Cheshire
Tourist Information Centre,
Sandbach Service Area, M6 Northbound
Tel: (0270) 760460 BB BABA

MID WALES
Open All Year

Aberystwyth, Dyfed SY23 2AR
Information Centre, Ceredigion District Council
Terrace Road
Tel: (0970) 612125/611955 BB BABA

Knighton, Powys LD7 1EW
Information Centre, Offa's Dyke Association
The Old School
Tel: (0547) 528753 BABA

Llandrindod Wells, Powys LD1 6AA
Information Centre, Radnor District Council
The Old Town Hall
Tel: (0597) 822600 BB BABA

Machynlleth, Powys SY20 8EE
Tourist Information Centre,
Canolfan Owain Glyndwr
Maengwyn Street
Tel: (0654) 702401 BB BABA

Welshpool, Powys SY21 7DD
Tourist Information Centre,
Vicarage Gardens Car Park
Tel: (0938) 552043 BB BABA

Open Summer Only

Aberaeron, Dyfed SA46 0BT
Information Centre, Ceredigion District Council
The Harbour
Tel: (0545) 570602 BB BABA

Aberdovey, Gwynedd LL35 0EO
Information Centre, Snowdonia National Park
The Wharf
Tel: (0654) 72321 BB BABA

Bala, Gwynedd LL23 7AB
Information Centre, Snowdonia National Park
High Street
Tel: (0678) 520367 BB BABA

Barmouth, Gwynedd LL42 1LU
Tourist Information Centre,
The Old Library
Tel: (00341) 280787 BB BABA

Blaenau Ffestiniog, Gwynedd LL41 3HD
Information Centre, Snowdonia National Park
High Street
Tel: (0766) 830360 BABA

Builth Wells, Powys LD2 3BL
Tourist Information Centre,
Groe Car Park
Tel: (0982) 553307 BB BABA

Cardigan, Dyfed SA43 1JY
Information Centre, Ceredigion District
Council, Theatre Mwldan, Bath House Road
Tel: (0239) 613230

Corris, Gwynedd SY20 9RF
Tourist Information Centre,
Corris Craft Centre
Tel: (0654) 761244 BB BABA

Dolgellau, Gwynedd LL40 1LF
Information Centre, Snowdonia National Park
The Bridge
Tel: (0341) 422888 BB BABA

Elan Valley, Powys LD6 2YA
Elan Valley Visitor Centre
Tel: (0597) 810898 BB BABA

Harlech, Gwynedd LL46 2YA
Information Centre, Snowdonia National Park
High Street
Tel: (0766) 780658 BB BABA

Llanfyllin, Powys SY22 5DB
Tourist Information Centre,
Council Offices
Tel: (069184) 8868 BB BABA

Llanidloes, Powys SY18 6ES
Tourist Information Centre, Longbridge Street
Tel: (05512) 2605 BB BABA

Newtown, Powys SY16 2PW
Tourist Information Centre,
Central Car Park
Tel: (0686) 625580

New Quay, Dyfed SA45 9NZ
Information Centre, Ceredigion District Council
Church Street
Tel: (0545) 560865 BB BABA

Presteigne, Powys
Tourist Information Centre,
Market Hall
Tel: (0544) 260193 BB BABA

Rhayader, Powys LD6 5AB
Tourist Information Centre,
The Old Swan
Tel: (0597) 810591 BB BABA

Tywyn, Gwynedd LL36 9AD
Tourist Information Centre, High Street
Tel: (0654) 710070 BB BABA

SOUTH WALES
Open All Year

Cardiff, South Glamorgan CF1 2EE
Tourist Information Centre,
8-14 Bridge Street
Tel: (0222) 227281 BB BABA

Merthyr Tydfil, Mid Glamorgan CF47 8AU
Tourist Information Centre,
14a Glebeland Street
Tel: (0685) 79884 BB BABA

Newport, Gwent NP9 1HZ
Tourist Information Centre, Newport Museum
& Gallery, John Frost Square
Tel: (0633) 842962 BB BABA

Pont Abraham, Dyfed SA4 1FP
Tourist Information Centre, Pont Abraham
Services, Junction 49, M4,
Llanedi, Pontardulais
Tel: (0792) 883838 BB BABA

Pontypridd, Mid Glamorgan CF37 3PE
Pontypridd Historical & Cultural Centre,
The Old Bridge
Tel: (0443) 402077 BB

Sarn, Mid Glamorgan CF32 9SY
Tourist Information Centre, Sarn Park Services,
Junction 36, M4 Nr. Bridgend
Tel: (0656) 654906 BB BABA

Swansea, West Glamorgan SA1 3QN
Tourist Information Centre, Singleton Street
Tel: (0792) 468321 BB

Open Summer Only

Abercraf, Powys
Tourist Information Centre,
Dan yr Ogof Showcaves,
Upper Swansea Valley
Tel: (0639) 730284

Aberdulais, West Glamorgan SA10 8ED
Tourist Information Centre,
Aberdulais Basin, Nr. Neath
Tel: (0639) 633531 BB BABA

Abergavenny, Gwent NP7 5HH
Tourist Information Centre,
Swan Meadow, Cross Street
Tel: (0873) 77588 BB BABA

Bagle Brook, West Glamorgan SA12 8DS
Tourist Information Centre,
Beefeater Restaurant, Sunnycroft Road, Baglan
Tel: (0639) 823049 BB BABA
(written and telephone enquiries on the
whole of South Wales)

Barry, South Glamorgan CF6 8TT
Tourist Information Centre,
The Promenade, Barry Island
Tel: (0446) 747171 BB BABA

Brecon, Powys LD3 9DA
Tourist Information Centre,
Cattle Market Car Park
Tel: (0874) 2485 BB BABA

Brecon, Powys LD3 7DF
Brecon Beacons National Park Centre,
Watton Mount
Tel: (0874) 4437

Broad Haven, Dyfed SA62 3JH
Pembrokeshire Coast National Park Centre,
Car Park
Tel: (043783) 412

Caerphilly, Mid Glamorgan CF8 1AA
Tourist Information Centre,
Old Police Station, Park Lane
Tel: (0222) 851378 BB BABA

Cardiff West, Mid Glamorgan CF7 8SB
Information Centre, Rank Motor Lodge,
Junction 33, M4, Pontyclun
Tel: (0222) 891878 BB BABA

Carmarthen, Dyfed SA31 3AQ
Tourist Information Centre,
Lammas Street
Tel: (0267) 231557 BB BABA

Chepstow, Gwent NP6 5LH
Tourist Information Centre,
The Gatehouse, High Street
Tel: (02912) 3772 BB BABA

Cwmcarn, Gwent NP1 5AL
Visitor Centre, Cwmcarn Forest Drive,
Nr. Cross Keys
Tel: (0495) 272001 BB BABA

Fishguard, Dyfded SA65 9HL
Tourist Information Centre,
4 Hamilton Street
Tel: (0348) 873484 BB BABA

Haverfordwest, Dyfed SA62 6SD
Tourist Information Centre,
40 High Street
Tel: (0437)763110 BB BABA

Hay on Wye, Powys HR3 5AE
Tourist Information Centre, The Craft Centre,
Oxford Road
Tel: (0497) 820144

Kilgetty, Dyfed Sa68 0YA
Information Centre,
Pembrokeshire Coast National Park
Kingsmoor Common
Tel: (0834) 813672 BB BABA

Llandovery, Dyfed SA20 0AR
Tourist Information Centre, Broad Street
Tel: (0550) 20695 BB BABA

Monmouth, Gwent NP5 3DY
Tourist Information Centre, Shire Hall
Tel: (0600) 3899 BB BABA

Newcastle Emlyn, Dyfed SA83 9AE
Tourist Information Centre, Market Hall
Tel: (0239) 711333 BB BABA

Newport, Dyfed SA42 0SY
Pembrokeshire Coast National Park Centre,
East Street
Tel: (0239) 820912

Pembroke, Dyfed
Pembrokeshire Coast National Park Centre,
Drill Hall
Tel: (0646) 682148

Pen y Cae, West Glamorgan SA9 1GL
Craig y Nos Country Park, Swansea Valley
Tel: (0639) 730395

Pont Nedd Fechan, West Glamorgan
SA11 5NR
Tourist Information Centre,
Nr. Glynneath
Tel: (0639) 721795 BB BABA

Porthcawl, Mid Glamorgan CF36 3DT
Tourist Information Centre,
The Old Police Station, John Street
Tel: (065671) 6639 BB BABA

St. David's, Dyfed SA62 6SB
Pembrokeshire Coast National Park Centre,
City Hall
Tel: (0437) 720392

Saundersfoot, Dyfed SA69 9HE
Tourist Information Centre, The Harbour
Tel: (0834) 811411

Swansea, West Glamorgan SA3 4DQ
Tourist Information Centre,
Oystermouth Square, Mumbles
Tel: (0792) 361302 BB

Tenby, Dyfed SA70 8AP
Tourist Information Centre, The Croft
Tel: (0834) 2402

Tintern, Gwent NP6 6TE
Tourist Information Centre,
Abbey Entrance, Tintern Abbey
Tel: (0291) 689431 BB BABA

Tredegar, Gwent
Tourist Information Centre,
Bryn Bach Country Park
Tel: (0495) 711816 BB BABA

BB
Bed Booking Service

BABA
Book-A-Bed-Ahead Service

BRITISH TOURIST AUTHORITY OVERSEAS OFFICES

Your enquiries will be welcome at the offices of the British Tourist Authority in the following countries:

Australia

British Tourist Authority, 4th Floor,
171 Clarence Street, Sydney, NSW 2000.
Tel: (02) 298627 Fax: (02) 2621414

Belgium

British Tourist Authority, 306 Avenue Louise,
1050 Brussels,
Bergatraat 52, B2–1000 Brussels.
Tel: 02/511 43 90
Telex: 23108 GBRAIL B

Brazil

British Tourist Authority, Avenida Nilo Pecanha
50 – Conj. 2213, Edificio de Paoli, 20040
Rio de Janeiro – RJ.
Tel: 220 1187
Telex: (38) 2130694 EINGBR

Canada

British Tourist Authority,
94 Cumberland Street, Suite 600, Toronto,
Ontario, M5R 3N3.
Tel: (416) 925 6326
Fax: (416) 9612175

Denmark

British Tourist Authority, Montergade 3,
116 Copenhagen K.
Tel: 01 1207 93 Telex: 15370 BTACPH DK

France

British Tourist Authority,
63 rue Pierre-Charron, 75008 Paris.
Tel: 42 89 11 11
Telex: TAGBAND 649 138 F MINITEL: 3616
code OTGB

Germany

British Tourist Authority, Taunusstraße, 52–60,
6000 Frankfurt 1.
Tel: 069–23 80 711 Telex: 4185 209 BTA D
Fax: 069–2380717 Btx: 22 00 20

Hong Kong

British Tourist Authority, BTA Suite 903,
1 Hysan Avenue, Causeway Bay, Hong Kong.
Tel: 5–764366
Telex: 80201 BTAHK
Fax: 5–8950045

Ireland

British Tourist Authority,
123 Lower Baggot Street, Dublin 2.
Tel: 614188 Telex: 91419

Italy

British Tourist Authority, Corso Vittorio
Emanuele II No 337,00186 Rome.
Tel: 654 0821 or 654 0464
Telex: 622690 BTA ROM I

Japan and Korea

British Tourist Authority,
246 Tokyo Club Bldg, 3–2–6 Kasumigaseki,
Chiyoda-KU, Tokyo 100.
Tel: (03) 581 3603 or (03) 581 3604
Telex: 2223235
Fax: (03) 581 5797.
Installation of new telephone system may
affect number.

Netherlands

British Tourist Authority, Aurora Gebouw
(5th Floor), Stadhouderskade 2, 1054 ES
Amsterdam.
Tel: 020–85 50 51 Telex: 13395 BTABR NL
Fax: 020–186868

New Zealand

British Tourist Authority, Third Floor, Dilworth
Building, Corner Queen & Customs Streets,
Auckland 1.
Tel: (09) 3031 446 Fax: (09) 776 965

Norway

British Tourist Authority, Fr, Nansens Plass 9,
0160 Oslo 1 (Visitors only),
Postboks 1554, Vika, 0117 Oslo 1 (Post only).
Tel: (2) 41 18 49 Telex: 76748 BTA N
Fax: (2) 33 53 79

Singapore

British Tourist Authority, 24 Raffles Place,
17–04 Clifford Centre, Singapore 0104.
Tel: 5352966, 5352967 (24 hr ansaphone)
Telex: RS28493 BTA 5IN Fax: 5344703

Spain

British Tourist Authority, Torre de Madrid
6º of 7, Pza España 18, 28008, Madrid.
Tel: 241 13 96 Telex: 49295 M BTA E

Sweden

British Tourist Authority, Klarra Norra,
Kyrkogarta 29, 5–111 22 Stockholm.
Tel: 08–21 24 44
Telex: 11537 BTA S

Switzerland

British Tourist Authority, Limmatquai 78,
CH-8001 Zurich.
Tel: 01/47 42 77/97
Telex: 45 817832 BTA CH
Fax: 01/251 44 56

United States of America

CHICAGO – British Tourist Authority, 625 N
Michigan Avenue, Chicago, IL 60611.
Tel: (312) 787 0490 Fax: (312) 787 7746

DALLAS – British Tourist Authority, Cedar
Maple Plaza, Suite 210, 2305 Cedar Springs
Road, Dallas, TX 75201.
Tel: (214) 720 4040 Fax: (214) 871 2665

LOS ANGELES – British Tourist Authority,
Room 450, 350 South Figueroa Street, Los
Angeles, CA 90071.
Tel: (213) 628 3525 Telex: 466695 BTA LSA CI
Fax: (213) 687 6621

NEW YORK – British Tourist Authority,
40 West 57th Street, New York,
NY 10019–4001.
Tel: (212) 581 4700 Telex: 237798
Fax: (212) 265 0649

Booking Conditions

1. Payment—A deposit of £25 per person per week is required on bookings or 25% of the total cost when booking a self catering unit or caravan. If required, your premium for holiday cancellation insurance will be added to the sum required as a deposit. The balance is payable 42 days prior to departure. If the booking is made within 42 days of departure full payment is required at that time.

2. Cancellation by you—Cancellation of your holiday may be made at any time by the person who signed the booking form. It must be submitted in writing through the office at which the booking was made. Your deposit will be retained to cover our administration costs, and there will be additional cancellation charges in accordance with the following scale.

Cancellation notice received in writing before departure	Cancellation Charge
More than 42 days (6 weeks)	Deposit
29–42 days	30%
15–28 days	45%
14 days	60%
Departure date or after	100%

N.B. If you have taken out Holiday Insurance through HWL, you may be able to recover these amounts subject to the reason for cancelling being covered under the policy.

3. Alteration or cancellation by us—Circumstances may arise where we have no alternative but to cancel your accommodation. If such an exceptional situation should occur, we will make a complete refund to you or offer suitable alternative accommodation.

In the event that we have to cancel your holiday at any time, we will be liable only for any money paid to us at the time of cancellation. Holidays Wales Limited accepts no further liability whatsoever.

4. VAT—is included in all prices at the current rate of 15%, where applicable. In the event of any changes in the VAT regulations, these will be passed on to the client (only applicable if VAT has been included in the price).

5. Outside Agencies—All bookings for accommodation and other facilities are made by us as agents for the establishment concerned upon the understanding that we shall not accept any liability whatsoever for injury, loss, damage, accident or delay caused by or in any way connected with the acts of defaults of any Company or person engaged in carrying out the bookings or any proprietor or servant, or any liability whatsoever arising in any way directly or indirectly in connection with the making of the booking.

6. Holidays Wales Limited cannot accept liability for losses, additional expenses or any claim whatsoever due to changes in accommodation establishment, sickness, weather, strikes or any other cause. All such losses, additional expenses or claims will be borne by the client.

Note: Bookings other than through Holiday Wales Limited are subject to the operator's own booking conditions.

Holiday Insurance

Every year we receive heartbreaking letters and phone calls from clients who have had to cancel their holiday at short notice or have had a mishap whilst away. These occurrences can be very costly if insurance has not been taken out.

Holiday Insurance brings peace of mind and we recommend that everyone in your party takes advantage of the special scheme we have arranged through **Accident & General Ltd,** with **Municipal General Insurance Ltd.** A full Statement of cover will be sent to you with your confirmation of booking which also includes claims notification procedures. If a specimen copy of this statement is required prior to booking, we will be happy to send one on request

Premiums per person which must be included with the Deposit:

	Serviced Accommodation	Self Catering Accommodation
Up to 3 nights	£3.75	£2.75
Up to 7 nights	£4.50	£3.50
Up to 14 nights	£6.00	£5.00
Each additional week	£3.00	£3.00

Once a booking is accepted, no refund of premium can be allowed. The cover and limits are:
1. Cancellation and curtailment up to holiday cost (excluding holiday premium).
2. Personal accident up to £5,000.
3. Personal baggage up to £1,000 (single article limit £200/valuables limit £200).
4. Personal money up to £200.
5. Personal liability up to £500,000.

Claims under sections 1, 3 and 4 are subject to an excess of £15.00 except loss of deposit where no deduction is made.

WALES – HOTELS & GUEST HOUSES 1991 BOOKING FORM

Send this booking form to the accommodation of your choice.
Note to applicants and establishments using this form.
It must be clearly understood that the Wales Tourist Board is in no way connected with the booking and accepts no liability whatsoever in any way connected with, arising out of the booking, or the use of this form. In the case of direct bookings applicants (or their agents as the case may be) should check direct with operators as to any Terms of Booking.

Booking Ref.

Client's Name and Address (or Agent's Stamp)

Tel No:_____

Accommodation

Accommodation name_____

Accommodation address_____

_____

Date of arrival / /   Length of stay ☐ Nights

Details of Party

Mr/Mrs Miss	Initals		Age if Under 16

Total Number in party ☐   Number of children ☐

Number of adults ☐   Number of children (under 2) ☐

Pets ☐

Type of accommodation required

HOTELS, GUEST HOUSES AND FARMHOUSES

Enter number of rooms in box.

Single rooms(s)	*Double-bedded room(s)*	*Twin-bedded room(s)*	*Family room(s)*
With bath/shower ☐	With bath/shower ☐	With bath/shower ☐	With bath/shower ☐
Without bath ☐	Without bath ☐	Without bath ☐	Without bath ☐

Special Requirements _____

_____

Payment

Payment Method ☐   Cheque ☐   Postal Order ☐

Cheque/Postal Order Number [   ]

If you wish to pay by credit card, please tick the appropriate box and enter your account number below.

Please check that the establishment of your choice accepts your particular card.

☐ American Express   ☐ Diners Card

☐ Access   ☐ Visa

[   ]

Basic Cost	£
Supplements	£
Holiday Insurance	£
Total Cost	£
Less Deposit	£
Balance Payable	£

I agree to the terms of the Booking Conditions of the operators concerned as advised to me at the time of booking.

I enclose a deposit of   £

Signed_____ Date_____

123

BOOKING FORM *Holidays* WALES 1991 HOLIDAYS

PO BOX 40, SWANSEA, WEST GLAMORGAN, SA1 1PX

Note: This booking form to only be used for holidays booked through Holiday Wales Reservation Service.

Booking Ref. _____

Your Name and Address

Your Tel No:_____

Details of your Party (This will be given when telephoning)

Mr/Mrs Miss	Initals		Age if Under 16

Total Number in party	☐	Number of children	☐
Number of adults	☐	Number of children (under 2)	☐
		Pets	☐

Mark NO in this box if holiday insurance is not required ☐

Accommodation

Accommodation Name_____

Accommodation Location_____

Date of arrival [/ /] Length of stay [ ] Nights

Type of accommodation required

Hotels, Guest Houses & Farmhouses (Enter No. of rooms in box)

SINGLE ROOM(S)

With bath/shower ☐

Without bath ☐

DOUBLE-BEDDED ROOM(S)

With bath/shower ☐

Without bath ☐

TWIN BEDDED ROOM(S)

With bath/shower ☐

Without bath ☐

FAMILY ROOM(S)

With bath/shower ☐

Without bath ☐

MEAL BASIS:

Bed and Breakfast ☐   Dinner, Bed and Breakfast ☐

Special Requirements_____

Help with your Travel Arrangements

Please give details of any travel arrangements you require us to make on your behalf.

_____

_____

_____

(If travelling in own car, please leave blank).

Touring Holidays (Pre–Booked)

Night	Hotel	Date of Arrival	Nights
1			
2			
3			
4			
5			
6			

Payment Method   Cheque ☐   Postal Order ☐

Cheque/Postal Order Number [ ]

If you wish to pay by credit card, please tick the appropriate boxes, enter your account number and sign below.

I authorise Holidays Wales Ltd. to charge to my account

☐ Full cost of holiday now   ☐ or my initial payment only

Please tick appropriate box.

☐ Access   ☐ Visa   ☐ American Express

(No other credit cards are acceptable).

No. [ ][ ][ ][ ][ ][ ][ ][ ][ ][ ][ ][ ][ ]

Card Holder's Name_____

Card Holder's Signature_____

Expiry Date _____

Basic Cost	£
Supplements	£
Holiday Insurance	£
Total Cost	£
Less Deposit (plus insurance)	£
Balance Payable	£

I understand that the BALANCE must be received at least 42 days before the holiday is due to start. I have read the booking conditions and agree on behalf of all persons named above to abide by these conditions.

Signed_____ Date_____

CASTELL DINAS BRAN, LLANGOLLEN

There are some sounds spoken in Welsh which are very different from their English equivalents. The following is a basic guide:

WELSH		ENGLISH EQUIVALENT
c	cath = *cat*	cat (never as in receive)
ch	chwaer = *sister*	loch
dd	yn dda = *good*	them
f	y fam = *the mother*	of
ff	ffenestr = *window*	off
g	gardd = *garden*	garden (never as in George)
h	het = *hat*	hat (never silent as in honest)
ll	llaw = *hand*	There is no equivalent sound. Place the tongue on the upper roof of the mouth near the upper teeth, ready to pronounce l; then blow rather than voice the l.
th	byth = *ever*	Three (never as in English the)

The vowels in Welsh are a e i o u w y; all except 'y' can be long or short:

long a tad *father*	similar to English hard
short a mam *mother*	similar to English ham
long e hen *old*	similar to English sane
short e pen *heard*	similar to English ten
long i mis *month*	similar to English geese
short i prin *scarce*	similar to English tin
long o môr *sea*	similar to English more
short offon *walking stick*	similar to English fond
long w sŵn *sound*	similar to English moon
short w gwn *gun*	similar to English look

y has two sounds:

1 – CLEAR

dyn *man*,	a long 'ee' sound almost like English geese
cyn *before*,	a short 'i' sound almost like English tin

2 – OBSCURE

something like the sound in English run

Examples:

y *the;* yn *in;* dynion *men.*

It is well to remember that in Welsh the accent usually falls on the last-syllable-but-one of a word, e.g. cadair *chair.*

A FEW GREETINGS

Bore da	Good Morning
Dydd da	Good day
Prynhawn da	Good afternoon
Noswaith dda	Good evening
Nos da	Good night
Sut mae?	How are you
Hwyl	Cheers
Diolch	Thanks
Diolch yn fawr iawn	Thanks very much
Croeso	Welcome
Croeso i Gymru	Welcome to Wales
Da	Good
Da iawn	Very good
Iechyd da!	Good health

USEFUL TRANSLATIONS

Aber	Estuary
Llan	Church
Caer	Fort
Mynydd	Mountain
Afon	River
Pont	Bridge
Castell	Castell

Tourism Wales

The Wales Tourist Board is the statutory authority for the promotion and development of Tourism in Wales. For further information about the Board and its services please write to:

Wales Tourist Board, Department TCAM,
Davis Street, Cardiff CF1 2FU

If you're still undecided on a place to stay, or you want to know more about an area, then take a look at our colourful, informative range of publications. Our guides are designed to help you get the most out of your holiday in Wales, offering plenty of useful information and advice. To order any of the publications listed simply write, enclosing the appropriate remittance in the form of a cheque, postal/money order in £ sterling to: Wales Tourist Board, Dept WTS, Davis Street, Cardiff CF1 2FU

Wales: Self-Catering Guide 1991 – £2.50

Guide to over 350 self-catering properties in Wales including cottages, flats and chalets, caravan holiday home parks and touring caravan and camping parks.

Wales: Bed and Breakfast Guide 1991 – £2.50

Guide to budget accommodation in Wales, featuring over 500 hotels, guest houses and farmhouses, all with one thing in common – they offer bed and breakfast at an all inclusive price of £16 or under per person per night.

All publications include 5 mile to the inch full colour maps of Wales.

Wales Tourist Map – £1.45

A real best-seller. Detailed 5 mile/1 inch scale, also includes a wealth of tourist information, town plans, suggested tours and information centres.

Wales: Castles and Historic Places – £6.95

This full colour guide is a joint publication produced by the Wales Tourist Board and Cadw: Welsh Historic Monuments. More than 140 sites are covered in the extensive gazetteer, including castles, abbeys, country houses, Roman and prehistoric remains – all regularly open to the public. An historic introduction sets the scene, and 12 pages of maps help visitors to plan their routes.

Videos

Three videos are available.

The Wonder of Wales Video (VHS)* – £10.50

A new 24 minute video encapsulating the breathtaking beauty and myriad attractions of Wales. Narrated by Siân Phillips, the film features prominently the cultural and architectural heritage of Wales and includes the most recent visitor attractions in the Principality.

Heritage of a Nation Video (VHS/BETA)* – £10.00

Narrated by Richard Burton, this 25 minute video presents the Heritage of Wales from prehistoric times through to the present day. Wales as a holiday country is vividly depicted with some memorable sequences.

South Wales Valleys Video (VHS/BETA)* – £10.00

The South Wales Valleys (approx. 15 minutes) is a lively short presentation of the culture and heritage of the area.

Posters

North Wales scenes	£1.30
Tal-y-Llyn	£1.30
Llangrannog Beach	£1.20
Great Little Trains	£1.30
Coracle Fisherman	£1.20
Mid Wales scenes	£1.30
South Wales scene	£1.30

NOTE: All prices quoted include postage and packaging.
*Please indicate clearly video format required when ordering.

TOWN INDEX

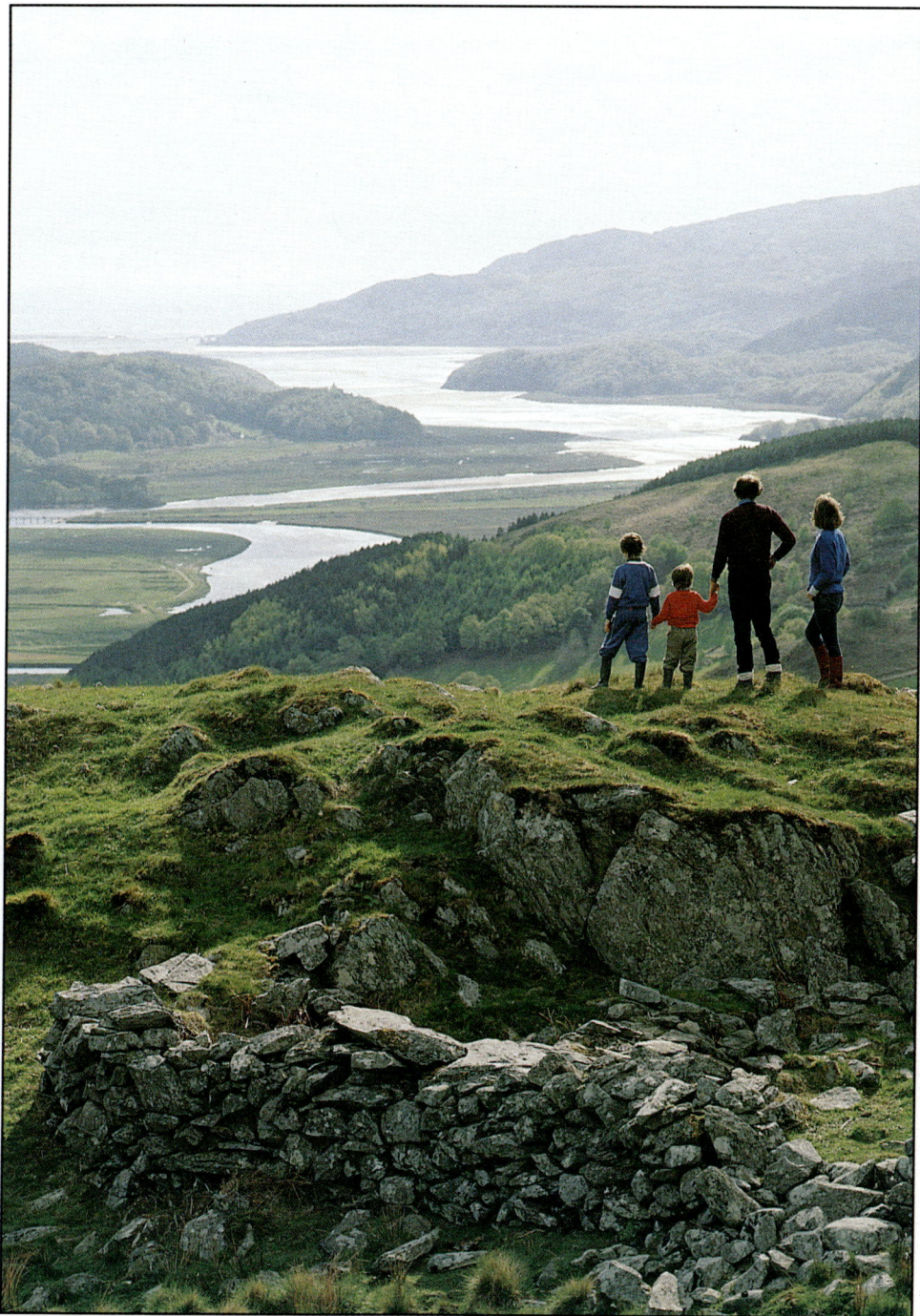

PRECIPICE WALK OVERLOOKING MAWDDACH ESTUARY, NEAR DOLGELLAU

Maps of Wales

The maps which follow divide Wales into twelve sections, each with a slight overlap. The grid overlaying each map will help you find the town or village of your choice for against the entry of each of them in this book is a reference number indicating the section of map and grid square. Simply turn to the appropriate map sheet, look for the grid square quoted in the code and pick out the place itself in that square. The maps are at 5 miles or 8 kilometres to one inch square.

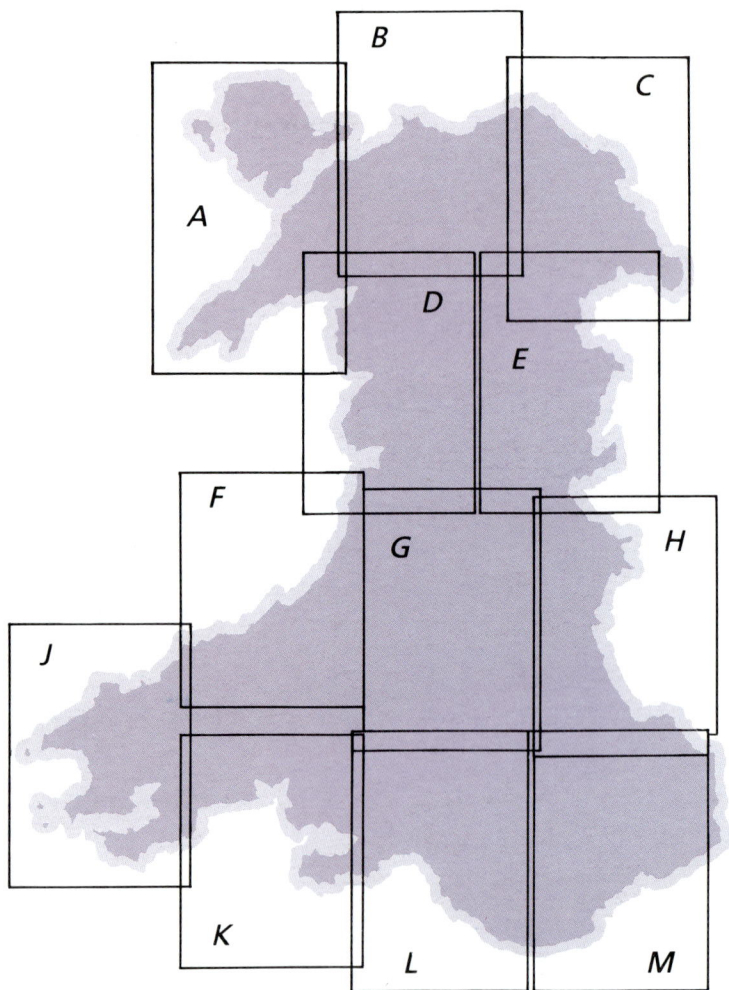

Miles 0 1 2 3 4 5
Kilometres 0 1 2 3 4 5 6 7 8

a b c d e

The Skerries
WYLFA NUCLEAR POWER STATION
Cemlyn Bay Neuadd Bull Bay
Hen Borth Porth-wen Porth-yr-ychen Porth-yr-ysgaw
Carmel Hd. Tregele Cemaes Bay Amlwch Llanelian Point Lynas

Llanfair -ynghornwy Bodewryd Penysarn Ynys Dulas
Llanfechell Llanwenllwyfo
Rhydwyn Llanrhuddlad Rhosgoch Rhos -y-bol Nebo Traeth-yr-ora
Church Bay Dulas Bay
Llanfaethlu CAPEL LLIGWY Moelfre
Parys Mountain Penrhos LLIGWY CROMLECH
Porth Trefadog Llanddeusant Penrhos Traeth Bychan
Porth Tywyn-mawr Llanbabo VISITOR CENTRE Llandyfrydog Din Lligwy
Dun Laoghaire and Dublin – Holyhead 3½ hrs Llannerch-y-medd Llanallgo
Llanfwrog Llanfihangel Traeth Lligwy
N.Stack Tre'r Beirdd Benllech
Holyhead Mount Porth Penrhyn Brynteg Ynys Sei
720ft. FORT mawr Red Wharf Bay Puffin I.
S.Stack Llanfachraeth Penmon PRIO
y Island Caergybi Traeth-y-dribin Llangwyllog Llanbedr-goch Traeth Coch DOVE
Holyhead Bodedern Trefor Pentraeth Llanddona Llangoed
Porthdafarch Caer -geiliog Llynfaes Beaumaris Llanfaes
Porth-y-post Four Mile Br. Bodffordt Rhos -meirch Llangefni Talwrn Traeth Lafan
Trearddur Bay Bryngwran A5 Penmynydd Llandegfan Garth
Rhoscolyn Gwalchmai Heneglwys Cerrigceinwen Porthaethwy Menai Bridge PENRHYN CASTL
Cymran Bay Groeslon Pentre -berw Llanfair PG Bangor Tan-y-bont
Rhosneigr Llanfaelog Gaerwen CATHEDRAL Rachub
Porth Nobla Ty Croes Bodorgan BRYN-CELLI DDU Glasinfryn Bethe
BARCLODIAD Y GAWRES Llandaniel Fab Pentir Rhiwlas Gerla
Porth Trecastell Aberffraw Hermon Llangaffo Llanddeiniolen PENRHYN SLATE QUARRIES
Llangadwaladr Bodowyr Malltraeth Y Felinheli Ca
Newborough Bryn-siencyn Port Dinorwic Penisa'r waen Cwm-y-glo LLANBERIS LAKE RAILWAY
Niwbwrch Bethel Clwt-y-bont DINORWIC PUMPED STORAGE SCHEME
Newborough Forest Dwyran Seion Deiniolen 3104ft.
Llanddwyn I. Caernarfon Bryn Brâs Llanrug Nant Peris 326
SEGONTIUM Llanberis 3279ft.
Aber Menai Pt. Caeathro Waunfawr Moel Eilio SNOWDON MOUNTAIN RAILWAY Glyder Fawr
Ty-hen Llandygwnning Mynytho Bont-newydd 2382ft. Betws Garmon 3560ft.
Porth-oer 999ft. Methlem Rhiw Llangian Llanwnda AIRFIELD Mynydd Mawr Y Garn Wyddfa
Rhoshirwaun PLAS YN RHIW Abersoch Groeslon 2290ft. Rhyd -ddu 2461ft. Y Aran
Mynydd Anelog 628ft. Llanfaelrhys Llanengan Dinas Dinlle Nantlle Y Garn SNOWDON
Aberdaron Porth Neigwl (Hell's Mouth) Llandwrog Mynydd Mawr 2080ft. FALL
Penygroes Tal-y-sarn Llyn Dinas
Pen-y-cil We Porth Ceir Pontllyfni Llanllyfni Nantlle Uchaf Garnedd goch 1984ft.
Trwyn Cilan Nebo Nazareth 2301ft. Beddgelert 2566ft. Beddgelert Forest
Aberdesach Moel Hebog FOREST PARK CENTRE ABERGLASLYN PASS
Clynnog Fawr 1996ft. Pant-glas Nantmor
1712ft. Cnicht
Trefor Gyrn Ddu 1670ft. Bwlch Mawr Mynydd Cenin 2265ft.
Yr Eifl 859ft. Bryncir Garndolbenmaen Moel Ddu nan-ian WELSH
Nant Gwrtheyrn 1850ft. Llanaelhaearn 1811ft. Garreg Tanyb
Llithfaen Dolbenmaen Penmorfa TREMADOG HIGHLAND RLY.
FFYNNON GYBI Dwyfor Pentre-felin OF
Porthdinllaen Nefyn Edern Garn Boduan 918ft. Bryncir Llangybi Cricieth Porthmadog Penr
Morfa Nefyn Boduan Y Ffôr Borth-y-gest Minffordd
Porth Ysgadan Llannor Chwilog Llanystumdwy Morfa Bychan Portmeirion Talsar
Porth Ychen Tudweiliog Efailnewydd Abererch BUTLIN'S HOLIDAY CAMP Black Rock Sands Llanfihangel -y-traethau
Traeth Penllech Dinas Aberech Penychain Morfa Harlech
Penllech Carn Fadryn Rhyd-y-clafdy Pwllheli Traeth Bach
Porth Colmon Llangwnnadl Penrhos South Beach Eisingrug
Llaniestyn Bryncroes Sarn TREMADOG BAY Harlech
Ty-hen Mynytho Llanbedrog SLATE CAVERNS Llanfair

PENINSULA LLYN
TREMADOG BAY

MAP B

Miles 0 1 2 3 4 5
Kilometres 0 1 2 3 4 5 6 7 8

a   b   c   d   e

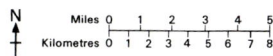

a   b   c   d   e

1

Formby
Skelmersdale
Wi

2

Bootle
Liverpool
St. Helen's
N
le

Wallasey
M E R S E Y S I D E

Hoylake
Birkenhead
Widnes

West Kirby
Garston
Runcorn

3

Point of Ayr
Talacre
Heswell
Bebington

Ffynnon
groew
tatyn
Llanasa
Trelogan
Mostyn
Neston
Ellesmere
Port
Frodsham

MAEN
ACHWYFAN
Whitford BASINGWERK
ABBEY
Greenfield
Hapsford

HALL
Lloc
Gorsedd
Carmel
Holywell
Bagillt
A5117

4

Caerwys
Tremeirchion
Babell
Halkyn
TEXTILE
MILL
Saughall
Chester
Kelsall

Moel
y-parc
Nannerch
Rhosesmor
Northop
Connah's
Quay
Shotton
Queensferry
C H E S H I R E

Rhydymwyn
Northophall
Sychdyn
Ewloe
Sandycroft
HAWARDEN
AIRFIELD
Tarvin

5

Cilcain
Pantymwyn
Buckley
Hawarden
Tarporley

Llys-y-coed
Gwernaffield
Mold
Llong
Broughton
Saltney

Moel Fammau
Tafarn-y-gelyn
Gwernymynydd
Nercwys
Pen-y-ffordd
Pant-blyddyn

Clwyd
Mashafn
Llanferres
Hope

Llanbedr
Hirwaen
Leeswood
Treuddyn
Rossett
Farndon

Dyffryn Clwyd
FOREST
Pant-y-
ffordd
Caergwrle
Trevalyn
Clutton

6

Rhuthun
Ruthin
Fryrys
Llanarmon
yn Ial
Llanfynydd
Llai
Gresford

Llanfair
Dyffryn Clwyd
Graigfechan
Rhydtalog
Frith
Cefn-y-bedd
Hope
Hugmore
Holt
Ridley Wood

Pentre-celyn
Llandegla
Moel Bwlch Gwyn
Gwersyllt
Brymbo
Minera
Coed-poeth
Wrexham
Malpas

Cefn-coch
World's
End
Rhostyllen
Marchwiel
No Man's
Heath

7

Gwyddelwern
Bryneglwys
Rhoslanerchrugog
Johnstown
Stryt-yr-hwch
Bangor-is-y-coed
Bangor on Dee
Higher
Wych

Moel
Morfydd
VALLE
CRUCIS
ABBEY
Pen-y-cae
Ruabon
Eyton
Tallarn Green
White

Carrog
Llantysilio
CANAL
MUSEUM
Acrefair
Cefn-mawr
Overton
Penley
Bronington

Corwen
Glyndyfrdwy
Llangollen
RAILWAY
Trevor
AQUEDUCT
Froncysyllte
Erbistock
Eglwys
Cross

133

MAP D

a   b   c   d   e

SNOWDONIA

NATIONAL

PARK

Forest
Beddgelert
ABERGLASLYN PASS
2566ft. Moel Hebog
Nantmor
Cnicht 2265ft.
Moelwyn Mawr 2527ft.
Moelwyn Bach 2334ft+
GLODDFA GANOL
LLECHWEDD SLATE CAVERNS
STWLAN DAM
Blaenau Ffestiniog
Bethania
Gylchedd 2059ft.
Cader Bronllyn 2194ft.
Carnedd-y-Filiast
Llangwm
Foel Goch 2004ft.
Mwdwr Eilan 1543ft.

Dolbenmaen
Moel Ddu 1811ft.
Tan-lan
Ffestiniog
Migneint
Arennig Fach 2259ft.
Moel Emoel
Cefn ddv

Penmorfa
Tremadog
Minffordd
WELSH HIGHLAND RLY.
Maentwrog
Penrhyndeudraeth
Graig Wen 1923ft.
Llyn Celyn
Fron-goch
Landderfel
De

Porthmadog
Borth-y-gest
fa Bychan
Portmeirion
Talsarnau
TRAWSFYNYDD NUCLEAR POWER STATION
TOMEN-Y-MUR
2800ft.
Arennig Fawr
Gwastadros 1182ft.
Bala
Llanfor
Llancil
VALE
TOMEN BALA

Sands
Traeth Bach
Llanfihangel-y-traethau
Morfa Harlech
Eisingrug
Trawsfynydd
2461ft.
Moel Llyfnant 2221ft.
Llyn Tegid
Rhos-y-gwaliau
BALA LAKE RAILWAY
Llangywair
Penllyn Forest

Llandanwg
Harlech
SLATE CAVERNS
Llanfair
Gwynfryn
Y Graig ddwyg 2046ft.
Crawcwellt
1766ft.
Moel-y-Fiedlog
Mynydd Bryn-llech
Llanuwchllyn
Moel-y-Geifr
Talardd 2054ft.

Llanbedr
Mochras (Shell Is.)
MAESARTRO CRAFT VILLAGE
R.A.F.
Rhinog-Fawr 2362ft+
MAESGWM FOREST VISITOR CENTRE
Rhinog Fach 2333ft.
Moel Hafod Owen 1428ft.
Coed y Brenin
Dduallt 2155ft.
Moel-y-Geifr
Cefn Tre-Ysbyty 1681ft.

Dyffryn Ardudwy
Moelfre 1932ft.
Y Llethr 2475ft.
Rhobell Fawr 2408ft.
Foel Ddu 1527ft.
Aran Benllyn 2901ft.
Dyrysgol 2397ft.

Llanenddwyn
Llanddwywe
Talybont
RURAL LIFE CENTRE
Diffwys 2462ft.
Llawr Llech
Y Garn 2063ft.
Cwrwch Moel Offrwm 1328ft.
Ganllwyd
Llanfachraeth
2970ft.
Moel Cors-y-garnedd
Aran Fawddwy
Rhyd-y-main
Llanymawddwy
Llanuwchllyn

Bontddu
Llanelltyd
ABBEY
Brithdir
Bwlchyfign
2149ft.
FALLS
Dyfnant

Llanaber
Abermaw
BARMOUTH
Barmouth
Penmaenpool
Dolgellau
Bwlch y Oerddrws
Aber Cowarch
Tir Rhiwiog 1787ft.
Carreg-y-fran
Dyfnant

BARMOUTH BAY
Ferry
Toll
FAIRBOURNE RAILWAY
Fairbourne
Arthog
Tyrau Mawr 2167ft.
CADER IDRIS
Mynydd Moel
Cross Foxes
Waen Oer 2197ft+
MEIRION WOOLLEN MILL
Dinas Mawddwy
Mallwyd
Foel

Penygarn Craig-y-llyn 1504ft.
2040ft.
Penygader 2927ft.
Mynydd Dolged
1708ft.
Tal-y-Meryn
1244ft.
Dugoed
Banwy

Llwyngwril
Llanfihangel-y-pennant
CASTELL-Y-BERE
Mynydd Pencoed Cau
Minffordd
Corris Uchaf
Aberllefenni
Dyfi Forest
CRAFT CENTRE
Cwm Llinau
Llyn Gwyddior
EFFORDD GLYNDWR

Llangelynnin
Rhoslefain
Abergynolwyn
TALYLLYN RAILWAY
NANT GWERNOL
Craig Goch 2186ft+
Tarenygesail
Corris
Esgairgeiliog
ALT. TECH. NAT. CENTRE
Cemmaes
Pandy

Tonfanau
Llanegryn
ROOD SCREEN
Dol-goch
FALLS
Foel Cocyn 1018ft.
Taren Hendre 2076ft+
Moelygeifr
Tal-y-llyn
Cemmaes Road
Llanwrin
Commins Coch
VALLEY
A470
Llanbrynmair
Twmpath Melyn 1444ft+
Rhy

Aber Dysynni
Bryn-crug
Pandy
Trum Gelli 1755ft.
Corlan Fraith Happy Valley
Machynlleth
Pennal
Penegoes
Aber Gwydol
Darowen
Llan
Pont-dolgadfan
Talerddig
A470

Tywyn
Cwrt
Forge
Dulas
Talywern
Pennant
Bryn Amlwg 1603ft.
Carno

Aberdyfi
Aberdovey
837ft.
914ft.
DOVEY
Derwenlas
Glaspwll
Aberhosan
Bryn y Fedwen 1784ft.
Pont Crygnant
Bryn yr Oerfa 1507ft.
Waen Garno 1293ft.
Bryn Crugog 1463ft.
Colwyn

Ynyslas
Traeth Maelgwn
Furnace
Glandyfi
Eglwys-fach
1467ft.
Pen Carreg-gopa
Llyn Conach
Pen-rhaiadr
Dylife
Fedw Ddu
Staylittle
Bryn Tail 1321ft.
Fan

Llancynfelyn
Tre'r-ddol
OLD CHAPEL MUSEUM
Rheidol
1703ft.
Moellylyn
1607ft.
Bryn Moel
Bugeilyn
Hafren Forest
Mynydd y Grois 1578ft.

Talybont
Tre Taliesin
Forest
Drosgol 1806ft.
Source of R. Wye
Pen Plynlimon-fawr 2468ft.
Or Du 1659ft.
Bryn Tail
Llanidloes

Borth
Dol-y-bont
Nant-y-moch Reservoir
PLYNLIMON
Drum Peithnant
Y Foel 1791ft.
Pen-Bwlch-y-groes 1487ft.
Cwm-belan

Bow Street
Llandre
Elerch
Disgwylfa Fawr 1661ft.
Eisteddfa-gurig

Clarach
Wallog
Penrhyn-coch
LLYWERNOG SILVER LEAD MINE
Dyffryn Castell
Cwm-belan

Aberystwyth
CLIFF RLY.
Waun-fawr
Capel Dewi
Capel Bangor
Goginan
Ponterwyd
Old

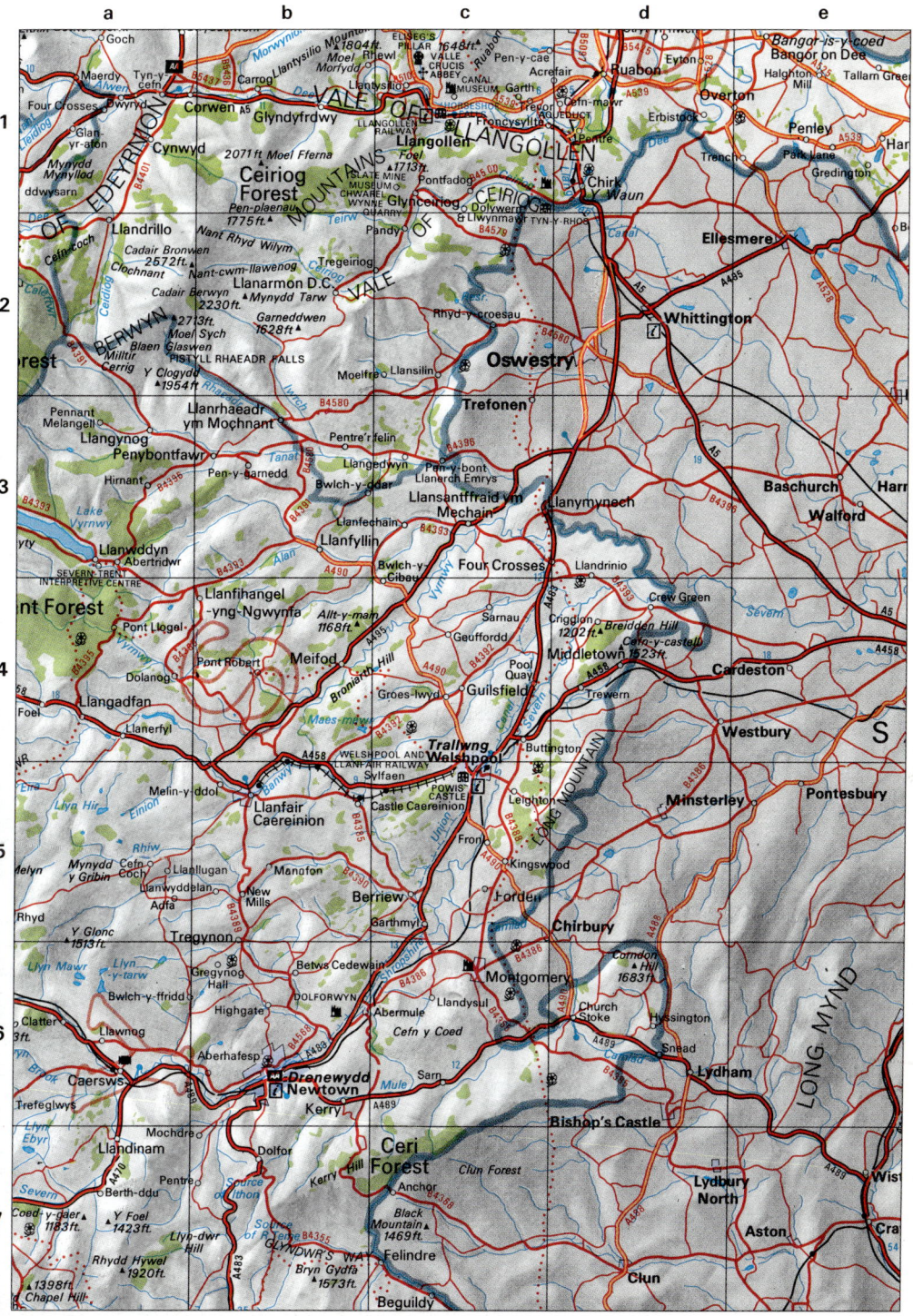

M A P F

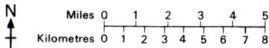

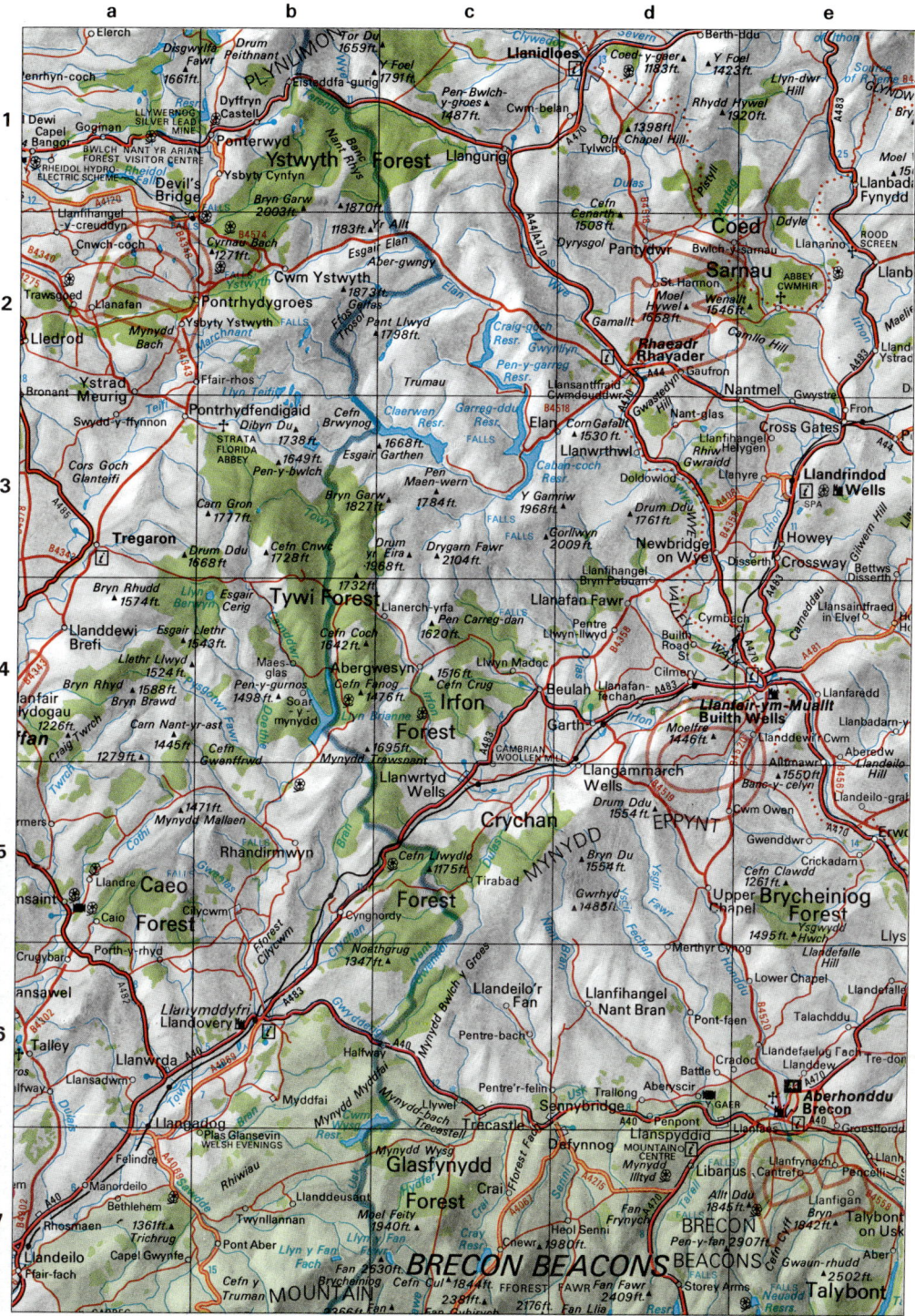

Miles 0 1 2 3 4 5
Kilometres 0 1 2 3 4 5 6 7 8

N

a b c d e

1

Elerch
Disgwylfa Fawr 1661ft.
Drum Peithnant
Tor Du 1659ft.
Y Foel 1791ft.
Eisteddfa-gurig
Clywedog
Severn
Llanidloes
Coed-y-gaer 1183ft.
Berth-ddu
Y Foel 1423ft.
Llyn-dwr
Source of GLYNDW
Bry
A483

Penrhyn-coch
Goginan
Llywernog Silver Lead Mine
Dyffryn Castell
Pen-Bwlch-y-groes 1487ft.
Cwm-belan
1398ft. Old Chapel Hill
Rhyd Hywel 1920ft.
Moel
25

St. Dewi
Capel Bangor
Bwlch Nant Yr Arian Forest Visitor Centre
Ponterwyd
Ysbyty Cynfyn
Ystwyth Forest
Llangurig
A44/A470
Dyrysgol
St. Harmon
Moel Hywel 1658ft.
Llanbadarn Fynydd
Moel
15

Rheidol Hydro Electric Scheme
Devil's Bridge
Bryn Garw 2003ft.
1870ft.
Cefn Cenarth 1508ft.
Pantydwr
Coed Sarnau
Ddyle
Llananno ROOD SCREEN
Llanb

2

Llanfihangel-y-creuddyn
Cnwch-coch
84574 Cyrnau Bach 1271ft.
1183ft. Yr Allt
Esgair Elan
Aber-gwngy
Wye
Dyrysgol
Gwnstadyn Hill
Wenallt 1546ft.
Nantmel
ABBEY CWMHIR

Trawscoed
Llanafan
Mynydd Bach
Cwm Ystwyth
1873ft. Gellas
Pant Llwyd 1798ft.
Elan
Craig-goch Resr.
Gamallt
Moel Hywel 1658ft.
Nant-glas
Camlo Hill
Fron
Gwystr

Lledrod
Pontrhydygroes
Ysbyty Ystwyth
FALLS
Marchnant
Gwynllyn
Pen-y-garreg Resr.
Rhaeadr Rhayader
A44
Gaufron
Nant-glas
Llanfihangel Rhiw Helygen Gwraidd
Cross Gates
Llandr
Ystrad

3

Bronant
Ystrad Meurig
Ffair-rhos
Llyn Teifi
Claerwen Resr.
Garreg-ddu Resr.
84518
Elan
Corn Gafallt 1530ft.
Doldowlod
Llanwrthwl
A470
Llandrindod Wells SPA
Gwystre

Swydd-y-ffynnon
Pontrhydfendigaid
STRATA FLORIDA ABBEY
Dibyn Du 1738ft.
Cefn Brwynog
1668ft.
Esgair Garthen
Caban-coch Resr.
Y Gamriw 1968ft.
Drum Ddu 1761ft.
Howey
Llanyre
Disserth
Crossway
Bettws Disserth

Cors Goch Glanteifi
1649ft. Pen-y-bwlch
Pen Maen-wern
Town
Gorllwyn 2009ft.
Newbridge on Wye
Carneddau
Llanfihangel Bryn Pabuan
Llansaintfraed in Elvel

4

Tregaron
Drum Ddu 1668ft.
Carn Gron 1777ft.
Cefn Cnwc 1728ft.
Bryn Garw 1827ft.
Drum yr Eira 1968ft.
Drygarn Fawr 2104ft.
FALLS
Llanfihangel-yr-yfa
Builth Road St.
Cymbach
Cilmery

Bryn Rhudd 1574ft.
Esgair Cerig
1732ft.
Tywi Forest
Llanerch-yrfa
Pen Carreg-dan 1620ft.
Llanafan Fawr
Pentre Llwyn-llwyd
Llaneir-ym-Muallt Builth Wells
Llanfaredd
Llanbadarn-y
Aberedw

Llanddewi Brefi
Esgair Llethr 1543ft.
Llethr Llwyd 1524ft.
Maes-glas Pen-y-gurnos
Cefn Coch 1842ft.
1516ft. Cefn Crug 1476ft.
Llwyn Madoc
Beulah
Garth
Moelfre 1446ft.
Llandewr'r Cwm
Llandeilo-grab

Llanfair Clydogau
1226ft.
Bryn Rhyd Bryn Brawd
Carn Nant-yr-ast 1445ft.
Soar y mynydd
Abergwesyn
Cefn Fanog
Irfon Forest
Llyn Brianne
Garth
CAMBRIAN WOOLLEN MILL
Irfon

5

Craig Twrch 1279ft.
1471ft.
Mynydd Mallaen
Cefn Gwenffrwd
1695ft.
Mynydd Trawsnant
Llanwrtyd Wells
Crychan
Bryn Du 1554ft.
MYNYDD EPPYNT
Cwm Owen
Gwenddwr
Crickadam
Ecw

Rhandirmwyn
Cefn Llwydlo 1175ft.
Tirabad
Llangammarch Wells
Drum Ddu 1554ft.
Gwrhyd 1485ft.
Cefn Clawdd 1261ft.
Upper Chapel
Brycheiniog Forest
Llys

Llandre
Caio Forest
Cilycwm
Ffawyddog
Forest
Cynghordy
Noethgrug 1347ft.
Bryn Du 1554ft.
Ysgwyd Hwch
1495ft.
Llandefalle Hill
Llandefalle

6

Talley
Llanymddyfri Llandovery
Llanwrda
A40
Halfway
Llandeilo'r Fan
Pentre-bach
Llanfihangel Nant Bran
Pont-faen
Cradoc
Lower Chapel
Talachddu
Llanddew
Tre-don

Llansawel
Crugybar
Porth-y-rhyd
A483
Myddfai
Pentre'r-felin
Sennybridge
Battle
Aberyscir
45
Aberhonddu Brecon
Groesffordd

Llansadwrn
Plas Glansevin WELSH EVENINGS
Llywel
Trecastle
Trallong
USK GAER
A40
Penpont
Llanspyddid
Llanfrynach
Cantref
Pencelli

7

Felindre
Manordeilo
Rhiwiau
Glasfynydd Forest
Defynnog
MOUNTAIN CENTRE
Libanus
Cantref
Llanhamlach

Rhosmaen
Bethlehem
1361ft. Trichrug
Twynllannan
Moel Feity 1940ft.
Crai
Mynydd Illtud
Fan Frynych
BRECON BEACONS
Pen-y-fan 2907ft.
Llanfigan
Bryn 1842ft.
Talybont on Usk
Aber

Llandeilo Ffair-fach
Capel Gwynfe
Pont Aber
Llyn y Fan Fach
Fan Brycheiniog 2630ft.
Cefn Cul 1844ft.
Fan Fawr 2409ft.
Cnewr
Heol Senni
Storey Arms
Gwaun-rhudd 2502ft.
FALLS
Nantlla Resr.
Talybont

MOUNTAIN
Cefn y Truman
2381ft.
FFOREST FAWR
Fan Llia
2176ft.

MAP H

a   b   c   d   e

1

Black Mountain ▲1469ft.
GLYNDWR'S WAY   Felindre
Bryn Gydfa ▲1573ft.
Moel Wilym ▲1568ft.   Beguildy
Llanbadarn Fynydd
Black Mt.   Duthlas
Beacon Hill ▲1796ft.   Llanfair Waterdine
Aston   Craven Arms
Clun
Bromfield
Leintwardine   Ludlow
A49   A4117

2

HILL CREEN
Bryn-melyn   Source of R. Lugg   Knucklas   Panpunton
Llanbister   Crug   Tref-y-Clawdd   S DYKE   Llanwen Hill
Llanddewi Ystradenny   Bleddfa   Glog Hill ▲1335ft.   Llangunllo   Rhos-y-meirch   Pilleth
Maelienydd   Whitton   Norton
Knighton
Wigmore   Richards Castle   Woofferton
A456

Radnor

Dolau   Llanfihangel Rhydithon   Maes Treylow   Discoed   Presteigne
Penybont   Radnor Forest   Beth Hill ▲2002ft.   Kinnerton   Mortimer's Cross   Luston
Bettws Disserth   Llandegley   Esgair Nantau   New Radnor   Evenjobb
Llandeilo-graban   Walton   Eardisland   Leominster

Forest

3

Llandeglas Rhos   Old Radnor   A44   Kington   Lyonshall   A4112   A44
Llanfihangel Nant Melan   Gwaunceste Hill ▲1778ft.   Dolyhir
Hundred House   Little Hill ▲1532ft.   Colva Hill   Gwaithla   Gladestry   Weobley   Bush Bank   Bodenham Moor

4

Red Hill ▲1666ft.   Newchurch   Brilley Mountain   Sarnesfield
Llanbadarn-y-garreg ▲1532ft.   Bryngwyn   Michaelchurch on Arrow   Eardisley
Llanbedr Hill   Rhos-goch   Willersley
Clandeilo Hill   Clyro Hill   Rhydspence   Clifford   Wye
Painscastle   Rhydbach   Sutton St. Nicholas

HEREFORD AND WORCESTER

5

Erwood   Clyro   Bronydd   A438   Lugwardine
Llanstephan   Hay-on-Wye   A438   A438
Llowes   Llanigon   Hereford   A465
Glasbury   Boughrood   GOLDEN   Madley
Llyswen   Aberllynfi Three Cocks   Hay Bluff ▲2220ft.   Vowchurch   Kingstone   Callow
Llandefalle   A4079   Felindre   VALLEY
Bronllys   Lord Hereford's Knob ▲2263ft.   Much Dewchurch

6

Tre-domen   Treffeca   Llaneleu   Wormbridge   Sandyway
Pengenffordd   Waun-Fach ▲2660ft. Pen-y-gader-fawr ▲2624ft.   Capel-y-ffin   Llangua   Grosmont
Llanfihangel Tal-y-llyn   Mynydd Troed   Llanthony   PRIORY
Llangorse   Llan-gors Lake   Mynydd Du   Pen-twyn-mawr ▲2504ft.   Cwmyoy
Cathedine   MOUNTAINS   Pandy   Cross Ash   Skenfrith   Llangrove

Forest

7

Scethrog   Llansantffraid   Cwmdu   Crug Mawr ▲1805ft.   Cwmwoy
Talybont on Usk   Llanhamlach   Bwlch   Pencerrig-calch   Partrishow   Ynysgynwraidd
Aber   Tretower ▲2301ft.   Sugar Loaf ▲1955ft.   Llanfihangel Crucorney   Llanvetherine   Newcastle   Whitchurch
Coed-yr-ynys   Llanbedr   Betws   Skirrid-fawr ▲1596ft.   WHITE CASTLE   Maypole
Crickhowell   Llangynidr   Garn Caws   Glangrwyne   Llantilio   Rockfield
Llangattock

138

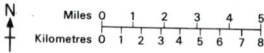

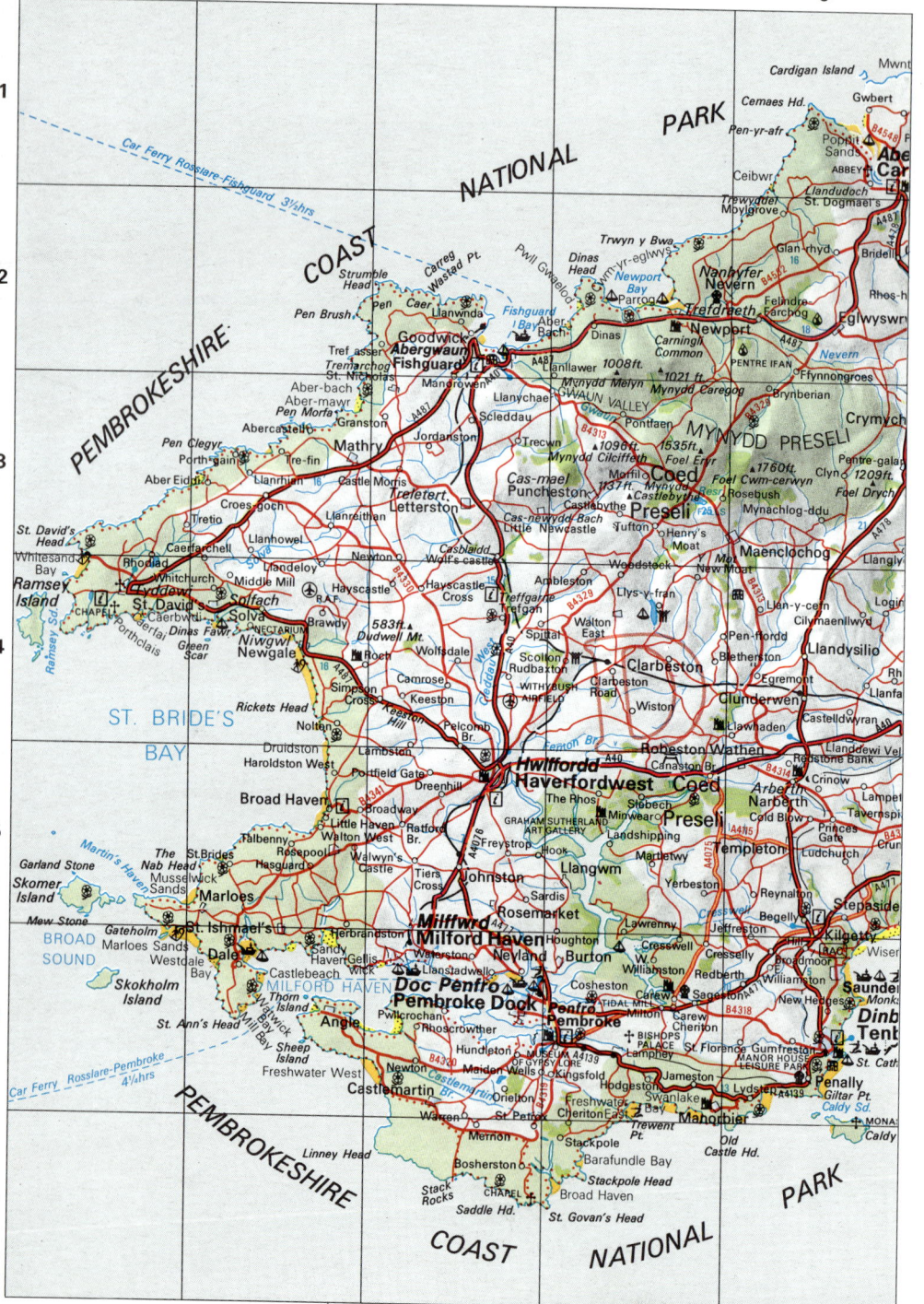

Miles 0 1 2 3 4 5
Kilometres 0 1 2 3 4 5 6 7 8

a   b   c   d   e

1

Car Ferry Rosslare-Fishguard 3½ hrs

PEMBROKESHIRE

COAST

NATIONAL PARK

Cardigan Island   Mwnt
Cemaes Hd.   Gwbert
Pen-yr-afr   Poppit Sands   Abe Car
ABBEY
Ceibwr   Llandudoch   St. Dogmael's
Trwyn y Bwa   Glan-rhyd   Brideli
Dinas Head   Mylgrove
Strumble Head   Carreg Wastad Pt.   Pwll Gwaelod
Newport Bay   Nanhyfer   Rhos-h
Pen Brush   Caer   Llanwnda   Parrog   Nevern   Eglwyswr
Tref assen   Goodwick   Fishguard Bay   Trefdraeth   Felindre Farchog
Tremarchog   Abergwaun   Aber Bach   Newport   A487
St. Nicholas   Fishguard   Dinas   Nevern
Aber-bach   Manorowen   A40   Carningli Common   PENTRE IFAN   Flynnongroes
Aber-mawr   Pen Morfa   Llanllawer   1008 ft.   Mynydd Melyn   Brynberian   Crymych
Abercastello   Granston   Scleddau   137 ft.   Mynydd Caregog
Pen Clegyr   Mathry   Llanychaer   WAUN VALLEY   MYNYDD PRESELI
Porthgain   Jordanston   Trecwn   Pontfaen   1096 ft.   1535 ft. Foel Eryr   Pentre-gala
Aber Eiddi   Tre-fin   Castle Morris   Mynydd Cilciffeth   173 ft.   1760 ft.   Clyn   1209 ft.
St. David's Head   Llanrhian   Croes-goch   Trefgarn   Cas-mael   Morfil   Rosebush   Foel Cwm-cerwyn   Foel Drych
Tretio   Caerfarchell   Llanhowel   Trelewydd   Punchestown   Castlebythe   Tufton   Mynachlog-ddu   Maenclochog
Whitesand Bay   Rhodiad   Whitchurch   Middle Mill   Hayscastle   Little Newcastle   Casblaidd   St. Henry's Moat   Llangly
Ramsey Island   Llanddewi   Solfach   Dudwell Mt.   Hayscastle Cross   New Moat   Llan-y-cefn   Logi
St. David's   Solva   Brawdy   Newton   Wolf's castle   Ambleston   Llys-y-fran   Cilymaenllwyd   Llandysilio
CHAPEL   Dinas Fawr   NECTARIUM   583 ft.   Wolfsdale   Spittal   Walton East   Pen-ffordd   Llanfa
Porthclais   Niwgwl   Green Scar   Roch   Camrose   Scollon   Rudbaxton   Bletherston   Egremont
Newgale   Simpson Cross   Keeston   WITHYBUSH   Clarbeston Road   Wiston   Clunderwen   Castellwyran
ST. BRIDE'S BAY   Rickets Head   Nolton   Pelcomb Br.   Clarbeston   Llawhaden   Llanfa
Druidston   Lambston   Fenton Br.   Robeston Wathen   Redstone Bank   Crinow
Haroldston West   Portfield Gate   Dreenhill   Canaston Br.   Arberth   Lampe
Broad Haven   Broadway   Hwlffordd Haverfordwest   Slebech   Narberth   Tavernsp
The Rhos   GRAHAM SUTHERLAND ART GALLERY   Slebech   Cold Blow   Prince's Gate   Ludchurch
Talbenny   St. Brides   Rosepool   Walton West   Freystrop   Landshipping   Martletwy   Templeton   Stepaside
The Nab Head   Musselwick Sands   Hasguard   Hook   Yerbeston   Reynalton   Begelly   Kilgetty
Garland Stone   Skomer Island   Marloes   Herbrandston   Tiers Cross   Sardis   Lawrenny   Jeffreston   Saunder
Mew Stone   Gateholm   St. Ishmael's   Sandy Haven   Johnston   Rosemarket   Cresswell   Williamston   Dinb
BROAD SOUND   Marloes Sands   Westdale   Milffwrd Milford Haven   Houghton   Burton   W. Williamston   Tenb
Skokholm Island   Dale   Castlebeach   Wick   Neyland   Cresswell   Carew   Redberth   New Hedges
St. Ann's Head   Warwick   Thorn Island   Doc Penfro Pembroke Dock   Lawrenny   Carew Cheriton   Gumfreston   Penally
Angle   Sheep Island   Pwllcrochan   Pentre Pembroke   TIDAL MILL   Milton   St. Florence   MANOR HOUSE LEISURE PARK   St. Cath.
Car Ferry Rosslare-Pembroke 4¼ hrs   Rhoscrowther   Hundleton   BISHOPS PALACE   Lamphey   Hodgeston   MONA
Freshwater West   Castlemartin   Newton   Maiden Wells   Kingsfold   Jameston   Lydstep   Caldy Sd.
PEMBROKESHIRE   Warren   Orielton   St. Petrox   Freshwater East   Swanlake   Giltar Pt.   Caldy
Linney Head   Merrion   Cheriton East   Manorbier   Old Castle Hd.
Bosherston   Stackpole   Trewent
Stack Rocks   CHAPEL   Barafundle Bay
Saddle Hd.   Stackpole Head
COAST   NATIONAL   Broad Haven
St. Govan's Head   PARK

N

Miles 0 1 2 3 4 5
Kilometres 0 1 2 3 4 5 6 7 8

a   b   c   d   e

Glog   Hermon
869ft   *Hermon*
09ft   Llanfymach   Waun-deg   Allt Walis   Halfwa
Drych   Glandwr   Dinas   Trelech   Cwm-duad   Mynydd Figyn
827 ft.   Llanllawddog   Brechfa

Hebron   Eglwys   Fair a Churig   Llanpumsaint   Pont ar Sais   Llanfynydd   Salem
Cynwyl   Elfed   GWILI   RAILWAY
1   Llanglydwen   Coed   Deuror   Cwm-bach   Trelech a'r   Betws   Talog   Blaen-y-coed   Rhyd-ar-gaeau   Pen-y-banc
Login   Cwmfelinmynach   Gelliwen   Abernant   Bwlch-newydd   Newchurch   Cwmdwyfran   Felin-gwm-uchaf   Broadoak   DINEFWR
Llanboidy   Ffynnon-ddrain   Peniel   Bronwydd Arms   Whitemill   Llangathen   Llangathen
Rhyd-y-wrach   Meidrim   Merthyr   Caerfyrddin   Carmarthen   AMPHITHEATRE   Felinwen   Felindre   DRYSLWYN   Llangathen
Llanfallteg   Llangynin   Bron-y-Gaer   Samau   Abergwili   Nantgaredig   Dryslwyn   Golden Grove
2   Hendygwyn   at Daf   Whitland   Pwll-trap   San Clêr   St. Clear's   Banc-y-felin   Llanllwch   Llangynog   Croes-y-ceiliog   Llangunnor   Capel   Dewi   Nant-y-caws   Llanarthney   Pen-rhiw-goch   Carmel   Pentre Gw
Brandy   Hill   Llandeilo   Abercywyn   Llangynog   Cwm-ffrwd   Llanddarog   Porth   Foelgastell   Gors-las   Pen-y-groes   Tir-y-dail
Red Roses   Llanddowror   Llanybri   Maesybont   Cross   Hands   Ammanford
Crunwear   Llandawke   Eglwysgymin   Laugharne   Llansteffan   Llangyndeyrn   Crwbin   Dre-fach   Pontyberem   Tumble   Capel   Hendre   Ty-croes
Llanteg   Eglwyscummin   Llansadyrnin   DYLAN THOMAS'   BOATHOUSE   Broadway   Llandyfaelog   Meinciau   Pont Henry   Llan-non   Craig Faw
3   Pentywyn   Pendine   Broadway   Ferryside   Broadway   Four Roads   Pontiets   Cynheidre   Five Roads   Hendy   Pontardul
Amroth   Marros   Ginst   Pt.   St. Ishmael   Llansaint   Kidwelly   Trimsaran   Horeb   Resr   Cefn
Wiseman's Bridge   Pendine   Sands   Towyn   Burrows   Bury Port   Felinfoel   Llangennech   Dafen   Groves   End   Bryn   Llwynhendy   Gorseinon
undersoot   Monkstone Pt.   CARMARTHEN   Pembrey   Forest   Pembrey   Pwll   Bynea   Loughor
Dinbych y Pysgod   Tenby   BAY   Cefn Sidan   Burry Port   Gowerton   Fforest   fach   Loughor
St. Catherine's Island   BURRY INLET   **Llanelli**   Penclawdd   Gowerton   Three   Crosses   Waunarlw   Cockett
4   Pt.   MONASTERY   Caldy Island   Whiteford Pt.   Llanrhidian Sands   Salthouse Pt.   Llanmorlais   Dunvant   Upper   Killay   CLYNE   VALLEY
Broughton Bay   Llanmadoc   Cheriton   Landimore   Llanrhidian   Parc le   Breos   SWANSEA   AIRPORT   Clyne   Common
Burry Holms   Oldwalls   Cefn Bryn   609ft.   Parkmill   Bishopston   Newton
Rhosilli   Bay   Llangennith   Reynoldston   Knelston   Penrice   Nicholaston   Southgate   Caswell Bay
5   Worms Hd.   Llanddewi   Rhosili   Pennard   Pobbles Bay   Pwll-du   Hd.   Pwll-du   Langla
Mewslade   Bay   Port-Eynon   Horton   Oxwich   Oxwich Pt.   Three Cliffs Bay   Slade

6

7

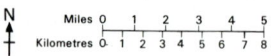

MAP L

N

Miles 0 1 2 3 4 5
Kilometres 0 1 2 3 4 5 6 7 8

a   b   c   d   e

1

Salem
Manordeilo
Bethlehem
Rhosmaen
Llanddeusant
Twynllannan
Forest
Craig
Allt Ddu
Llanfigan
BRECON
Trichrug 1361ft.
Pont Aber
Llyn y Fan Fach
Fan Brycheiniog
Moel Feity 1940ft.
Fan Foel 2630ft.
Fan Fawr 2409ft.
Pen-y-fan 2907ft.
Talyb on
Llandeilo
Capel Cwynfe
Cefn y Truman
MOUNTAIN
Cefn Cul
FFOREST FAWR
Fan Fawr 1592ft.
Storey Arms
Gwaun-rhudd 2502ft.
Ffair-fach
Trapp
CARREG CENNEN
Foel Fraith 1982ft.
Fan Hir
Garreg-goch
2366ft.
Fan Gyhirych
Fan Nedd 2071ft.
Talybont
Derwydd
BLACK
Garreg-lwyd 2028ft.
DAN-YR-OGOF SHOW CAVES
Gwaen Nant-ddu
Forest
Llandybie
1506ft.
Tair Carn Isaf
Craig-y-nos
Nant-ddu
Glyn-hir
Brynaman
Penycae
Ystradfellte
Coed Taf

2

Garnant
Gwauncaegurwen
Cwmllynfell
Cwm-giedd
HENRHYD FALLS
Coelbren
Cader Fawr
Pontsticill
Betws
Ystradgynlais
Pen-rhos
Onllwyn
Coed y Rhaiadr
VISITOR CENTRE
Ty-croes
Ystalyfera
968ft.
Gurnos
Seven Sisters
Nedd Fechan
Penderyn
A465
Merthyr Tydfil
Crynant Forest
Glyn Neath
Aber Pergwm
Hirwaun
Mynydd Aberdare

3

Coed Abertawe
Pontardawe
Rheola Forest
DEEP COAL & STEAM
Resolven
Forest
Rhondda Aberdare
Aberdare
St. Gwynno Forest
Clydach
Penscynor
Cefn Mawr
Blaen-Rhondda
Gyncorrwg
Treherbert
Morriston
Castell-nedd Neath
Cymmer
Treorchy
Abercynon

4

Swansea
Margam Forest
Maesteg
Ogmore Vale
Pontypridd
Port Talbot
Margam
Blackmill
Llantrisant

5

Mumbles
Margam Sands
Pyle
North Cornelly
Bridgend
Tair Onen Forest

6

Porthcawl
Ogmore
Cowbridge
Llancarfan
Tusker Rocks
Southerndown
Llantwit Major
St. Donat's
Aberthaw
Rhoose

7

HERITAGE COAST

MAP M

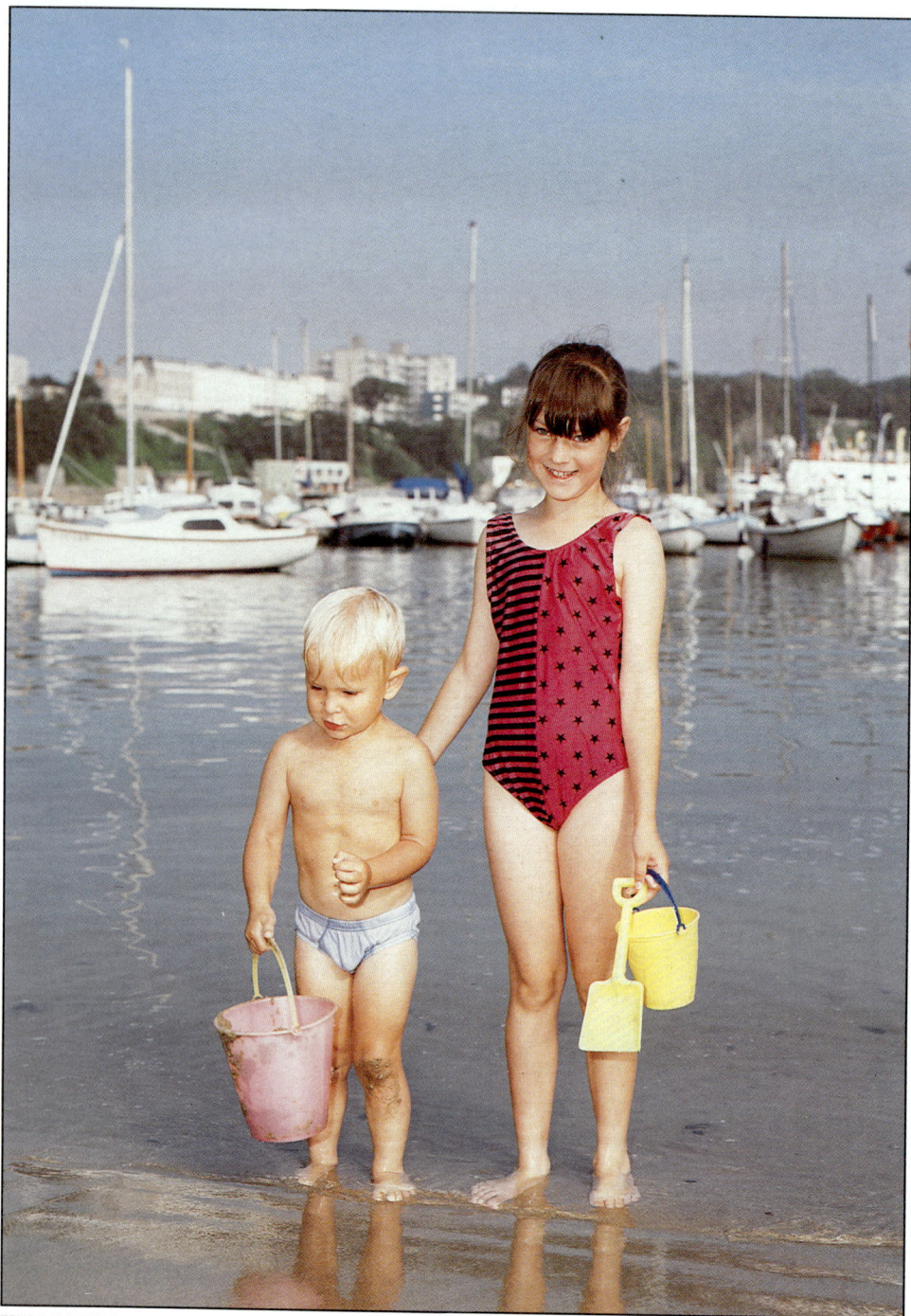

TENBY HARBOUR

OGWEN VALLEY, SNOWDONIA